Lawn Beauty
The Organic Way

LAWN BEAUTY
The Organic Way

By the editors of

Organic Gardening
and Farming

J. I. RODALE, *Editor-in-Chief*
ROBERT RODALE, *Editor*
JEROME OLDS, *Executive Editor*
M. C. GOLDMAN, *Managing Editor*
MAURICE FRANZ, *Managing Editor*

Compiled by
GLENN F. JOHNS

RODALE BOOKS, INC. EMMAUS, PA. 18049

Distributed by David McKay Co., Inc.

STANDARD BOOK NUMBER 87596-077-4
LIBRARY OF CONGRESS CATALOG CARD NUMBER 72-106060
COPYRIGHT MCMLXX BY RODALE PRESS, INC.

SECOND PRINTING — NOVEMBER, 1971

OB-66

Preface

"I DON'T EAT THE GRASS! Why shouldn't I use crabgrass killers or dandelion destroyers? Why should I break my back pulling out weeds when all I have to do is sock them with a little spray or powder and my lawn problems disappear."

Why not use chemicals on the home grounds? Why not indeed! The sudden concern over our malignant environment has taught us that the delicate chain of nature doesn't stop until it reaches our front door. The lesson is overwhelmingly clear: the selfish use of technology has a cumulative and harmful effect. Pesticides and commercial fertilizers with their tremendous staying power find their way into our drinking water and our food cycle. Ultimately, the poison or other complex chemicals carelessly spewered around nestle in the organs of our body or the marrow of our bones. Indirectly, but with as much certainty as though we poured arsenic into a coffee cup, we are poisoning each other.

Let's set the record clear right from the start. Using chemicals on the front lawn is an easy way to try to cope with your lawn frustrations. But the organic way to lawn care is not always as careless as

[v]

dumping some lethal solution into a spray bottle or lawn spreader. However, the end result is still a beautiful carpet-like green that you'll be mighty proud of.

One other thing. Years before our environmental dilemma came into strong focus, many homeowners discarded commonplace lawn advice and decided to apply natural organic lawn care to their home grounds. They stopped using DDT and other weed wreckers because they could see the danger in those lethal compounds. They shunned commercial fertilizers because they saw how they jazzed up the normal balance of the soil.

In deciding upon the organic way to lawn care they often endured the wrinkled brows and turned up noses of their friends and neighbors who could see no danger in using commercial concoctions.

Now, decades later, it's beginning to look like those organic kooks were pretty smart after all.

A special thanks to Mr. William Merritt whose editorial assistance was valuable in preparing the initial stages of this manuscript.

Contents

[vii]

Lawn Mower—136; The Reel Mower—136; The Rotary Mower—137; The Sickle Bar and Accessory Mowers—138; Mow-How—142; Before You Mow—143; When Mowing—143; A Rotary Mower Makes Fast Compost—145; Meanwhile, Back at the Scythe—146.

CONTENTS

[x]

[xi]

CONTENTS

Introduction

Well, for Lawn's Sake...

IF THERE'S ONE THING today's homeowner wants around the house, it's a lawn he can live with! As a matter of fact, most folks really want a dreamy, unique combination—a lawn that looks great, takes all the play and wear any family can give it, yet needs a ridiculous minimum of care.

So what happens? There's more fussing, fretting, nervous energy and money expended by home-garden enthusiasts on their lawns than on anything else that grows. Still, the wide majority of them remain almost continually dissatisfied. Why? They fail to apply the one thing most needed: *common sense.*

The big advantage that successful organic lawn-growers have is that this method gets them to look at their *soil—first—*not at pretty pictures on a package, nor at fancy gadgets or combination weed-killer-fertilizers, and so forth. Whether it's Al Piccioli of Needham, Mass., who rebuilt his bulldozed lawn soil into shape by growing a "cover crop" of potatoes in the front yard; or Herman Benioff of Allentown, Pa., whose cottonseed meal-granite

[xv]

dust-bone meal-phosphate rock formula turned his envious neighbors the same kelly-green as his grass; or George Pool of Lehigh Parkway near Emmaus, Pa., whose practically impregnable and maintenance-free Zoysia lawn is so "Persian-carpet" thick your shoes disappear as you walk across it—these people all have something vital in common.

The book you're holding does two important things for the lawn-lover: It concentrates on the ideas, methods and results of actual gardeners—folks who've put organic how-to into practice. And it conveys their experiences, their techniques and discoveries in terms every gardener can both understand and put into his own situation. No matter where you live—from the salty sea-spray home sites along East or West Coasts; to the icy sectors frozen over much of the year; to hot, dusty, stony, muddy or desert-dry areas—you can find people with your soil problems who have used organic ways to turn out a fine lawn. And regardless of what type of lawn you want—anything from a perfect golf green to a turf that withstands the jumping-est, tumbling-est bunch of kids—again, there are folks who've faced the same puzzles and worked out practical, successful ways to get just what you're after.

Without being over-technical, the chapters which follow provide direct detail on lawn varieties for different needs and climates, on the all-important soil-building to get a strong lawn going, on questions about mowing and watering and controlling bugs, weeds or disease, on improving a lawn already established, on just enjoying your lawn with a lot less work or trouble — and no poisons or chemicals.

By meeting the people and facts in these pages, we're confident you'll be doing what they've done: succeeding with the lawn you want by organic methods. Happy lawnscaping!

The Editors

CHAPTER 1

Soil — The Heart of All Good Lawns

It's What's Underneath that Counts

SOIL IS THE FOUNDATION of any lawn, and the kind of soil you have will largely determine the quality of your lawn. No one knows that any better than Alfred Piccioli. Most of his Cape Cod neighbors looked at him a little strangely that spring when the construction of his house was completed. After he carefully put back the topsoil that he had removed before construction began, Mr. Piccioli, with the help of his family, planted his lawn area, not in grass seed, but in potato seed!

He took some good-natured ribbing from his friends when the potato seed sprouted into plants — and his home being in a residential area, the front lawn did look a little odd.

[1]

But Mr. Piccioli knew what he was after and the important thing was not some temporary inconvenience but the end result. He knew that the constant hoeing his potatoes would require would stir up many beneficial minerals and aerate the soil. It also was a form of crop rotation that would give a bundle of benefit to the soil.

When the potato plants blossomed, curiosity mounted. Even passing motorists stopped to inquire about the strange crop on the front lawn. Mr. Piccioli patiently explained his organic plan to all who asked.

That summer, the lawns of New England sweltered under a widespread drought. Although many of his neighbors' lawns dried up and burnt out, Mr. Piccioli's potatoes continued to flourish, and his "lawn" remained one of the greatest in town. At fall harvest time, he and his family dug up a healthy crop of potatoes and stored them away for good winter eating. Plant roots were left in the ground to rot and become organic food, while the tops were cast into the compost heap. He then rotary tilled and added more compost, after which he sowed a quality lawn seed. Before frost set in, he coaxed the seed along and established his lawn.

Early the next spring, his lawn continued to grow and by early summer it was flourishing. Today his organic-fed lawn is one of the finest in the neighborhood, and the Piccioli family is well-pleased with the results of their efforts.

[2]

Many homeowners, like Mr. Piccioli, have found that their lawn soil is the light-colored, infertile subsoil excavated from the cellar or what is exposed after topsoil is pushed around in grading the site. And although they aren't all growing potatoes as a prelude to grass, many of them do know that the soil they have is not all bad. With proper organic treatment, it can be made productive enough to grow a good lawn. The key lies in the soil.

Soil is not a lifeless mass of inert mineral material, but is a living, dynamic body. About 90 different soil series have been identified and named. Each soil has characteristics that makes it different from other soil and each will respond differently

An all-too-familiar sight to many homeowners are lumps of clay soil that make up their home lot. With proper organic treatment clayey soil can be made productive enough to nourish a good lawn.

depending on how it is treated and managed. Each can support a satisfactory lawn when these differences are taken into consideration.

Soils consist largely of sand, silt, clay, organic matter, air and water. Most soils contain all 6 of these components. Their proportions influence a soil's capacity to absorb and hold water, air and fertilizer. The relative proportions of the particles such as clay, silt and sand give a soil its textural classification such as fine sandy loam, clay loam or any of the other 10 textural classifications.

The texture of the soil is more important than its fertility. Fertilizer and limestone can easily change the fertility of a soil, but poor texture, such as excess sand or clay, is not easily remedied.

Most homeowners spend enough money to have a good lawn but never have one because they plant a layer of soil with the wrong grass. In addition they do not stop to consider the questions of soil type, depth of preparation and fertilizer which are also important.

Therefore, the first thing to determine is how deep is your topsoil. Unless you are dealing with virgin topsoil, a foot or more deep, further preparation is probably necessary. If it happens to be only three or four inches deep, it should be scraped off to one side. Its fertility will not be lessened if a few inches of subsoil are included with it to increase its bulk. The biggest mistake would be to prepare just a few inches of topsoil which might camouflage a hard layer of debris and packed clay.

In the case where existing topsoil is eight inches or more deep, then the stripping is unnecessary and the entire layer may be considered and treated as one, with the quantities of humus, lime, and fertilizer thoroughly worked into the top eight or ten inch layer.

The subsoil for a lawn is just as important as the topsoil. The subsoil should be broken up if it is of a hardpan nature. If on the contrary, it is loose and sandy, it would be wise to include a layer of clay soil that would tend to stiffen that bottom layer. In any case, the subsoil foundation for a good lawn should be not less than eight inches deep.

It is in this subsoil that your lime will do the most good. Use from 25 to 50 pounds of ground limestone per thousand square feet according to the acidity of the soil to bring the soil reaction up to pH 6.5. Sandy soils require less and clay soils require more lime to alter the acidity of the soil. When that layer is properly prepared, grade it to form the desired contours of the land.

WHAT'S WRONG WITH THE SOIL YOU'VE GOT?

Subsoil taken from the basement of a new house — often containing plaster, cement, lumber and other debris — is a poor soil for a lawn. Every house-building contract should provide for all topsoil to be piled separately for the final grading and for debris to be removed — not buried on the site.

[5]

For most homeowners, the problem will be one of using the soil they have. Soils are generally poor because of lack of plant nutrients, a condition which can be cured by applying fertilizer. Poor physical makeup of the soil is a much more serious matter.

Soils of the average graded lawn contain a high proportion of clay. They dry into hard crusts. They are sticky and impervious when wet, slow to absorb water when dry, and furnish little water to plants. Drought quickly affects plants growing on those clay subsoils.

Lawns can be grown on clay, even subsoil clay, but they will be less vigorous and satisfactory. They will require more skill and more work than lawns on soils of good physical makeup.

Even on good soils, a lawn requires work and care. You can't sit back and expect a perfect lawn to appear!

The Soil Test—A Must for Proper Lawn Care

Playing by ear may be all right for an accomplished musician, but when it comes to the gardener who wants to improve his soil—and his lawn—guesswork doesn't pay. The more he finds out about his soil, the better he will be able to provide for his lawn.

Soil testing is one very practical way to learn more about the makeup of any soil. The two big steps to making the most of this idea are:

[6]

1. *Test Your Soil.* Dig into it and find out what's there and what isn't. By any one of several available testing methods (which are discussed a little further on), get a dependable analysis of the essential lawn nutrients your soil contains — how much or how little of each. Check, too, on its acid-alkaline status (pH) to be sure this condition is favorable. And, if at all possible, determine the percentage of organic matter it now holds, since this factor is also a mighty important one in any soil. Make the tests periodically, often enough to stay aware of changes and how well your treatment is working.

2. *Treat Your Soil.* Treat it according to the test results. Decide on a program of fertilizing that matches up supply with demands shown in your soil's check-up. Add whatever is needed to overcome any extreme of acidity or alkalinity. Work to increase the soil's organic matter content, which is literally its "lifeline" and exerts the greatest influence on desirable tilth, good drainage and moisture-holding capacities, response to other fertilizers and all-round richness. Treat your soil right — with natural materials. Plan and prepare to use organic sources of the nutrients your soil and plants need, along with natural ground rock supplies of the minerals. Make your treatment program one that builds the soil and lasting fertility — not an artificial stop-gap measure that temporarily treats symptoms rather than causes of deficiencies in the land.

[7]

Few soils have all the right nutrients in just the right amounts for ideal lawn growth. Some may be deficient in one element; others may lack two or more. Even within a single lawn plot, different sections often have varying levels of the same nutrients. Then, too, each time your lawn is grown, changes take place, depending on what practices are followed. Just standing idle will alter a soil's makeup from year to year.

TYPES OF TEST AVAILABLE

There are two basic ways to test soil accessible to the average homeowner. First and simplest of them is the home soil-test kit, which is marketed commercially and has been used successfully by many thousands. The kit provides solutions and guides for determining the approximate content of the 3 major soil nutrients—nitrogen (N), phosphorus (P) and potash (K)—plus a similar means of establishing the pH standing. Home testing kits are easy to use, require no knowledge of chemistry or laboratory procedure. One of their biggest advantages is that they permit you to make frequent on-the-spot tests of your soil (whereas other methods are often delayed) and help you adapt a fertilizing program in accord with your soil's prime needs.

The test is made simply by putting a small portion of the soil sample in a test tube and then introducing one or two "reagents." A reagent is a chemical which reacts with the nutrient being tested, and shows the quantity of the nutrient available by changing color. Color charts are supplied with the kits, and the final analysis is made by checking the color of the solution in the tube with the test chart for the nutrient being tested. Although they do not analyze for closely detailed percentages, home soil-test kits used with moderate care do give the gardener a good estimate of the state of his soil—and are a valuable tool in better gardening and soil care.

The other general way to have soil tested is to send a sample to a laboratory offering this service or to your state experiment station. Farmers, rural homesteaders and city gardeners frequently get help and information through their county agent. Most state experiment stations charge a small fee for the soil test report, which in addition to an NPK and pH analysis may include indications of trace element levels and organic matter content. One note of planning: stations do not usually reply quickly, especially during seasonal planting and fertilizing periods when they have many requests.

Other testing methods—mostly used only in technical or specialized agricultural research—include plant tissue or leaf analyses in determining nutrient deficiencies. A reliable humus-testing kit, which costs about $25.00, is also available for those who would like to keep a constant record of their soil's organic matter status. The great majority of lawn owners, though, will find either the home soil-test kit or state station testing best for their requirements, since these will answer the two big questions: Does my soil have a sufficient amount of the major nutrients — nitrogen, phosphorus and potassium? Is my soil too acid or alkaline?

A test for nitrogen, incidentally, can be used as a rough guide to the humus or organic matter condition of the soil, as there is a very close relationship between nitrogen content and humus content. High nitrogen generally means a high humus rating.

TAKING A SOIL SAMPLE

Whether it is for your own home-kit test or for use by the extension station or an independent laboratory, the soil sample you take is all-important. What any test shows, obviously depends on the sample, and so this small part that is to represent your soil in the examination must be taken carefully. Briefly, here are the steps in taking a soil sample:

Assemble your tools, making sure they and the containers to hold samples are clean and free of foreign matter. Be especially sure there are no residues or fragments of fertilizer, which can throw the test results completely off. Your digging or sampling tool may be a spade, trowel, garden dibble, narrow shovel with straight sides, or a soil auger or probe. For gathering samples, use a large bucket or similar container. Coffee cans or small cardboard boxes which will hold about a pint of soil will serve for the final samples.

Soil samples can be taken at any time during the year that weather conditions permit. The soil should be free of frost and fairly dry. If the lawn is quite large, taking a composite, or mixed, sample from several points will provide more information than a spot sample. (Note, however, that a combined sample from two distinctly different soil types would not be a suitable representative of either one. In a case like that, individual samples would be better.)

For a composite sample, start at one end of the plot and with the garden tool cut straight down about 6 to 8 inches and lift out a narrow slice; lay that to one side. Then take another thin slice, about ½ inch, from the same section and put it in the bucket or collecting container. Shovel the first slice back in place. Now move about 6 feet in any direction and repeat the operation. Continue until the plot is given an over-all sampling. On a field of an acre or more, samples can be taken several rods apart.

Once you've covered the area to be tested, mix the samples thoroughly in the bucket and remove one pint of soil. Spread this "homogenized" sample where it can continue drying, and when completely dry and without lumps, place it in the sam-

[11]

ple container. Damp or wet soil will give false test readings. Next, label the soil sample, indicating where and when it was taken.

Remember, soil tests can be no better than the samples tested. To reflect an accurate picture, they should be as representative of the area as possible; otherwise the story told by the test will not be true. A pint of soil—the size of the composite sample recommended—is about 1/150,000,000 part of an acre. A level teaspoonful—the amount actually tested—is 1/100 part of a pint.

WHAT TEST RESULTS MEAN

No matter which way you get your soil tested, the results can be of value only if you understand and use them. NPK readings secured with a home soil-testing kit are generally expressed as "high," "medium" and "low" or as "abundant," "adequate" and "deficient" for each major nutrient. Acid-alkaline tests range from neutral to slightly or highly acid, or slightly to very alkaline. Laboratory and extension tests usually report percentages of the major elements and a pH reading expressed in acidity-alkalinity scale figures. (7.0 is neutral; readings below that are progressively acid; above, increasingly alkaline.)

Some test kits and most station or laboratory reports also make recommendations for improving weak or very deficient nutrient levels shown in the test. The important point for lawn

[12]

keepers who want their soil enriched in a way that does the most good is that they translate any general or chemical recommendations into natural fertilizers—organic materials that deliver long-lasting benefits and improve the soil's composition at the same time. Happily, there is nothing complicated about following that method. Actually, it is the easiest, most effective and economical system to make soil fertile and gardening both more fun and more rewarding.

Convert Your Soil Test into Action

Let's look at the major nutrients and consider how each one can be supplied when a soil test shows a deficiency. Nitrogen of course is one of the most vital elements for a productive soil, and one which must be constantly renewed. It is directly responsible for the vegetative growth of plants above ground. With a good supply, the plant grows sturdily, matures rapidly and has good foliage color, food value and flavor. On the other hand, excess nitrogen—such as is forced into the plant by chemical "shot-in-the-arm" fertilizers —causes weak watery growth, lowered disease and pest resistance, and poorer color, taste and nutritional value. Moreover, synthetic nitrogen supplies are quickly leached or washed out of soils, and the plants soon become starved for that essential element.

If your test shows a low nitrogen level, start ap-

[13]

plying one or more of the rich natural sources. Fresh or dried manures are basic fertilizers relatively high in nitrogen, and should be included in an organic fertilizing program whenever available. Cottonseed meal and other vegetable meals, such as those from soybeans and linseed, are especially rich in nitrogen (cottonseed meal has 7 per cent) and are excellent for overcoming deficiencies. Activated and digested sludge, available in many cities from the sewage processing plants, are both good sources. The first contains about 5 per cent nitrogen; the second approximately the same as barnyard manure—two per cent.

Bone meal is another good supplier of nitrogen, as well as a phosphorus-rich material. Raw bone meal has between two and 4 per cent nitrogen, 22 to 25 per cent phosphoric acid. Steamed bone meal contains one to two per cent nitrogen, up to 30 per cent phosphorus. One of the richest sources of nitrogen is blood meal or dried blood— materials collected in slaughter-houses and later dried and ground. Blood meal analyzes 15 per cent nitrogen while dried blood has 12 per cent. Either of those can be used directly in the soil or composted, but because of their high nitrogen content, they should be applied gradually and sparingly over a period of time.

Our fertilizer preferences includes processed sewage sludge which will yield two pounds of pure nitrogen for each 34 pounds of sludge spread to

1,000 square feet. Check with your local sewage disposal plant. You probably can get all the sludge you want free—if you do the hauling.

When using manure, compost or bone meal, 100 pounds per 1,000 square feet will add 2 pounds of nitrogen to the soil.

But be guided by what you can get locally at the best price. Don't hesitate to substitute soybean meal for cottonseed meal if you can get lots of it cheap. And, above all, don't forget to check with the local authorities about sewage sludge—it's ideal for lawn building.

PHOSPHORUS

Phosphorus plays a leading role in plant nutrition. It's essential for healthy growth, strong roots and resistance to diseases. Phosphate deficiency is considered by many agronomists to be the prime factor in limiting crop production.

When a soil test points to phosphorus shortage, get busy adding a healthy natural supply. Best source is rock phosphate, ground to a meal or powder, which contains about 30 per cent phosphoric acid. Colloidal phosphate, also a natural mineral product, is found chiefly in Florida in sedimentary deposits of soft phosphate with colloidal clay. It contains from 18 to 25 per cent phosphoric acid.

Other good sources of phosphate include bone

[15]

meal (22 to 25 per cent), dried shrimp wastes (10 per cent), raw sugar wastes (8 per cent), dried ground fish (7 per cent), activated sludge (2½ to 4 per cent), dried blood (one to 5 per cent) and wool wastes (two to 4 per cent). Humus and organic matter, especially manures, team up to make natural phosphates more available to plants.

POTASH

Potash is the mineral that concerns itself mainly with plants' carbohydrate manufacture. As one of the "big 3" soil nutrients, it is essential for the development of strong plants, particularly in overcoming disease susceptibility and maintaining balanced nitrogen use. Plants lacking potash do not resist heat or cold well, and their process of photosynthesis is slowed down.

If a potassium deficiency shows up in your soil test, look to one of the naturally occurring materials rich in potash to bolster it. Granite dust or granite stone meal—often called ground rock potash—is a highly recommended source. Its potash content varies from 3 to 5½ per cent, sometimes more. Modern machinery can pulverize rock materials to such fineness that nutrients become available for lawn assimilation in relatively short periods of time, depending on the condition of the soil to be treated. Potash rock helps supply both a short-term and long-range release of its mineral

[16]

content and is one of the most effective potassium fertilizers.

Greensand or greensand marl, an undersea mineral deposit, is an excellent potassium supplier (7 per cent) and also contains beneficial quantities of many trace elements, some lime and phosphorus. Plant residues, manures and compost also bring potash to the soil in a free and available form. This is important because even in fertile soils the supply of free potassium is seldom enough to meet the needs.

Wood ashes are another potash-rich material. Broad-leaf wood ashes contain as much as 10 per cent; coniferous ashes, about 6 per cent. Other sources include tobacco stems (4½ to 7 per cent), millet and buckwheat straw (3.2 and 2.0 per cent respectively), cocoa shell residues (2.6 per cent) and wool wastes (up to 3½ per cent). An analysis of garbage in N.Y. City showed from 2.3 to 4.3 per cent potash.

STEADYING THE pH

The acid-alkaline (pH) balance of your soil is important because a lopsided pH will block the release of major and minor plant foods. A soil that is too acid will not release "unavailable" nutrients properly; neither will a soil that is too alkaline. Most lawns do best on soil that is slightly acid to neutral — a pH reading of about 5.9 to 6.9.

[17]

If a test indicates your soil is too acid, use natural ground limestone, about 4 to 8 pounds for every 100 square feet. If tests show your soil is quite acid and you want to raise it by one full unit — such as from pH 5.5 to 6.5, then lime as follows:

Sandy Soil . . . . 35 lbs. per 1,000 square feet
Sandy Loam . . . . . 45 lbs. per 1,000 square feet
Medium Loam . . . 70 lbs. per 1,000 square feet
Silt or Clay . . . . . . 75 lbs. per 1,000 square feet

Sprinkle the lime by hand or with a cart-spreader, but be sure to work from two different directions at right angles. This is the way to seed and spread fertilizer, too, because it guarantees you even distribution. It is also wise to do these operations on comparatively windless days.

Although the general word on liming is to go slow and only lime when the soil is overly acid, liming has definite value to the lawn maker. When the soil is too acid, it impedes the growth and activity of bacteria necessary to convert raw fertilizing substances into forms the grass can absorb.

When that happens, the grass is literally starving in the proverbial land of plenty. More fertilizing will not correct that as it will in a soil with a pH of 6.0 or better.

The situation worsens in very acid soils, those with a pH below 5.0, because in them organic matter does not decay at a normal rate and roots tend to congest the turf. That prevents air and water

[18]

from getting into the topsoil which further aggravates the acid condition. You may also use materials like wood ashes, bone meal, dolomite, crushed marble and oyster shells, all of which contains liberal amounts of lime.

For alkaline soils, materials such as cottonseed meal and acid peat moss are very effective. Leaf mold, sawdust, wood chips and other acid mulching materials will also help. Actually, organic matter is the best way to remedy either a highly acid or alkaline soil because it tends to neutralize both excesses and acts as a buffer against adverse pH levels at the same time.

Keep in mind, of course, that a soil test is not the only reliable check on the soil's needs and the requirements of the lawn growing in it. A soil test reveals the available, soluble nutrients, and these constitute about 3 per cent of the total minerals present in the soil. Many people feel that testing the actual tissue of a plant is a better method, since it reveals what the plant is lacking. But the trouble with tissue testing is that it shows the hunger after it exists and by that time the damage has been done. An accurate soil test can help prevent deficiencies, and thereby serve as a valuable tool for the average gardener.

HUMUS TEST HELPFUL

A test for the humus content of your soil, by the way, is a good idea because it will show how successful you've been in adding vital organic matter. Soils in the U.S. today average 1.5 per cent humus, but our country's virgin soil contained 4 per cent. In an *Organic Gardening and Farming* magazine survey a few years ago, we found the average organic gardener has about 2.5 per cent organic matter. You can see there's room and need for improvement.

The more you know about your soil, the better you can use it. Soil tests and intelligent treatment as a followup to what they show can do a lot for your lawn success.

TYPES OF SOIL AS INDICATED BY WEED GROWTHS

It may be possible for you to tell something about your soil from the type of weeds that favor it. This may be particularly true when you have bought a vacant or suburban lot that has not been worked for some time.

1. Wet Land: Ferns, horsetail, sedge, rush, cattail, buttercup, pennywort. The surface may be dry but these weeds are a sure indication that the land is wet below.

2. Sour Land: (Acid) sorrel, dock, wild strawberry, bramble.

3. Poor, Dry: Devil's paint brush, spurge.

4. Tight, Compressed: Knotwood, poa annua.

5. Deep Clay: Wild onion.

6. Limestone: Chicory, teasel.

[20]

Topsoil

GROW YOUR OWN TOPSOIL

Maybe your builders took away your topsoil or buried it so deep you can't find it. And maybe you don't want to buy topsoil which is full of seeds and of dubious fertility. You can still start a lawn and build your topsoil as you go. It's not too hard, but it takes time — at least a year. Here's how it's done: Sow a green manure cover crop right into your subsoil after you have enriched it with sludge, cottonseed meal, tobacco stems and bone meal.

This is the common-sense advice of Thomas H. Everett, Curator of Education and Horticulturist, New York Botanical Garden. In his handbook on lawns, Mr. Everett makes this sound suggestion: after liming and fertilizing the subsoil, sow two quarts of winter rye to each 1,000 square feet of soil or the same quantity of Canada field peas.

"Green manuring means growing cover crops especially for the purpose of turning them under and converting in the soil to humus," notes Mr. Everett, adding that "humus is formed by the decay of the extensive root systems as well as the tops. . . When top growth is 6 to 12 inches tall, spade the cover crop under or bury it with plow or rotary tiller and immediately refertilize and sow another cover crop. Don't turn the last of the cover crops under later than 6 weeks before sow-

[21]

ing the permanent grass seed." In other words, give the cover crop at least 6 weeks to decay and form humus.

To that sound counsel to lawn builders who are willing to build their own topsoil from scratch, we should like to add this word to residents of the Deep South. The fall is an excellent time to plant crimson clover, hairy vetch, winter rye or ryegrass. Here, again, you are providing excellent green manures which you can turn under prior to your spring lawn planting. These crops also provide a cover for the soil during the fall and winter.

Where there's poor soil in an area planned for a lawn, a temporary cover crop may be the solution. When the time comes for the lawn to be planted, turn under the soil-improving cover.

Clover seed, for example, may be sown on poor soil, and a dwarf mat will soon cover the section. Although a rich, moist soil would cause rank growth, impoverished clay or sand will produce a much better clover mat. It can be cut with a mower in the summer and kept short and thick enough for children to play on.

While growing, clover sends its strong roots down into the soil to depths of 30 inches or more —deep enough to break up hardpan and compacted earth. At the same time, clover roots carry hundreds of small lumps, called nodules which provide a home for nitrogen-producing bacteria. These little workers enrich the soil continuously while the clover is growing.

Only in extreme drought will clover show signs of needing water. It takes just one pound of dwarf white Dutch clover seed to sow each 1,000 square feet. Late summer to early autumn or spring are suitable planting times.

If you lack the time or patience to build your own topsoil, you may prefer to buy it. Try to find a source of good topsoil. Plan to add at least 4 inches of topsoil even though it is expensive. That is the surest and often the most economical way to produce a good lawn.

The top 6 inches from a farm pasture or crop land is good topsoil. Do not accept river-bottom silt or soil dug from a hill with a power shovel or untreated factory waste, regardless of how "rich" it looks.

The texture of your top 4 to 6 inches of soil is perhaps more important to the health of your lawn than are the nutrients which it contains. A very sandy soil is too "light" in texture. It is like a mass of tiny stones, with too few smaller bits of soil between the sand grains to hold water and fertilizer materials. Grass cannot do its best for lack of water and lack of nourishment. To improve a very sandy soil, work organic matter into it. An inch or more of heavier soils helps, too, if it is mixed thoroughly with the top 4 inches of sand. A sandy soil is improved more if you add both organic matter and heavier soil than if you add either material alone.

A clay soil is a "heavy" soil. It is slippery and

[23]

sticky when wet and shrinks and cracks open as it dries. Grass cannot do its best in a heavy clay, for there is not enough air in the soil for good root growth. Heavy traffic, where people walk or play, packs a clay soil even more tightly. Work organic matter into a heavy clay soil to improve it. Do not work sand into a clay soil; it will only pack harder than before.

If your soil needs organic matter, any one of several materials will do. Choose the one that is handiest and cheapest. For each 1,000 square feet of new lawn, use 3 large (7½ cubic feet) bales or the equivalent of peat; from 2 to 3 cubic yards of well-rotted manure or cultivated peat; from 3 to 4 cubic yards of spent mushroom soil; from 1 to 2

Screened loam or topsoil (left) costs more than the unscreened kind, but it is free of rocks, roots and other debris. Both kinds, however, are just as apt to contain weed seed.

[24]

cubic yards of digested sewage sludge; or from 100 to 250 pounds of compost. Smaller amounts of organic matter are of little value.

Beside its function of holding moisture, humus in the topsoil improves aeration. Grass cannot grow unless it has a supply of air around its roots. The rough humus texture holds soil particles apart, providing spaces where oxygen can reach the roots and soil microorganisms.

KINDS OF TOPSOIL

Screened loam is much more expensive and is so "fluffed up" in the process of screening that a ten-yard load at the screening source will end up to be about 7 yards by the time it reaches you, but an advantage is that it will contain no debris such as roots and stones. However, it is just as apt to contain weed seed as any other soil, including the little "nuts" of the noxious weed, "Nutgrass," (grasslike but not a grass). Topsoil from swamps and other low wet places is also apt to contain that weed. Such soil should be avoided.

Be suspicious of excessively black soil. It may have come from the bottom of a bog or swamp and will generally be of poor physical structure, very acid, and apt to bake like brick when exposed to dry conditions, or it may be "trash"—cleanings from gutters and manholes.

Unscreened loam is less expensive and is called "run-of-the-pile." Some may be very good, with very few roots, stones, etc., and others may be full of debris. It is best to visit the pile from which you will receive your soil to be sure you get what you want. Ordering "sight-unseen" is not a good idea. A cubic yard of soil contains 27 cubic feet, in the event that you want to check your delivery truck dimensions. Length times width times height will give you cubic feet. Unscreened soil will pack much less during transport as compared to screened loam. There is some labor involved in raking out the debris.

You will need 4 inches of topsoil as a minimum amount after it is rolled or settled. By applying 6 inches at construction, you'll end up with about 4 inches. Needless to say, the deeper your topsoil, the better lawn you'll have. Three cubic yards of soil will cover a thousand square feet an inch deep. You will be wise not to buy a piece of land from which the topsoil has been removed, unless the seller is willing to return the soil which has been removed.

Subsoil is that which will immediately underlie your "topsoil" or "loam," whichever you prefer to call it. For non-technical purposes, these two terms can be used synonymously.

If your topsoil has been pushed to one side in piles, and if trucks and other vehicles have driven over your intended lawn area, then that subsoil is probably packed hard. It should be harrowed well, or otherwise broken up, 6 inches deep. The grass roots need to penetrate deeply. A hard compacted layer will prevent this and the plant will suffer from lack of oxygen and water.

PEATS FOR SOIL CONDITIONING

Soils that are not in good physical condition for turf establishment, either because of excessive sandiness or high silt and clay content, can be improved by additions of organic materials. They will increase the moisture and fertilizer retaining capacity of sandy soils and improve the rate of air and water movement through silts and clays. Where subsoils are exposed by grading operations it is often just as satisfactory and more economical to use good organic material to condition them than to apply a 4 to 6 inch layer of topsoil of indifferent quality.

Many kinds of organic materials can be used for physical conditioning. Their value depends not only on the initial job they will do but on their persistence in the soil. Such materials as raw sewage sludge, rotted manure and spent mushroom soil will do a very good temporary job. Their rate of decomposition is so rapid, however, that their effectiveness usually is limited to one to two years. Well-rotted sawdust is much more permanent, but the residual cellulose which it contains often is so high that materially more fertilizer must be used for several years after the turf is established to prevent nitrogen deficiency.

[27]

Because of its many desirable characteristics, good quality reed-sedge peat or reed-sedge and moss peat mixtures are excellent organic materials for soil modification. When clean and properly processed, peat handles easily and can be spread uniformly. If its minimum moisture absorptive capacity is 500% and its organic matter content 90% or better (dry matter basis), it can be depended upon to give satisfactory results, providing application rates are adjusted to the character of the soil and the use that is to be made of the turf. Its resistance to decomposition insures that adequate residues will persist in the soil for a period of 10 years or longer.

Where soils are to be modified for general lawn use, applications of 1 to 1½ cubic yards of peat per 1,000 square feet of area are adequate unless soils are in exceptionally poor condition (high sand or clay content). On athletic fields or play areas subjected to severe trampling, rates should be increased to 2 to 3 yards per 1,000 square feet. Application rates for golf greens where very high soil resiliency is required can go as high as 4 to 5 yards per 1,000 square feet.

Peats always should be thoroughly mixed with the soil to full tillage depth. Uneven mixing or the presence of solid layers may cause serious trouble, both in grass root development and uniform movement of moisture. On large areas this can be done by thorough disking or with equipment such as the rotovator. Offsite mixing is quite common for small areas such as golf course greens because of the greater assurance of a thorough mixing job. Manures can be used in the place of the peats, but they generally carry a lot of weed seeds and often make for a weedy lawn. The peats are not apt to contain any weed seeds and are generally preferred.

A MOSSY SOIL IS NOT ALWAYS ACID

Moss does not always indicate an acid soil. We have learned from experience with soil analysis that moss grows on soils of many qualities. Lack of available plant food and lack of competition from higher plants most often encourage growth of moss. The presence of moss is not necessarily a sign that the soil is extremely acid, or even that it is mildly acid. We have discovered many growths of moss on alkaline or overlimed soils. Moss will develop on a dry soil as well as a wet soil.

No one can lose by incorporating plenty of organic matter with the soil; but a general recommendation for heavy liming, based on the presence of moss, is going to bring grief to many persons, in the form of overlimed and undernourished soils.

Compost for Lawns

Wouldn't you like a lawn that stays green all summer, has no crabgrass and rarely needs water-

[29]

ing? Then use compost liberally when making and maintaining it. You want a thick sod with roots that go down 6 inches, not a thin, weed-infested mat laying on a layer of infertile subsoil.

In building a new lawn, work in copious amounts of compost to a depth of at least 6 inches. If your soil is either sandy or clayey (rather than good loam), you'll need at least a two-inch depth of compost, mixed in thoroughly, to build it up. The best time to make a new lawn is in the fall. But if you want to get started in the spring, dig in your compost and plant Italian ryegrass, vetch or soybeans, which will look quite neat all summer. Then dig this green manure in at the end of the summer and make your permanent lawn when cool weather comes.

To renovate an old, patchy lawn, dig up the bare spots about two inches deep, work in plenty of finished compost, tamp and rake well, and sow your seed after soaking the patches well.

Feed your lawn regularly every spring. An excellent practice is to use a spike tooth aerator, then spread a mixture of fine finished compost and bone meal. Rake this into the holes made by the aerator. You can use a fairly thick covering of compost—but not so thick it covers the grass. That will feed your lawn efficiently and keep it sending down a dense mass of roots that laugh at drought.

Where compost is desired to aid a growing crop, there are cautions necessary to avoid injuring plant roots growing near the surface. In order not

[30]

to disturb these roots of established plants, the compost may be mixed with topsoil and together applied as a mulch. This is the best means of adding what is often termed a top dressing. It serves a double purpose in that at the same time it is providing plant food which will gradually work itself down to the growing crop, it also affords an effective mulch to the soil, giving protection from extremes of temperature, hard rains, and so forth.

In the past two decades there has been a great amount of research in composting, anaerobic methods and many more variations of these. Behind them all, however, lies the original Indore method, invented by the father of organic gardening, Sir Albert Howard. The Indore method is still the most widely used and is still practical and productive.

Sir Albert Howard found that by layering different organic materials, decomposition took place more quickly and more completely. He first placed down a 5- or 6-inch layer of green matter, then a two-inch layer of manure (blood meal, bone meal, sewage sludge or other high-protein material may be substituted), and a layer of rich earth, ground limestone and phosphate rock. That simple formula produced a rich, crumbly compost, rich in nutrient value and valuable as a soil structure builder. In further research, Howard found that a heap 5 to 10 feet wide, and 5 feet high, was ideal (the length is optional). He also found that decomposition was facilitated by aeration, and so

[31]

he placed pipes or thick stakes through the pile as it was being built, then pulled them out when the heap was 5 feet high. He then lightly pressed the entire outside surface to prevent blowing, formed a shallow basin on top to catch rainwater, covered the entire surface with a thin layer of earth, and left it to decay.

Organic gardeners have taken Howard's core of compost research and produced beautiful compost and beautiful lawns. Take the example of O. A. Severance of Watertown, New York, who transformed a completely unproductive piece of land into a lush garden spot, all through the use of compost. Mr. Severance makes compost in a pit, surrounded by a wall of loose field stone seven feet square on the inside and two feet high. The wall is laid on top of the ground and the soil inside is dug out a foot deep.

Into this pit go hen and stable manure, leaves, weeds, garbage, lawn clippings, sunflower stalks, some sod and ground limestone. This pit, layered according to Howard's Indore process, is level with the top of the stones when it is completed. Severance turns the pile in three weeks when he estimates the temperature has reached 150 degrees. Four weeks later he turns the pile again, in order to be sure all material has a chance to get into the center of the heap where decomposition is proceeding most rapidly. In a total of three months he takes out well over two tons of finished compost. In that way he can make two piles each season.

Here are some important things to keep in mind when you try composting:

1. Nitrogen is essential to fast composting. Manure, by supplying nitrogen, performs the wonderful service of heating up a compost heap quickly. Although satisfactory compost can be made without manure, it will take longer to rot up. Dried manure, cottonseed meal, dried blood, bone meal — available in garden stores — will work well as a heating-up agent.

2. Shredding of the material is essential. If a compost shredder is not available, a rotary mower can be used efficiently. We were able to cut up the material for our average test heaps in 30 minutes with a rotary mower.

3. Sufficient moisture in the heap is needed if composting is to take place quickly. If your heap is made of predominantly dry materials, it is good to water it liberally when it is first made. But it is usually not necessary to water it again for ten days or two weeks (if the heap is made of shredded material).

Fall is just about the best time of the year for composting. Leaves and dry weeds are available in plentiful supply. And the soil needs compost in the fall and winter months to help it rebuild fertility lost during the past growing season. Compost applied in the fall will have plenty of time to work into the soil and will not in any way interfere with growing grass.

Leaves would be a good basic raw material for you to start with, because most gardeners have not yet learned how to use them properly and will be glad to give you theirs. In a matter of a half hour you can cut up a tremendous pile of leaves with your rotary mower. Use the leaf mulching attachment if you want them cut up in small pieces (which will speed up the composting).

Leaves alone are quite resistant to decay, because they are relatively low in nitrogen. Mixing in grass clippings will help, but you still should add manure for optimum composting. A good formula is this:

100 pounds of leaves
100 pounds of grass clippings
100 pounds of manure — fresh or dried

If you don't have grass clippings, you can substitute weeds, garbage or spoiled hay. But I would recommend that you do not use just leaves and manure. Even though shredded, leaves tend to mat together and need some other material to separate them.

Shred everything — even the manure — with your compost shredder or rotary mower. We have found that the average well-made mower will wade through lumpy and stringy cow litter with ease, and with no undue wear on the machine.

Shred a little of each type of material at a time. Pile it together and water the heap as it accumulates. It is not necessary to layer the materials if they are shredded. And do not wait until the pile is complete before starting to water it.

[34]

When you have shredded up everything organic you can get your hands on that you want to put in your heap, there is nothing more that you can do for several days. You probably won't want to put your material in a bin or enclosure, as that will just make turning more difficult. And, after all, your heap will only be around for ten days.

The 24-hour period just after your heap is made is the most crucial period in its life. If it doesn't start heating up actively by the second day, there is not much hope for it. You probably have not put enough manure or highly nitrogenous material in it. If your heap doesn't heat up, your best bet is to add more manure or organic nitrogen fertilizer. If you don't, you may have to wait 6 months to a year for decay to take place.

Three days after you have made your heap of shredded material, it should be turned. Turning will not be difficult, because the heap will be fluffy and easy to handle. Turning should be continued at three-day intervals, until ten days have passed. If the weather is hot and your heap begins to dry out, keep watering it. Don't let it get soggy, however.

If at the end of 10 days your heap begins to cool, you can feel satisfied. You have made compost in the minimum period possible under home gardening conditions.

One thing to remember: You can improve the quality of your compost greatly by adding natural rock fertilizers to it as you make it. For every hundred pounds of compost material, you can add several shovels of rock phosphate, colloidal phosphate, granite dust, greensand and/or ground limestone. The intense bacterial activity in the heap will help break down the nutrients in the rock and make them available faster.

COMPOSTED LAWNS WITHSTAND DROUGHT

Roy Clark of Topeka, Kansas, has an old stand of Kentucky bluegrass in his lawn that has withstood all that the weather and bugs could throw at it and is still thriving. His formula for a beautiful lawn: start with the right compost, mow at the right height for drought conditions and maintain proper tilth with plenty of earthworms.

Mr. Clark was faced with a problem of starting a lawn in hardpan, a soil badly depleted and low in mineral content. A compost for proper treatment would have to contain just about all the 16 elements necessary for good plant growth. Tilth was very poor since hardpan baked badly after rains and plowing turned it up in large chunks.

Plenty of material for a good compost was available in the area and Mr. Clark set out to assemble the kind he wanted. Base was fresh cow manure from a fattening lot for beef cattle. Feed lot manure was chosen over dairy farm manure since it contained a high percentage of undigested and partly-digested grain. Several bales of moldy alfalfa were located at a very reasonable price. The

[36]

hay was no good for feeding, but was ideal for adding to the compost.

The manure and hay comprised the larger bulk of the 12 by 7 foot compost pile. Mineral for the compost was readily available. Mr. Clark brought several tons of limestone dust, cheap by-products of local rock crushers. Since the limestone dust was very fine, it could be distributed very thoroughly throughout the compost and the large amount used would make it readily available for plant use. Experience has also proved the value of other natural rock products — ground potash, marl and phosphate rock — in supplying these important minerals.

A smaller amount of leaf mold was needed. Mr. Clark looked over several timber patches until he found some at just the stage of decomposition he wanted. Commercial blood meal, bone meal and an activator were purchased for adding to the compost. During the time the compost was processing, garbage, shrub clippings, and garden surplus-material were added.

When the compost was ready for application, Mr. Clark began working it into the hardpan. The soil was plowed to a depth of about 6 inches and compost mixed thoroughly into the loosed soil. Care was used to keep the mixing uniform to prevent low-fertility spots from developing after a few seasons. Composting changed the hardpan into a mellow, easily workable soil with texture fine enough for grass seeding.

[37]

There has been a crying need in that area for lawns that can survive dust storms, excessive heat, insect infestation and 60 mile an hour winds with only a minor amount of watering, and often none.

Many cities have been forced to restrict or prohibit entirely the watering of lawns. Water conservation in the area has come in for national attention, and Kansas is one of the midwestern states asking for federal assistance to stop wind erosion. Lawns have become expendable in the face of drought emergency, but Roy Clark's drought-resistant lawn is living proof that the problem can be licked with organic methods.

CHAPTER II

What Is a Lawn?

A LAWN is more than a collection of grass plants. It is also something other than grass plants cut short. It is made up of grass, primarily, but so is a pasture. It is mowed at intervals, but so is a hay field. Webster's dictionary says it is "ground covered by fine grass kept closely mown." L. H. Bailey is more specific in *Hortus,* where he defines it as "an area of the landscape carpeted with a greensward designed as a foundation setting for buildings," etc. According to Bailey, the greensward may consist of grasses, usually perennial, or ground cover plants. Webster is not so lenient. He says that greensward is a "cover of green grass." Fine grass, presumably. Perhaps it is the texture of the grass that makes a lawn. Or perhaps it is one of the following considerations advanced by Heinrich Meyer:

1. Lawns are a cultivated crop. Lawns are an artificial enterprise that has no counterpart anywhere in nature.

2. Lawns owe their quality to vegetative rather than sexual reproduction.

3. Lawns must stay put, while grasses in nature can migrate.

Rarely do gardeners and house owners stop to think what makes a lawn such a unique enterprise and rarely do they, therefore, reap the rewards for their efforts and expenditures; for, let that be understood, there is no costlier crop than a lawn. It produces neither food nor flowers, but it must be watered and mowed, it must be trimmed and fertilized like no other crop.

Under natural conditions, grasses grow and form meadows and mats and carpets. These grasses are interspersed with different plant species, so that to each plant of grass a relatively large territory is allotted. Here, the various plants, including the grasses, attain flowers and produce seeds. These seeds propagate the species in question while, at the same time, a moderate amount of asexual expansion takes place through runners which set up new plants with flowers and seeds. The residues from these plants stay on the spot and produce a natural fertilizer. But if the soil should gradually change, the grasses can move on and find unexplored and undepleted land. For their seeds spread and their runners run. Yet, all these natural processes must not take place in a lawn.

Here we want a dense mat of grasses only, possibly with a slight admixture of clovers. We cannot allot much space to the individual plant, because we want a dense stand. It can immediately be seen that this in turn determines the need for watering and fertilization. For while the dense stand shades the soil and checks evaporation, the numbers of plants to be lushly supported (on a relatively small space for each individual) requires top-most fertility and under average conditions, additional watering.

We cannot permit lawn grasses to go to seed because we are not interested in grass flowers, beautiful and interesting and variable though these may be; we want the utmost of vegetative growth. It is well known to thoughtful plant physiologists that there is a constant conflict between vegetative and reproductive processes. If you allow a plant to go to seed, if you permit another generation to develop, the mother plant may have completed all or part of its job. It will cease growing, it may even die. If you prevent it from flowering and seeding by constant cutting or mowing, you force the plant individual to spread itself, as if it had the secret idea of an escape. It will send out shoots and runners, it will expand itself by vegetative regeneration. True enough, these offsets are part of the same plant, even if ultimately they cease to be connected with the mother stock; but

[41]

the new plants to all intents are complete and could reproduce themselves. But we will oppose this most eminent urge, because we want a lawn.

Everyone who has a big lawn knows of the task that trimming the edges may involve. And if he does not do the tedious job himself, he knows of the time it takes when he pays the bill. Let us look at this bill from a botanical angle! The grasses merely follow the natural urge that has made them the most common plant on earth, they follow their migratory need. They want to escape competition with other grasses and get to where the perennial border or the lusty beds of annuals seem to enjoy their territory so exclusively.

Grasses are among the most reproductive plants, and at the same time, among the most boldly suckering and self-perpetuating beings. If given half a chance, they throw out runners—not to perpetuate the kind, but to perpetuate the individual. This fine habit helps them along. They can intrude quickly and then take over with persistency. But do we let them follow this ingrained urge? On the contrary, we trim the edges and force the lawn to stay put. Monoculture at its peak!

Grass—What a Life Saver!

When most folks think of grass, they immediately think of a lawnmower. Of course the making of a lawn is an important use of grass. On an acreage basis, however, more grass is eaten by livestock than is mowed by lawnmowers. When a cow eats grass, she makes either milk or meat for us.

It may be truthfully said that all animals eat grass in one form or another. Those animals that don't eat grass directly, live on other animals which do eat grass.

The value of grass was first recognized when savage men hunted wild game to eat. Many of the large animals eaten by man were grass eaters. Our American Indians also obtained their food by killing bison, deer, elk, moose, and other grass-eating animals.

In olden times people had flocks and herds of domestic animals. These people drove their herds and flocks of goats, sheep, and cattle before them —always in search of nutritious grass. In the summer the Nomads drove their animals higher and higher into the mountains in search of grass as it became green in the spring. In the fall as snow flurries dominated the weather and grass became more scarce, the herds and flocks were driven to lower elevations for protection from the severe climate. In many parts of the world today, including areas in western United States this same nomadic practice is carried out.

Dependence on grass as a source of food for livestock is perhaps even greater today in the Atomic Age than it has been in all ages past. At least we have more cattle depending upon grass. Now, however, in the world, stockmen improve the grasses by scientific management. On improved pastures high quality animals have access to nutritious grazing at all times without the necessity of transferring the herds from place to place.

GRASS — GUARDIAN OF WATER

One way that grass conserves water is by hastening the movement of rainwater into the soil. Experiments near Guthrie, Oklahoma, showed that 30 inches, or 98 per cent, of the annual precipitation went into the soil when the cover was native grass. This corresponds to 26 inches of precipitation that soaked into the soil under cultivated and terraced conditions.

Grasslands are very effective in increasing infiltration of water into the soil. They also permit runoff water to flow over watersheds without eroding the soil. This protection results in clean water and prevents siltation of the reservoir. In contrast, forests encourage more water to enter the soil and less to flow over the surface as runoff. Grasslands generally yield more surface runoff than do forests on comparable land. For that reason, grass usually is the better watershed cover for areas which drain into reservoirs.

There's more in praise of grass. It protects bare soil from the beating raindrops and shades the soil from excessive heating by the sun. Another important function is to furnish food for earthworms and insects whose burrows permit the soil to "breathe" and "drink" more freely. Holes made in the ground by worms, insects, and grass roots, increase the amount and rate of water entering the soil. Some of the water is stored in the soil for use by plants. That reserve supply of soil moisture enables plants to withstand dry weather. Another portion of the water which enters the soil percolates deeper and increases the supply of ground water. Some of the ground water emerges as springs and some raises the water level in wells.

Probably no crops grown in the United States have more conservation uses or more all-around value than do the grasses. Grasses protect land from wind and water erosion and maintain or improve soil quality. In addition the same grasses produce pasture and hay. Grasses are being seeded to restore badly eroded land to useful production, to heal gullies, to prevent damage by runoff water on steep slopes, and to line waterways so that excess water from cultivated fields can be disposed of without erosion.

Grass shelters the bacteria, molds, fungi, and the unknown sources of life in the top few inches of the earth's surface. Live grass roots bring minerals to the topsoil and let water soak into the subsoil. Dead grass roots are even more effective as water channels. Grass is a most important link in the miracle of life's chain. It is the pipe line through which flow the minerals, proteins, and carbohydrates from soil to animals and man.

Grass provides our table with nutritious steaks and life-giving milk. Grass also carpets and cushions the soil against violent winds and lashing rains. Yes, grass is indeed a life-saver; it helps to save your life and mine.

A CLOSEUP OF GRASS

Here are a few technical terms that will help you understand the way grasses grow.

sheath—the part which encloses the stem.

blade—the part above the sheath.

collar—the area on the outer side of the leaf at the junction of the sheath and blade.

ligule—the thin appendage or ring of hairs inside the leaf at the collar.

culm—the jointed grass stem.

node—joint of the stem.

internode—the part of the stem between two nodes.

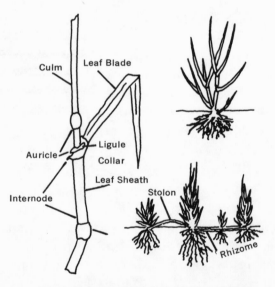

Credit: Dr. Jess L. Fults, Colorado State College

Diagrams showing the parts of a grass (left) and the growth habits of bunch grasses (top right) and sod forming grasses (bottom right).

[46]

rhizome—an underground stem.

stolon—a propagative stem creeping above ground with roots at the nodes.

decumbent stem—a stem which curves upward from a horizontal or inclined base.

A brief explanation of the way grass grows is given by Dr. Jess L. Fults, Head of the Botany Department at Colorado State University, as follows:

Growth in grass is unlike that in trees or herbs of a higher order, but they all have this in common—pruning stimulates new growth. When you mow your grass, you are pruning it, and within limits, it will respond by the development of new buds and shoots. But there is a limit to how close and how frequent clipping can be done without starving the plant to death. The function of the grass leaf, like that of any other plant, is to manufacture food for the use of the whole plant. Too frequent or too close clipping of the top may interfere with that function. Turf grasses are selected because they will endure closer and more frequent mowing than most other plants because their growth is localized at the base. But they differ in the amounts of clipping they can take and still remain vigorous.

Lengthwise growth of a grass stem takes place between nodes. If a corn plant (which is a grass) a few inches tall is dissected and viewed under a microscope, it is possible to see all the joints that

[47]

will be present when the plant is fully mature. The same is true of many other grasses.

Grass leaves grow in length at the base rather than equally throughout, as is true in most other kinds of plants. This character allows the leaves of good turf grass to be renewed continually in spite of repeated clipping. Few if any of the leaves of our perennial turf grasses live over winter. Most new growth starts in the spring from previously formed buds at the basal nodes.

Grasses may be annuals, germinating, seeding and dying in a single season, like the annual brome grasses, crab grass or green bristle grass. Or they may be perennials, the individual grasses living several years and seeding year after year. The perennial grasses are of 3 basic types—bunch grasses, sod formers with rhizomes and sod formers with stolons.

Whether a given grass is a bunch grass or a sod-forming grass depends on the manner in which new shoots grow from the basal buds. If new shoots grow up inside the sheath of the previous stem growth, the result is a bunch grass such as crested wheatgrass or ryegrass. If the new shoots push through the sheath and run along the surface of the ground followed by rooting at the nodes, the result is a sod-forming grass like creeping bent. If the new shoots run along under the surface followed by repeated shoot and root formation underground, the result is a sod-forming grass such as Kentucky bluegrass (rhizomatous).

[48]

There are, of course, some intermediate types with decumbent stems that root at the nodes. Some of the creeping red fescues and nimblewill, a weedy grass that gets into bluegrass lawns are intermediate types.

The "openness" or "tightness" of a turf is partly determined by mowing, fertilizing and watering practices. Basically it is a matter of the length of the internodes of the rhizomes or stolons and the number of buds which are formed. Long internodes, such as are found in western wheatgrass, make for an open sod; short internodes and many basal buds, such as are found in Kentucky bluegrass, make for a tight sod.

GRASS IS EASY ON THE EARDRUMS

You may want to plant more grass to cut down neighborhood noises. A recent study by the Riverbank Acoustical Laboratories in Geneva, Ill., revealed that it's a highly efficient absorber of sound. The use of grass and foliage for their acoustical properties is seldom considered because they are known to be poor sound barriers. This may be an oversight, according to William Siekman, manager of Riverbank. Their test found grass—and trees to a lesser extent—are good sound absorbers, even though they are not effective sound barriers.

"Our study indicates that grass would be useful as a sound-absorbing material in closed areas such as courtyards," Siekman said.

[49]

Before measurements were made, the grass was trimmed to two-inch length, a standard height for lawns. The sod was saturated with water to remove any acoustical effect due to the earth, insuring true results. The examination also included evaluating the sound-absorbing qualities of Canadian balsam firs, commonly used as Christmas trees, and found they possess enough to merit further study.

According to Siekman, one reason people enjoy being in parks and forests is that the grass and trees cause a soothing change in everyday sounds, such as children playing.

CHAPTER III

Lawns of Many Kinds

A LAWN can become a complicated and dynamic thing that can take different forms to serve different purposes, so it is as well to be clear at the outset just what it is you want. For example, do you want a lawn to rival a putting green and perhaps actually to be used as such, or a piece of grass to show off the flower borders? Will it be much used, or mainly looked at? Above all, how much time are you prepared to devote caring for it?

It is necessary to know all these things and some others as well before one even begins to choose the grasses with which the lawn will be made. If it is to be the finest of fine lawns with a billiard-table surface, it must be made of slow-growing, narrow-leaved grasses such as the fescues and bents. These grasses also need the most attention since they are slow to germinate, are easily invaded by weeds and are intolerant of poorly drained soils.

At the other extreme, lawns made of perennial ryegrass or smooth-stalked meadow grass — which is sometimes known as Kentucky bluegrass — will grow rapidly in any reasonable soil and give a good green carpet of grass. Their main drawback is that they do not like frequent hard mowing and cannot therefore be made into really smooth lawns.

Then there is rough-stalked meadow grass, which grows well in places too shady for many other grasses, crested dogstail, which survives even on poor chalky soils, and timothy, which stands a lot of hard wear.

There is no need to become an expert on grasses or to attempt to sow particular kinds even if they could be obtained separately, which usually is not possible. The best lawns are nearly always made from mixtures of grasses and not from one kind of grass, but it is as well to know that these different grasses exist and that the seedsmen make use of them in preparing lawn seed mixtures for particular purposes. Some clearly state what grasses are in each mixture and in what proportions. It is a pity that more do not adopt this practice.

But seed is not the only way in which a lawn can be produced. You can do it much more quickly by laying sod, and possibly more cheaply by treating the natural grass of the site, though it is by no means certain this will save money in the long run.

There is also the possibility of planting sections of creeping grass turf and leaving them to spread over the site, but that takes time and does not always result in the type of lawn that is desired.

The major difficulty with sod is to get good pieces that contain the right grasses for the kind of lawn you want to make. If they are simply cut from a meadow or a building site, it is improbable that they will contain the best lawn grasses, but some turf contractors now grow their own turf from seed, and that can be very satisfactory. Area for area, turf is a good deal more expensive than grass seed, and that may prove the decisive factor.

If one decides to make do with the grass that happens to be growing on the site, there is the same problem that it may contain undesirable grasses, but at least they will be grasses that naturally grow well in that particular place. Mowing can make a difference to the grass composition of a lawn after a year or so, because if it is close and frequent the coarser grasses will tend to die out and the finer grasses will take over, while less-severe mowing will have the opposite effect.

Don't forget to consider the problem of levels. Field grass left by builders is seldom level. That may not matter much if the garden is to be planned informally, perhaps with irregular areas of grass between beds of shrubs and perennials, but in most small gardens that is not the case. Small hollows can be filled in gradually with top-dressings of peat and soil worked in with a rake and broom, but there is a limit to what can be done in that way. The only remedy for large irregularities is to strip off all the turf, level the underlying soil with spade, fork and rake and then relay the turf. And that can be a big operation.

The major drawback to growing a lawn from turf, apart from the fact that it may take several months to get a complete cover, is that only a few creeping grasses are suitable and those tend to make rather lush, springy lawns that cannot be mown closely. Some form of creeping bent, *Agrostis stolonifera,* is often used but it varies greatly in the fineness of its leaves and the type of turf it produces. It is therefore important to get a really good variety. Moreover, it roots very close to the surface, sometimes right on the surface, which makes it rather susceptible to drought and easily damaged by careless mowing.

All in all, there is nothing to beat a lawn made from a good seed mixture chosen to suit the site and the purpose for which the lawn is required.

One of the best ways to build up poor soil where you want a strong foundation for permanent lawn growth is with green manure—an inexpensive cover crop that does a concentrated job of incorporating plenty of needed humus. Start with a winter rye or wheat crop sown any time from early September to mid-October. Turn this under in the spring and follow it with a planting of soybeans, barley, vetch or clover, dug in during late summer when it's in a succulent, bacteria-stimulating stage.

Of course, with access to enough organic materials, the basis for a fine lawn can be built more quickly, but the green-manure technique is a sound, economic way.

Temporary Grasses and Their Uses

Temporary grasses are those which do not make permanent sods because they are short lived. However, they usually are cheap and provide pure stands until the seeding date arrives for planting the desired permanent grass. Annual or Italian ryegrass lends itself to such use better than other species. It has a wide tolerance of extremes, and as a seedling is more aggressive.

It will grow when seeded as late as mid-November, or even later if the weather remains mild. If it does not germinate soon after seeding, it will do so early in spring. An early spring or summer seeding will carry over until time for a September seeding of a cool season permanent grass.

A late fall seeding can be followed by a May to July planting of a warm season grass, in which case the entire lawn must usually be ripped up and replanted.

GRASSES FOR PARTIAL SHADE

Although bentgrass is normally considered suitable for a sunny lawn, it also does well in some shade. But bentgrass in full sun is more subject to

[55]

disease than when under shade. This disease problem can be controlled, but the treatment is not practical for the average homeowner. Bentgrass also is very susceptible to the sod webworm, more so in the sun than under shade. Bentgrass is recommended for use in lawns with partial shade, and at elevations of 1,500 feet or more.

RED FESCUES

Red fescues are not tolerant to sun in southern areas. The problem is complicated because most shady lawns are not uniformly shaded. A mixture of Kentucky bluegrass and red fescue to solve such a problem usually results in a thinning of both species because they are not compatible. The answer may be to seed the shady lawn to red fescue only, then the following September seed the thinned areas to bluegrass or bent.

Red fescue seedlings are vigorous. The seed can be planted in the fall or spring with equally good results. Recommended varieties are Pennlawn, Illahee and Chewing's. Ranier is now making a good showing. All are in the seed trade.

Like bentgrasses, red fescues are tolerant to a wide range of soil conditions, but are more easily starved or thinned by low fertility or excessive competition by trees on which they depend for shade. They must be fertilized regularly, clipped high and watered. When the sod is thinned by improper management, it does not heal.

[56]

PLAYGROUNDS, BANKS AND TRAFFIC AREAS

There is an increasing need for specialized turf areas, such as athletic fields, playgrounds, public building grounds, parkways, fairways, cemetery and highway rights-of-way. The basic needs of all grasses used on such areas are covered in this publication. The basic recommendations apply to all types of turf, except to golf greens. There is always a grass best for any situation.

The factors to consider in grass selection should include degree of traffic, slope, light intensity, nature of soil, desired appearance, clipping height and exposure. The characteristics of each grass must be understood to make the proper choice. For example, tall fescue for a football field is a mistake because it requires a high clip. But tall fescue, as well as Common Bermudagrass, is well adapted to heavy traffic areas and playgrounds. Common Bermudagrass is the best for football and baseball fields.

However, no one can anticipate what the constitution of your lawn might be in the future. An insect or disease which previously was harmless may become a problem from one season to the next. A sunny lawn may ultimately be a shady one, or a shady one may suddenly become sunny. In either case the lawn may have to be renovated and a different grass established. Here is a general classification of lawngrasses as recommended by the Tennessee Agricultural Extension Service:

[57]

Classification of Lawngrasses

I. Temporary species

A. Winter annuals (sun or shade)
1. **Italian ryegrass***
2. **Balbo rye**

B. Summer annuals
1. **German millet (Useful under special conditions)**

II. Perennial species and varieties

A. Cool season grasses
1. **Colonial bentgrass,** *Agrostis tenuis* (sun or shade)
   Astoria
   Highland
   Rhode Island

2. **Creeping bentgrass,** *Agrostis palustris* (sun or shade)
   Penncross
   Seaside (Start both from seed. Vegetatively produced varieties are unadapted.)

3. **Velvet bentgrass**
   Kernwood
   Piper
   Raritan

4. **Kentucky bluegrass,** *Poa pratensis* (sun and partial shade)
   Arboretum* (Missouri)
   Common* (Kentucky and Missouri grown)
   Delta (Canada)
   Merion (Pennsylvania)
   Newport or C-I*
   Park (Minnesota)
   Windsor (Ohio)
   (All European strains are unadapted.)

5. **Rough-stalk bluegrass,** *Poa trivialis* (shade)

6. **Red fescue,** *Festuca rubra* (all shady lawn)

   *Recommended for the habitat that it is best suited.

[58]

Chewing's* (bunch type)
Columbia County (creeping red)
Illahee* (creeping red)
Olds (creeping red, Canada)
Pennlawn* (creeping red)
Oregon (creeping red)
Quebec (creeping red, Canada)
Rainier (creeping red, Oregon)
Trinity (creeping red)
(All European strains are unadapted.)

7. **Meadow fescue or English bluegrass,** *Festuca elatior*

8. **Tall fescue,** *Festuca elatior* var. *arundinacea*
   Alta fescue*
   Kentucky 31 fescue* (both sunny and partial shade)

B. **Warm season grasses**

   1. **Bermudagrass,** *Cynodon dactylon* and other species (all sunny
      lawn)
      African*
      Common* (Unmixed with NK-37—a very coarse, very aggres-
      sive variety)
      Everglade No. 1
      Genetift* (Bayshore)
      Ormond
      Sunturf*
      Texturf*
      Tiffine
      Tifgreen* (328)
      Tiflawn
      Tifway*
      U-3*
      Uganda

   2. **Zoysiagrass** (all sunny or partial shade)
      *Z. japonica** (Japanese lawngrass)
      Meyer 52*
      *Z. matrella** (Manilagrass)
      Z. tenuifolia (Mascarenegrass)
      Emerald* (Japanese lawngrass x Mascarenegrass—hybrid)

   3. **St. Augustinegrass** *(Stenotaphrum secundatum)*

   4. **Carpetgrass** *(Axonopus compressus)*

   5. **Centipedegrass** *(Eremochloa ophiuroides)*

[59]

Grass Zones

A grass zone map would show 5 big growing areas in the country. Most important to the lawn is the dividing line which runs from east to west — the Bluegrass Line.

Dr. Ralph E. Engel, research specialist of the

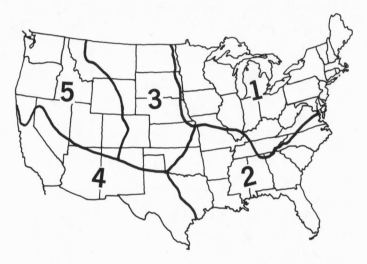

Credit: Crops Research Division, USDA

Map showing regions of the United States in which the following grasses are suitable for lawns: 1 and 5 — Colonial bentgrass, common Kentucky bluegrass, Merion Kentucky bluegrass, red fescue, Chewing's fescue; limited areas: Bermudagrass, Meyer zoysia. 2 — Bermudagrass, zoysia grasses; limited areas: carpetgrass, centipedegrass, St. Augustinegrass, common Kentucky bluegrass, Merion Kentucky bluegrass. 3 — Nonirrigated areas: blue gramagrass, buffalograss, crested wheatgrass; irrigated areas: common Kentucky bluegrass, Merion Kentucky bluegrass. 4 — Bermudagrass, zoysia grasses; limited areas: common Kentucky bluegrass, Merion Kentucky bluegrass, Chewing's fescue, red fescue.

[60]

Agricultural Experiment Station at Rutgers University, New Jersey, in reviewing the importance of the Bluegrass Line, has this to say:

"The line indicates the transition regions between the cool-season grass area of the northern United States where Kentucky bluegrass usually dominates and the warm-season grass region where Bermudagrass dominates in the South. The imaginary line is not a sharp dividing zone; either type of grass may be found growing 200 miles north or south of it, according to local conditions and needs."

But essentially, bluegrass is the dominant lawn strain north of the line and Bermudagrass is the main lawn grass in the Deep South.

Zones 1 and 5 favor the growth of the same grasses: colonial bents, common Kentucky bluegrass, also the Merion Kentucky bluegrass, the red fescues and the Chewings fescue. Bermudagrass and the Meyer zoysia can be grown in certain limited areas

As those residing in the Deep South know, the Bermudagrasses prevail there, also the zoysia. In limited areas, carpetgrass, centipedegrass, St. Augustinegrass do well, also the common and Merion Kentucky bluegrasses.

Moisture assumes real importance in the Great Plains—Zone 3—where only the two bluegrass strains can be grown in the irrigated sections. In the nonirrigated areas, plant blue gramagrass, hardy buffalograss and crested wheatgrass.

[61]

In Zone 4—the Southwest—Bermudagrass and the zoysia have a good chance of success. In limited areas with great care try the bluegrasses, Chewing's fescue and red fescue.

Adaptation of the proper grass to the climate is most important. Dr. Engel stresses that a good rule to follow is "to avoid taking a grass too far from its natural growing area." Neglect of this principle may "not always lead to failure, but it makes lawn culture unnecessarily difficult."

Choosing a grass in the middle latitudes (near the Bluegrass Line) may be "confusing," he notes. Because "elevation, turf need, soil conditions and maintenance potential influence the choice in this region where neither the cool-season nor the warm-season grasses are ideal at all times. If conditions are very severe (cold rather than hot), winter-hardy warm-season grasses" should do better than other varieties.

Bluegrass Line lawns may be seeded and planted with both summer-and-winter-growing grasses, if the preferences of both are considered. J. K. Underwood at the University of Tennessee Agricultural Experiment Station recommends that the following rules be observed:

Although incompatibility is the usual thing among grasses, there are exceptions. Pure Bermudagrass sod soon gets infested with winter annuals such as chickweed, henbit, field pansy and speedwells. It is therefore advisable to overseed with a hardy base grass such as bluegrass before the weed

[62]

seeds germinate in the fall. Bluegrass and bent have a different growing season from Bermudagrass and, therefore, are compatible with it. Using Italian ryegrass on Bermuda sod is permissible, but this requires reseeding every fall. The use of perennial ryegrass is not recommended because it thins out during the first summer after seeding.

The zoysias, like Bermudagrass, die back with frost. However, zoysia sod is so dense that results of overseeding are not as good as on Bermuda sod.

To overseed Bermuda and zoysia sods, clip them 1 inch high or less in August or early September, rake clean, and then seed bluegrass immediately. Overseed at one and one-half times the regular seeding rates. Water the seeding as previously directed. Continue clipping at the 1 inch height until the Bermudagrass stops growth in late October. Then raise the mower to 2-3 inches.

CHAPTER IV

After the Builders Leave

The Right Spot for Your Lawn

As a FUTURE home builder, you're likely to give ample consideration to picking your building plot to the standard factors—schools, churches, transportation and neighbors to your liking. You'll also want to consider how your house is going to fit on the lot and how much room will be left to create the kind of surroundings you like. And in planning that home environment, give the consideration right in the beginning to the lawn.

For instance, you'll want to be sure that your piece of ground has the right exposure, elevation, soil and contour for your lawn plus adequate wa-

[64]

ter. The house must be the center of your property, but the lawn will be its setting and should be encumbered as little as possible by drives and walks and be as large as conditions permit. You'll get that type of a lawn by planning well in advance. In fact, if you can completely lay out your lawn roughly in outline form a year before the building contractors arrive, you'll be extremely fortunate.

No hard and fast rules can be given to apply to all properties, when landscaping plans are made except this: *make a plan*. Make a minute plan in which all elevations, plantings, and uses and preferences are considered. Make your *own* plans —do not attempt to copy another. It will never work. No two plots are exactly alike, even in developments where houses are all the same and bulldozers have leveled the landscape. And no two families have the same needs, or the same gardening appetite or ability.

If your house is already built, you can still do a fine job of relating site, house and landscape, but with greater difficulty than if both were planned before building begins. Sometimes with a little alteration of the house itself, plus renovation of the home grounds, an old house in an outmoded style can be modernized and its aspects can be completely altered. But you need very careful planning to achieve such effects.

Perhaps you already have natural trees on your

[65]

property and intend to save some of them. Be sure
to plan which ones will remain and protect them
from the ravenous appetite of bulldozers and
earth movers.

When the bulldozers do come in, have them
move 4 to 6 inches of topsoil from the entire
building area and push it into a corner for replacement over the lawn after the building is completed. For that topsoil has organic matter, bacteria and available nutrients which will produce better lawns than basement excavation material. The
old rocky or clay fill can be used to establish and
provide lawn shape and give any slopes you feel
your lawn contour may need. Haul away all the
extra unneeded fill. In preparing the contours of
the lawn, try if possible to have a sagging slope
from the building to the grades of the adjacent
property and sidewalks or road. That means terraces are out unless the slope has more than one
foot fall in each 16 feet of distance. Terraces reduce the appearance size of the lawn and require
much more maintenance. And the turf on a terrace is usually poorest and most quickly noticed.
Remember that slopes which are fairly steep will
need approximately 20 to 30 per cent of a fast
germinating timberly grass in the mixture to hold
the soil. Annual or perennial ryegrass may be
used. For steep slopes the best fescue to use is
creeping red fescue rather than Chewing fescue.
It's a good idea to cover the slope directly after

seeding with salt marsh hay, regular hay (it carries weed seed, however), or with used tobacco cloth or other coarse mesh cloth, such as cheesecloth. Peg it down here and there to hold it. Usually if it is left in place it will rot away in a season or two. If burlap is used, it must be removed as soon as the seed germinates. Otherwise, it will smother the seedlings.

If your home site requires a major change in grade, make it on the subsoil. The topsoil having been pushed aside opens up the subsoil for a change. Here you can see if subdrainage problems exist. If they do, perhaps they can be eliminated by the use of tile drains.

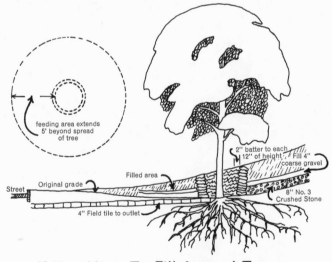

feeding area extends
5' beyond spread
of tree

2" batter to each
12" of height
Fill 4"
coarse gravel

Filled area

Street
Original grade

8" No. 3
Crushed Stone

4" Field tile to outlet

If You Have To Fill Around Trees

If fills are made, provide extra drainage and air to the old roots of trees.

[67]

Surface drainage is taken care of during grading. Always try to slope the grade away from the dwelling. The slope of the finished topsoil grade should be no less than a two inch drop in 100 feet. In preparing that final grade, more topsoil should be brought in if needed. Rake out any debris.

If the existing soil is very sandy in texture, the addition of native peat or peat moss will increase its water-holding capacity. Do not allow that organic matter to form layers. Mix it thoroughly with the top soil. That preliminary grading need not be table smooth, since fertilizer has yet to be spread and worked in. However, it is advantageous to add and work in your lime and phosphate at that time, since those should be incorporated into the upper 4 to 5 inches of topsoil.

CHAPTER V

Seeding the New Lawn

THOROUGH PREPARATION is the secret of success with many gardening operations and never more so than in the seeding of a new lawn. A lawn is a permanent feature and, once established, it is very difficult to do anything about it if the site has been badly prepared. Often it has to withstand a lot of hard wear and in many instances much misuse if children are about. So give it a really good start by paying careful attention to all stages of preparation.

Perhaps the first step is to consider the best time to seed a new lawn. In the North it is best to seed a new lawn from late August to late October, because grasses grow in the cool weather of fall and become well established before spring. If the lawn is to be a mixture of grasses and clover, such a mixture can be purchased. Some persons plant clover in the following spring. The inclusion of clover will make a heavy cover and inhibit the growth of quack grass but it also stains children's clothes and attracts bees and other insects.

Some definite advantages of fall seeding include:

1. The warm soil, adequate rainfall, and cool nights combine to establish an ideal growing condition for lawngrasses.

2. Fall-sown grasses root more deeply. Also the plants tend to stool more freely and thus produce a thicker, healthier sod. Fall-grown plants develop more extensive root systems and are thus able to better withstand dry, hot weather of the summer months.

3. Fall is a dormant period for weeds. During their inactivity, the lawngrasses have a chance to establish themselves without the competition of weeds.

4. The soil can be more easily prepared in the fall than in the spring. In the spring the soil is usually too wet to prepare in time to give the lawn grasses a start ahead of the weeds. Also spring soil is so cold that the seeds will germinate more slowly than in the warm soil in the fall.

LAWN GROWTH CYCLES

MARCH		APRIL		MAY		JUNE		JULY		AUGUST		SEPTEMBER		OCTOBER
15	1	15	1	15	1	15	1	15	1	15	1	15	1	15

WHEN DOES YOUR GRASS GROW BEST?

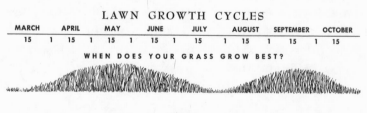

Timing is an important consideration in lawn seeding. Because grasses are cool weather plants, they grow fastest during the cool-moist months of spring and fall. From late June until mid-August they tend to become dormant. By planting in the fall the grass will have two favorable periods of growth—fall and spring—before it has to fight off the summer heat.

Selecting a Seed Mixture

WHY MIXTURES?

It is common knowledge that a good sod of a single grass is more uniform and thus usually more attractive than a sod composed of several species. Why then do we use mixtures? R. R. Davis of the Ohio Agricultural Research Center discusses below some of the "reasons," real or imaginary.

1. "A mixture has a wider adaptation to soil and climate conditions than a single grass." This is a legitimate reason for mixtures if we don't know local conditions and have no means of modifying the climate such as irrigation. With additional information about the capabilities of the grass, soil characteristics, fertilizer requirements and a good irrigation system, this reason for using a mixture largely disappears.

2. "A mixture has more tolerance to pests—dis-

[71]

eases, insects, weeds." There is no doubt that varieties of Kentucky bluegrass and other species have different reactions to diseases caused by fungi. Merion Kentucky bluegrass, for example, is well known for its resistance to melting out (*Helminthosporium vagans*) and its susceptibility to stripe smut, rust and powdery mildew. Common Kentucky bluegrass and many named varieties have a reverse reaction to these diseases. A pure stand of Merion is not recommended because of the strip smut problem. However, Merion blended with other varieties of bluegrass can make a very valuable contribution to the sod. Merion's aggressive nature makes it inclined to "take over" but other bluegrasses appear to remain in the sod where only 10-15 per cent Merion is used in the seed mixture. Red fescue is often used with bluegrass and the two are somewhat inclined to mask each other's weaknesses. The problem here may be too much aggression on the part of the red fescue.

Any problem that weakens the sod is an invitation to weeds. In this indirect manner, a mixture or blend may be more resistant to weed invasion.

3. "A mixture makes a good sod sooner after seeding." It is no secret that Kentucky bluegrass is slower in emergence and seedling growth than the ryegrasses, fescues, and redtop. This is particularly true with a spring seeding. There are at least two reasons other than impatience for wanting a quick cover, (a) beat the summer annual weeds

A good bluegrass mixture will produce the fine-textured permanent turf seen to the right, whereas the "cheap" mixtures so often an ill-advised "bargain" contain coarse weedy grasses such as are pictured planted to the left. It is usually best to avoid ryegrass and tall fescue in a seed mixture in favor of the various bluegrasses and fine-leaved fescues.

[73]

that are sure to come with spring seedings and/or
(b) lessen the danger of erosion on steep slopes.
With late summer and fall seedings, annual weeds
are not a serious problem. Both mechanical and
chemical aids for erosion control can be used to
hold the soil until grass appears if judgment dic-
tates that the fast-growing grasses should be omit-
ted.

4. "Seed cost is less when using a mixture."
Large grass seed, i.e., ryegrass, tall fescue, red fescue, cost less per pound than Kentucky bluegrass
or bentgrass. Cost per unit area is another matter
since less weight of the small seed is needed for a
stand. At any rate, selecting grasses based on seed
cost is poor economy that can be very expensive in
the long run.

WHAT GOES INTO A MIXTURE?

Bentgrass quickly dominates any grass commonly
seeded with it if given water, fertilizer and short
mowing. When mowed two inches high, bentgrass
moves slower against the other grasses but still
dominates. Too bad it is not able to keep *Poa annua*
out of fairways and greens without skillful management! Fortunately, packagers of lawn seed
have heeded experimental results and the practice
of putting a small percentage of bentgrass in lawn
mixtures is largely history. Unfortunately, many
homeowners must live with past mistakes.

Ryegrass starts most rapidly of the grasses com-

[74]

monly used in mixtures. It seriously competes with the slower grasses in the mixture. In fact, if a mixture contains a high percentage of ryegrass seed, the ryegrass will nearly eliminate the other grasses. Annual or domestic ryegrass is usually short lived and may leave the sod very thin when it suddenly goes. The thin sod is an open invitation for a weed invasion. There are usually enough perennial types in ryegrass seed lots to leave a few unsightly clumps that remain for years. Their course texture and the whitish cast (due to the inability of the mower to cut the tough fiber cleanly) are constant eyesores.

Common Kentucky Bluegrass is the most widely used lawngrass. It is well adapted to good soils in full sunshine and grows well even on a low fertility program. The grass cuts easily but needs frequent mowing in the spring, particularly if it is well fertilized. It is probably the best all-around grass. Leaf spot diseases may cause severe damage in the late spring, but it is moderately resistant to most other diseases. Since this grass is a cool-season grass, it tends to become dormant and brown-off during the hot dry mid-summer months.

Merion Kentucky Bluegrass is a high quality bluegrass that requires a high level of fertility and good management. Merion needs almost twice as much fertilizer as Common Kentucky bluegrass. It will withstand closer mowing than Common Kentucky bluegrass. When properly managed, it produces a dense sod which resists weed invasion.

[75]

Merion is highly resistant to leaf spot diseases, but it is susceptible to dollar spot, rust, stripe smut and certain soil-borne diseases, especially when poorly managed.

Windsor, Park, Delta, and Newport Kentucky Bluegrass have not been outstanding, despite the many claims for their superiority over other bluegrasses. They vary in susceptibility to diseases, summer injury, etc. The mediocre performance of these varieties does not justify the current high cost of the seed when they are compared to Merion and Common Kentucky bluegrasses.

Red Fescues (Pennlawn, Illahee, creeping red, and Chewing's) are good grasses for shady areas with droughty soils. They are fine textured, have bristly leaves, and produce dense sod in moderate shade. Red fescues cannot take much watering or heavy nitrogen fertilization and will not tolerate mowing below 1½ inches. Pennlawn is probably the best variety for most areas. It tolerates leaf spot diseases while the other red fescues may be severely injured by it. All are creeping types except Chewing's, which is a bunch type.

Tall Fescue is a coarse perennial grass. It tolerates a wide variation of soil and shade conditions. Because of its coarseness, it is not generally recommended for lawns. However, when seeded at a heavy rate, it produces excellent turf for play areas, athletic fields and utility areas. It is very resistant to wear. Tall fescue is a bunch type grass and should be mixed with a creeping type such as bluegrass or red fescue. Kentucky 31 is a better variety than Alta for most areas.

Roughstalk Bluegrass (Poa trivialis) is ideal for wet, shaded areas. It will not tolerate full sun and may disappear during the summer.

Bentgrass should not be used for lawns in Maryland and nearby states except in unusual cases. They are fine textured perennial grasses that are not shade tolerant and may be severely injured by diseases. Maintenance requirements are extremely high. Two types can be found — Colonial (bunch type) and creeping.

Redtop is a fast-germinating, short-lived perennial bunch grass. Although it is often used in seed mixtures as a companion grass to provide quick coverage and protection for the slower permanent grasses, it provides unwanted competition for the desirable grasses. No more than five per cent redtop should be included in the seed mixture if an area must be seeded in late summer or spring.

Ryegrass is a fast growing bunch grass that may be annual, perennial, or a combination of both. It may be used as a temporary cover for desirable grasses planted out of season but could smother the permanent grasses. Mixtures should never contain more than five per cent ryegrass. This seed is usually the major component of cheap seed mixtures. Ryegrass can be seeded alone as a temporary cover as discussed previously.

Zoysias are perennial grasses which should be established from plants rather than seeds. You may buy planting material in the form of sprigs, stolons, plugs or sod. They are excellent summer grasses for areas with full sunshine and heavy wear. The chief disadvantages are that they are slow to become established, and that they turn straw-colored with the first heavy frost and do not regain color until late spring. Four varieties are available: Meyer (Z-52), Emerald, Zoysia matrella, and Midwest. Meyer is the preferred variety in some areas. Emerald makes a slightly thicker turf but is less winter hardy. Midwest is a new variety which is coarse and fast-growing and should be used only on rough areas or where there is heavy traffic such as on athletic fields.

Zoysias require a completely different type of management than bluegrasses and fescues.

Bermudagrasses may occur naturally in some areas. Native Bermuda, often called "wiregrass," is usually found on dry soils where it is difficult to grow cool-season species such as bluegrass and red fescue. Bermudas are not shade tolerant and like zoysias, turn straw-colored with frost in the fall and remain brown until late spring.

Several varieties of improved, fine-leaved, high quality turf Bermudas are available. All Bermudas except Common must be sprigged, plugged or sodded. The best ones for use in Eastern Shore States are Tufcote and U-3. These spread rapidly and produce a high quality turf when managed properly. High rates of nitrogen are required to maintain vigorous growth and good green color.

Bermudas should be planted only in full sunlight. They are especially useful in areas which receive heavy wear. These grasses grow very fast and may invade flower gardens or your neighbors' lawns if not properly managed.

There are many other Bermudagrass varieties, including Tiflawn (57), Tifgreen (328), Tifway (419), Tifdwarf, and Sunturf which were developed in the South.

Bermudas, like zoysias, require an entirely different type of management. Generally, things such as close mowing and summer fertilization which cause failures of bluegrass lawns, are essential for Bermudas and zoysias. And such procedures as fall fertilization which are essential for bluegrasses, may prove fatal to Bermudas and zoysias.

UNDESIRABLE SPECIES FOR LAWNS

Orchardgrass is a bunchy type of grass that is very undesirable in lawns. It does not blend well with other grasses because of its color, rapid growth, broad leaves, and bunch-type growth habit.

Timothy is a fairly fast-growing grass that is undesirable in lawns because of its color, broad leaf, and bunch-type of growth. It gives a lawn a spotty appearance.

Tall Fescue has a coarse, broad leaf that is hard to cut. It grows in clumps and does not blend well with finer grasses if seeded at a light rate. It is a common component of cheap lawn mixtures. Tall fescue can be seeded at a heavy rate on problem soils that tend to remain too wet or too dry for most other grasses. In such areas a small amount of bluegrass or red fescue should be included in the mixture. When given good management and seeded heavily, such a mixture does well on athletic fields and rough areas.

When you buy lawn seed, be sure to ask for the seed best suited to your use by its correct name. Both of the above are fescues; the slender one is red fescue, the other, tall fescue.

[80]

RECOMMENDED SEED MIXTURES

Here are some recommended seed mixtures suggested by the Agricultural Research Center at Penn State University.

1. Unless otherwise indicated, all recommended seed mixtures are designed to produce permanent turf.

2. Seeding rates are in pounds per 1,000 square feet. To convert to an acre basis multiply rate given by 43.

3. For late spring and late fall seedings or for seeding on sloping areas 3 per cent redtop or 15 to 20 per cent Pelo, NK-100, or Manhattan ryegrass may be added to all lawn and heavy duty seed mixtures (Section I and II).

I. Lawn Seed Mixtures

A. Open, sunny location

1. Merion Kentucky bluegrass............ 40–65%
Kentucky bluegrass (Pennstar, ... 35–60%
Fylking, Prato, Delft, Cougar,
Campus, Newport C-1, Windsor,
Common) (Use 2 or more)
Seed at 2½–3 lbs. per 1,000 sq. ft.

2. Kentucky bluegrass (Pennstar, ... 100%
Fylking, Prato, Delft, Cougar,
Campus, Newport C-1, Windsor,
Common) (Use 3 or more)
Seed at 3–3½ lbs. per 1,000 sq. ft.

[81]

3. Pennlawn red fescue.................. 35–65%
   Kentucky bluegrass (Merion,........... 35–65%
   Pennstar, Fylking, Prato, Delft,
   Cougar, Campus, Newport C-1,
   Windsor, Common) (Use 2 or more)
   Seed at 3–4 lbs. per 1,000 sq. ft.

B. Shaded and partially shaded areas

1. Heavy shade
   Pennlawn red fescue 60–70%
   Rough bluegrass (*Poa trivialis*) 30–40%
   Seed at 4 lbs. per 1,000 sq. ft.

2. Moderate to partial shade
   Pennlawn red fescue.................. 50–60%
   Kentucky bluegrass (Merion,........... 15–25%
   Pennstar, Fylking, Prato, Delft,
   Cougar, Campus, Newport C-1,
   Windsor, Common) (Use 2 or more)
   Rough bluegrass (*Poa trivialis*) 15–25%
   Seed at 4 lbs. per 1,000 sq. ft.

C. Sunny and moderate shade areas where coarse texture and 2-inch minimum cutting height is not objectionable.

1. Kentucky 31 tall fescue................   100%
   Seed at 8 lbs. per 1,000 sq. ft.

II. Heavy-Duty Turf Seed Mixtures (Athletic Fields, Playgrounds, Parks)

1. Kentucky 31 tall fescue...............   100%
   Seed at 6-8 lbs. per 1,000 sq. ft.
2. Merion Kentucky bluegrass............ 40–65%
   Kentucky bluegrass (Pennstar, ... 35–60%
   Fylking, Prato, Delft, Cougar,

Campus, Newport C-1, Windsor,
Common) (Use 2 or more)
Seed at 3–4 lbs. per 1,000 sq. ft.

3. Pennlawn red fescue.................. 35–65%
   Kentucky bluegrass (Merion,........... 35–65%
   Pennstar, Fylking, Prato, Delft,
   Cougar, Campus, Newport C-1,
   Windsor, Common) (Use 2 or more)
   Seed at 4–5 lbs. per 1,000 sq. ft.

III. **Temporary Turf Seed Mixtures** (Quick erosion control
or temporary cover during summer periods when
seedings of permanent grasses are hazardous)
For temporary cover prior to seeding permanent
grasses in the current season.

1. Common ryegrass 100%
   Seed at 4–5 lbs. per 1,000 sq. ft.

IV. **Special Areas** (Highways, Slopes, Banks, Dikes, Dams,
Levees)

A. Mowed Areas

1. Kentucky 31 tall fescue............... 100%
   Seed at 4 lbs. per 1,000 sq. ft.

B. Non-mowed Areas

1. Penngift crownvetch 25%
   Kentucky 31 tall fescue, or Creeping ... 75%
   red fescue, or Perennial ryegrass
   Seed at 2 lbs. per 1,000 sq. ft.

2. Kentucky 31 tall fescue............. 100%
   Seed at 4 lbs. per 1,000 sq. ft.

[83]

Recommended Seed Mixture
Suburban Brand Grass Seed Mixture

Lot 410-11

FINE TEXTURED GRASSES

39.04% Kentucky Bluegrass
80% germination

19.50% Creeping Red Fescue
80% germination

38.96% Merion Kentucky Bluegrass
85% germination

COARSE KINDS
None Claimed

OTHER INGREDIENTS

0.25% Other Crop Seed
2.16% Inert Matter
Tested: May 1970
0.09% Weed Seed

Suburban Seed Company
99 Westland Avenue
Seedville; Maryland

Poor Seed Mixture
Suburban Brand Special Grass Seed

Lot SP24

FINE TEXTURED GRASSES
None or None Claimed
COARSE KINDS

70.62% Kentucky 31 Tall Fescue
85% germination

19.00% Perennial Ryegrass
90% germination

5.00% Annual Ryegrass
90% germination

OTHER INGREDIENTS

3.10% Other Crop Seed
1.78% Inert Matter
Tested: May 1970
0.50% Weed Seed

Noxious Weeds
3 garlic per ounce

Suburban Seed Company
99 Westland Avenue
Seedville, Maryland

[84]

The Best Seed for You

It would be folly to plant certain grasses that take tremendous care if you haven't the time to give that care. On the other hand, if a beautiful lawn is a hobby with you, a kind of showcase to your home, then the grasses that need pampering are the ticket.

Kentucky bluegrass is the "Old Faithful" of the grass kingdom. It best fits the needs for the "average" lawn. With moderate fertilization and high mowing (two to two and one-half inches), it will make a satisfactory lawn with little effort. One of the red fescues such as creeping red or Chewing's, may be used in a mixture with bluegrass. Red fescue should be 70 to 80 per cent of the mixture in shaded areas.

In spite of these findings at the Wooster Experimental Station, many of the state bureaus recommend mixtures that contain both bluegrass and bents. A sampling of a few of the mixtures recommended from different parts of the country are listed below. If you wish, you can make up your own lawn mixture from one of them. Or make the mixture that appeals most to you.

Turfgrass Varieties

The section of adapted turfgrasses is essential to the development of a good turf. Planting turfgrass species unadapted to a particular site, environment,

[85]

soil condition, management level or use will result in failure or an inferior turf.

Permanent turfgrasses such as Kentucky bluegrass and red fescue should compose a major portion of most seed mixtures planted in Michigan. Cheap, quick growing seed mixtures are generally a poor buy since they may contain large quantities of temporary and weedy perennial grasses which are unsuited for a high quality, permanent turf.

Only quality seeds which meet certain minimum purity and germination percentages should be used. Most state laws require proper labeling for germination, purity, and composition of grass seed mixtures. However, the buyer is responsible for selecting the properly adapted variety or mixture. Here is a rating of lawngrasses compiled by the University of Michigan Agricultural Extension Service.

Permanent Lawn Grasses

KENTUCKY BLUEGRASSES

Kentucky bluegrass (*Poa pratensis*), the most widely used turfgrass, is best adapted to well-drained, heavy, fertile soils. It is a perennial, cool season turfgrass having good sod forming characteristics due to its rhizomatous growth habit. Generally the Kentucky bluegrasses are not adapted to intense shade. There are a number of varieties of Kentucky bluegrass, some having dis-

[86]

tinctly different management requirements. It is important to carefully select the variety best suited to the particular management level desired. Kentucky bluegrasses should be mowed high. Cutting shorter than 1½ inches will seriously weaken the turf. Kentucky bluegrasses are widely used on lawns, athletic fields, institutional grounds, fairways, tees, roadsides, cemeteries and airfields.

Cougar — Is a moderately low growing variety with a similar leaf texture to Merion. Numerous leaves are oriented horizontally. It tends to have a blue-green color. It is highly susceptible to leafspot and is moderately susceptible to stripe smut and powdery mildew. Use of this variety is suggested only for areas where leafspot is not a problem. The outstanding attribute of Cougar is the excellent drought tolerance and drought recovery on sandy soils.

Delta — This variety of Kentucky bluegrass is similar to Kenblu. It is as susceptible to leafspot as Kenblu Kentucky bluegrass but recovers from injury much more rapidly. It is fairly resistant to stem rust and powdery mildew. The variety is outstanding in establishment vigor. Delta can recover from drought fairly quickly. The growth habit of Delta is quite erect.

Fylking — It has a dense, low growing habit of growth of relatively fine leaf texture. Its establishment rate is satisfactory. Fylking is reported to have good resistance to leafspot and stripe smut and a moderate resistance to stem rust. It is

[87]

moderately susceptible to powdery mildew. Fylking has had only limited testing.

Kenblu — It has superior early spring and late fall growth and color but becomes dormant in midsummer. This turfgrass is highly susceptible to leafspot diseases which cause severe thinning and browning in early summer. Although resistant to leaf rust, it is quite susceptible to powdery mildew which can cause severe injury in shaded areas. Kenblu Kentucky bluegrass withstands traffic moderately well and should be a basic component of a majority of lawn mixtures in Michigan which are to be maintained at a medium to low fertility level. In the past this variety has been known as Common. However, Common is a category of seed and not a specific variety.

Merion — This Kentucky bluegrass variety produces a turf of high quality and density when properly managed. It forms a medium textured sod having a wide, dark green leaf. Its chief attribute is resistance to leafspot disease, which results in superior summer growth when compared with Kenblu, Delta, Park, Newport, etc. It is highly susceptible to powdery mildew which can cause severe thinning under intense shade. Stem rusts are also a problem with Merion but can be overcome by a good nitrogen fertilizer program. Merion is highly susceptible to stripe smut, which is most prevalent under heavy thatch conditions. Stripe smut has been found in Michigan, but it has not as yet become as severe a problem as in states to the south. Merion also shows considerable susceptibility to a new disease which has been called *Fusarium* blight. With the advent of cool fall weather, Merion shows a reduced growth rate and turns a characterisic purplish-green color. Merion has superior ability to tolerate and recover from droughts and therefore would be better adapted, than most bluegrass varieties, to light sandy soils. Merion is comparatively slow to establish. It demands a high management level compared to most other bluegrass varieties and requires twice the rate of nitrogen fertilization (6-8 of actual nitrogen per 1,000 square feet per year). Merion tends to thatch more than other bluegrasses due to its vigorous, dense growth habit. Merion should be used only by individuals interested in investing the extra time and money required for a high quality turf.

Newport—A Kentucky bluegrass variety similar to Merion in growth habit which blends well with Merion. Its main virtue is excellent fall vigor which is desirable for football fields. It is not as vigorous in rhizome production and sod formation. The leafspot resistance of Newport is not adequate with severe thinning frequently occurring in the third and fourth years. Newport is moderately susceptible to stripe smut. It has shown some resistance to the current races of leaf and stem rust as well as to powdery mildew. It should not be used on droughty sites since it is very poor in drought tolerance and drought recovery capability. Newport seems to prefer a medium high nitrogen fertility level. It has a medium rate of establishment. Newport tends to become very stemmy at seedhead setting in June.

Park — It has an erect growth habit and a rapid growth rate. Its rate of establishment is superior. Park has shown good resistance to stem rust and stripe smut but is highly susceptible to leafspot.

Prato — Is a Kentucky bluegrass of superior density and relatively fine leaf texture. It has a fairly rapid rate of establishment. Prato has moderate susceptibility to leafspot but is quite susceptible to stripe smut. It is a moderately low growing variety with rather horizontal leaf blades. This variety was originally selected in Holland.

Windsor — Is a dark green, moderately low growing Kentucky bluegrass. It has moderate susceptibility to leafspot, powdery mildew and rust. Windsor responds to high nitrogen fertilization similar to Merion. It has had only limited testing.

BLUEGRASS BLENDS

The blending of several bluegrass varieties which possess varying disease resistant characteristics is preferred. The blend is suited to a broader range of adaptation and disease tolerance than a single variety. In general, blending reduces the incidence on any one disease on any one bluegrass variety contained in the blend.

Red fescue (*Festuca rubra*) is a perennial, cool season turfgrass of fine texture particularly adapted to light, sandy soils, shaded conditions and lower management levels. It is superior to the bluegrasses in establishment vigor and when mixed with bluegrasses, often serves as a valuable companion grass. Excessive nitrogen or water will cause severe thinning of red fescue. Normally 1 to 2 pounds of actual nitrogen per 1,000 square feet per year is adequate. All commercially available varieties of red fescue are susceptible to the leaf-spot diseases which can cause extensive parchy, areas of dead turf in mid-summer. Available varieties include Pennlawn, Rainier, Illahee, and Trinity red fescue which spread by underground creeping stems and Chewing's red fescue which has a bunch type growth habit. All of these varieties are similar in turfgrass performance with a slight edge to Pennlawn and Rainier in terms of overall quality. Pennlawn is the preferred red fescue variety in Michigan due to a superior drought recovery capability and better low temperature tolerance. Chewing's red fescue has a rapid establishment capability on sandy soils. A minimum cutting height of 1½ inches is recommended. If any percentage of "other crop" is listed on the label when purchasing red fescue seed, be sure it is not tall fescue.

SPECIAL PURPOSE TURFGRASSES

Rough Bluegrass (Poa trivialis) is a light green, prostrate growing, perennial turfgrass which is adapted to moist, shady conditions. It is superior to Kentucky bluegrass in establishment vigor but will not tolerate traffic or hot, dry conditions due to its shallow rooting habit. The light green colored rough bluegrass does not blend well with most turfgrasses; therefore, is not used to any extent.

Bentgrass (Agrostis sp.) is a vigorous perennial turfgrass with the ability to withstand close cutting (down to one-quarter inch). It is used primarily on putting greens and fairways of golf courses. It requires extensive, costly management including the use of fungicides due to its high susceptibility to diseases (dollarspot, brown patch, snow mold, etc.). As a result of the high cost and specific management requirements, its use is limited as a lawn grass. Stoloniferous bentgrasses are a serious weed in Kentucky bluegrass turfs. Bentgrasses are favored by wet soils, close mowing and high fertility.

TEMPORARY TURFGRASSES

Perennial ryegrass (Lolium perenne) is a short-lived perennial due to its susceptibility to winterkill. A major portion of a perennial ryegrass stand will be killed during the initial winter with complete killing by the end of the third winter. It has a bunch type, no creeping growth habit.

Perennial ryegrass is susceptible to rust and is difficult to mow due to the tough, fibrous nature of the leaves. Its main attribute is rapid germination and establishment which makes it an ideal grass to be used as a temporary lawn or as 20% of a mixture to serve as a soil stabilizer and cover until the slower permanent turfgrasses become established. The problem is to avoid excessive competition from the ryegrass which may crowd out the desired permanent turfgrass contained in the mixture.

Italian Ryegrass (Lolium multiflorum) is an annual, bunch type turfgrass. It is slightly superior to perennial ryegrass in germination and establishment vigor. It has a lighter green color and coarser leaf texture. Its use is similar to that of perennial ryegrass.

Redtop (Agrestis alba) is a gray-green, short-lived perennial grass which tends to thin out under turf maintenance. As a result, it persists as scattered tufts which disrupt turfgrass uniformity. Its main advantage is rapid germination and tolerance to wet, acid soils. However, it is of little value in quality turfs.

Tall Fescue (Festuca arundinacea) is a grass that is frequently misused. It is a coarse-textured, perennial which resists heavy wear, high temperatures, and drought. Tall fescue is vigorous in establishment but susceptible to snow mold and subject to winterkilling under close mowing and high fertility. The two most common varieties are Kentucky 31 and Alta which are very similar in perform-

[93]

ance. Due to the coarse leaf texture, tall fescue is generally not suited for home lawns. If planted as less than 70 per cent of the mixture, it becomes clumpy and undesirable. Tall fescue is used on athletic fields and heavy use areas where wear is excessive.

Which Is the Best Turfgrass?

No grass variety is perfect; all have good and bad features. We must learn these characteristics, decide what is required in the turf to be planted, and then choose the variety which most nearly meets these requirements.

Following is an evaluation of some of the most important characteristics and requirements of common turfgrasses compiled by the Agricultural Research Service at Penn State University. Under any one category a grass may differ little from those immediately above or below. However, it may be vastly different from those further away in the list.

The grasses in these lists may change order slightly as more is learned about them. Their positions also may vary according to climate, weather, soils, and other environmental factors. However, their general location (high, low, or intermediate on a list) is not likely to change and should be carefully noted when selecting varieties for planting.

I. TEXTURE – LEAF-BLADE WIDTH

Coarse — Tall fescue
↑   St. Augustine
         Meadow fescue
         Perennial ryegrass
         Common bermuda
         Kentucky bluegrass
         Zoysia
         Improved bermudas
         Colonial bentgrass
↓   Creeping bentgrass
Fine   Red fescue

II. HIGH TEMPERATURE TOLERANCE

High   Zoysia
↑   Improved bermudas
         Common bermuda
         St. Augustine
         Tall fescue
         Dichondra
         Meadow fescue
         Kentucky bluegrass
         Colonial bentgrass
         Red fescue
↓   Ryegrass
Low   Creeping bentgrass

III. COOL TEMPERATURE TOLERANCE
     (winter color)

High   Perennial ryegrass ⎫
↑   Kentucky bluegrass ⎪
         Creeping bentgrass ⎬ Tempera-
         Colonial bentgrass ⎪ ate
         Red fescue   ⎪ climate
         Tall fescue   ⎭ grasses
         Meadow fescue
         Dichondra   ⎫
         St. Augustine   ⎪ Subtropi-
         Improved ber-   ⎬ ical
           mudas   ⎪ climate
↓   Zoysia   ⎪ grasses
Low   Common bermuda   ⎭

IV. TOLERANCE OF CLOSE CLIPPING

Low cut Creeping bentgrass, ¼″ or less
↑   Improved bermudas
         Common bermuda
         Colonial bentgrass
         Zoysia
         Dichondra
         St. Augustine
         Tall fescue
         Red fescue
         Meadow fescue
↓   Perennial ryegrass
High cut Kentucky bluegrass, 1½″ or more

V. NITROGEN FERTILITY REQUIREMENT

Low   Zoysia
↑   Red fescue
         Tall fescue
         Meadow fescue
         St. Augustine
         Kentucky bluegrass
         Perennial ryegrass
         Improved bermudas
         Common bermuda
↓   Colonial bentgrass
         Dichondra
High   Creeping bentgrass

VI. SALINITY TOLERANCE

High   Improved bermudas
↑   Common bermuda
         Creeping bentgrass
         Zoysia
         St. Augustine
         Tall fescue
         Perennial ryegrass
         Meadow fescue
         Red fescue
         Kentucky bluegrass
         Colonial bentgrass
Low   Dichondra

VII. DROUGHT TOLERANCE

High   Improved bermudas
↑   Zoysia
         Common bermuda
         Tall fescue
         Red Fescue
         Kentucky bluegrass
         Perennial ryegrass
         Meadow fescue
         Colonial bentgrass
         St. Augustine
↓   Dichondra
Low   Creeping bentgrass

VIII. COMPACTED SOIL TOLERANCE

High   Tall fescue
↑   Improved bermudas
         Common bermuda
         Zoysia
         Kentucky bluegrass
         Perennial ryegrass
         Meadow fescue
         St. Augustine
         Red fescue
         Dichondra
         Colonial bentgrass
Low   Creeping bentgrass

IX. DISEASE TOLERANCE

High   Tall fescue
↑   Zoysia
         Improved bermudas
         Common bermuda
         St. Augustine
           Meadow fescue
           Perennial ryegrass
            Red fescue
↓   Kentucky bluegrass
           Colonial bentgrass
           Dichondra
Low   Creeping bentgrass

X. SHADE TOLERANCE

Shade Red fescue
↑   Zoysia
         St. Augustine
         Dichondra
         Colonial bentgrass
         Tall fescue
         Creeping bentgrass
           Meadow fescue
↓   Kentucky bluegrass
           Perennial ryegrass
           Improved bermudas
Sun   Common bermuda

XI. WEAR RESISTANCE

High   Zoysia
↑   Improved bermudas
         Tall fescue
         Common bermuda
           Perennial ryegrass
           Meadow fescue
           Kentucky bluegrass
           Red fescue
↓   St. Augustine
             Colonial bentgrass
             Creeping bentgrass
Low   Dichondra

XII. RECOVERY FROM MODERATE WEAR

Fast   Improved bermudas
↑   Common bermuda
         Creeping bentgrass
         St. Augustine
           Tall fescue
           Kentucky bluegrass
           Perennial ryegrass
           Meadow fescue
↓   Red fescue
             Dichondra
             Colonial bentgrass
Slow   Zoysia

XIII. RECOVERY FROM SEVERE INJURY

Complete Improved bermudas
↑   Common bermuda
            Zoysia (but slow)
            Dichondra
            Creeping bentgrass
            Kentucky bluegrass ⎫
            Colonial bentgrass   Tends
              Red fescue   ⎬ to
↓   Meadow fescue become
              Tall fescue   ⎭ bunchy
Partial   Perennial rye-
               grass

XIV. RATE OF TURF ESTABLISHMENT

Fast   Improved bermudas (stolons)
↑   Common bermuda
         Creeping bentgrass (stolons)
         St. Augustine
           Perennial ryegrass
           Meadow fescue
             Tall fescue
           Kentucky bluegrass
           Bentgrasses (seed)
↓   Red fescue
           Dichondra
Slow   Zoysia

What Lawn to Plant Where

Most northern lawns and many seeded southern ones are planted to a mixture of grasses. This extends the adaptability of the turf. The classic example is compounding of Kentucky bluegrass and fine fescues, two similar species responding to the same general care. With all the new varieties of these grasses, mixtures can take advantage even further of the special attributes of several components. Basically, the bluegrasses provide an outstanding sod, strong and recuperative, aesthetically pleasing. Bluegrass is at its best on fairly rich soils, in reasonably open locations. The fine fescues (Chewing's Illahee, Pennlawn and Rainier) are equally attractive. They tolerate shade, poor soil and dry locations. Fescue seeds are quick to germinate and make a good initial showing.

Between them, the bluegrasses and fine fescues make a widely useful turf for most of the country, under just simple, ordinary maintenance. For those able to provide somewhat more intensive care, Merion bluegrass can be increased (Merion requires heavier feeding than most bluegrasses, may need occasional thatch removal). On turfs that must be mowed short (such as the half-inch clipping customary on many fairways), a bentgrass might be preferred. Bentgrasses should be mowed, fertilized and watered a bit more attentively than is generally required with bluegrass-fescue. The more erect bentgrasses, such as Highland, are easier to care for than are the creeping sorts.

In the south, the situation is complicated by the diversity of environments and useful grasses. There seems to be increasing demand for a simple, easy-to-care-for seeded turf in the south. In the upper south this may be Bermuda, or in the lower south, mixtures in which Bahia predominates. Perhaps regular seeding with a combination of southern and northern grasses may prove easier than maintaining a single grass such as St. Augustine. St. Augustine is subject to severe disease and insect attack (clinch bugs), making it an unending bother in some parts of Florida.

Ex-northerners retired to the south would probably welcome a seed mixture that contained old-favorite northern grasses (such as Kentucky bluegrass, fine fescues and bentgrasses) as well as southern types (Bahia, zoysia, Bermuda, perhaps centipede). Whatever time of the year this was sowed there would be something suitable. Additional seedings from time to time might prove less taxing than repeated maintenance sprayings. The lawn might not look the equal of pampered Bermuda or zoysia varieties, but might suit those interested in take-it-easy retirement.

For Transition Area Lawns: Kentucky 31

Kentucky 31, a variety of tall fescue (*Festuca arundinacea*), may solve lawn problems in the eastern areas of the United States not suitable to either northern or southern grasses.

Such lawngrasses as Kentucky bluegrass and bentgrass are adapted to the cool-season area in the North, and zoysia and Bermudagrass grow well in the warm-season area in the South. However, none of them fare especially well in the zone that separates the two major areas. This zone, called the transition region, covers an area extending roughly from Washington, D.C., to northeastern Kansas.

In research to find a grass suitable for lawns in the problem area, Agricultural Research Service agronomists F. V. Juska, A. A. Hanson, and A. W. Hovin found that Kentucky 31 was well adapted for the region and that it would provide hardy, manageable, and attractive lawn turf.

Though tall fescue had been used on athletic fields, roadsides, airfields, and other areas where tough turf is desirable, it was considered too coarse and bunchy for lawns. And previous research had been directed primarily toward the use of tall fescue for forage.

In studies spanning 9 years, the scientists tested two seed mixtures, three cutting heights, and time, source, and rate of nitrogen for their effects on turf quality. They obtained the best results with Kentucky 31, seeded at about 6 to 8 pounds per 1,000 square feet, fertilized as indicated by grass color throughout the growing season, mowed to a height of about 2 inches. The experiments also

[99]

showed that a pure seeding of Kentucky 31 tended to prevent undesirable clumping that developed in tall fescue-bluegrass mixtures.

Generally, Kentucky 31 is well adapted to the transition zone for several reasons. It has good persistence under mowing, it has satisfactory winter color, is shade tolerant, grows well in heavy soils, will tolerate wet or dry conditions and either acid or alkaline soils.

It is especially suited for large, expansive lawn areas and parks where a uniform wear-resistant cover is more important than very fine texture.

Preparing the Seedbed

Much of the success of a new lawn depends on how well you prepare the seedbed. Therefore, allot ample time and care to this phase of lawn establishment. The seedbed preparation establishes the final grade and makes a firm, smooth soil surface ready for seeding.

SLOPES AND GRADES

On most lots are some fixed grade points. These points are the house foundation, sidewalks, driveways, terraces and established trees. In grading, both rough and finish, the problem is to spread the soil evenly so that the changes in elevation between fixed points are gradual. In general, the best grades slope gently away from the buildings

[100]

in all directions. A slope of 6 to 12 inches per 100
feet is the most desirable.

DRAINAGE

Some soils are naturally wet because of location
of poor internal and subsoil drainage. Therefore,
it may be desirable to install a tile drainage system.
Before starting any drainage job it would be well
to consult a competent drainage contractor. The
homeowner or contractor should make sure there
is a suitable outlet to carry off the water. In the cities and larger towns permission must be secured
to connect to the storm sewer. In rural areas the
outlet may be an open ditch. Drainage work
should be done after the rough grade has been
established but before the topsoil is put in place
for the final grading.

SOIL PREPARATION

After the bulldozer has spread the topsoil, or if
the area was worked up by plowing or rotary-till-
ing, then rake the area. Raking should remove
stones and other debris as well as smooth out high
and low spots.

Next, add the desired organic material, fertilizer
and limestone. A second raking will thoroughly
mix these materials in the soil.

It is usually desirable to roll the seedbed before
seeding. However, you may seed directly in this

[101]

loosened soil if it is firm under the first inch or two. The depth of your footprints will reveal the firmness of the soil.

If you roll the soil before seeding, rake the area over lightly to loosen the surface.

After sowing the seed, rake the surface again lightly to cover most of the seed and roll it again. This compact seedbed will offer the best condition for germination of the seeds and development of the young grass after germination. If the seedbed is too loose and deep, moisture may not be sufficient for germination and early growth of the grass.

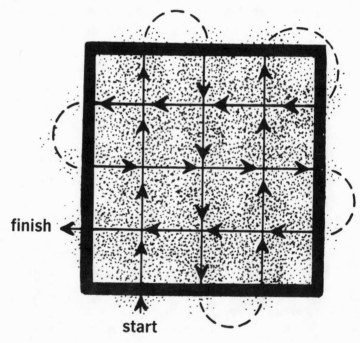

The ideal time to sow grass seed is early in the morning on a calm day. Never seed on a windy day as the seed will be carried away by the wind. Scatter the seed evenly over a measured area. This may be done by use of a seed-spreading machine or by hand. With either method, divide the seed for a given area into 2 equal parts and sow one half of it by going across the area from north to south. Plant the other half by walking across the area east to west.

To distribute the seed by hand, swing the arm in a wide arc and let the seed slip out of the hand while the arm is in motion. The wider you swing your arm, the more even the distribution. A wire broom or rake, pulled lightly over the surface following the seeding, will do a good job in covering the seed.

WAITING FOR THE GREEN GRASS

It's natural to be impatient for green grass after seeding a new lawn. One may even envy the neighbor who has used an inexpensive haygrass mix. Such envy will be only temporary, rest assured, for the large seeds which sprout so quickly give grass that is neither permanent nor attractive. In addition to getting more seeds for the money in each pound of a good bluegrass-fine fescue blend, the purchaser also gains grasses that are permanently satisfying. But they *are* a little slow to make their appearance in springtime. The reason is

[103]

simple. Grass seed needs both warmth and humidity in order to sprout. Spring soils are usually damp enough, but also residually cold from winter. Watering can correct dryness, but not much can be done about soil temperatures other than to await warmer weather.

The seeds of quality species average smaller than those of inexpensive haygrasses. Although they contain all the hereditary stuff for fine turf performance, they don't contain so much initial energy as is packed into a larger seed. Thus a good lawn shows substantial growth more slowly than some of quick-come quick-go plantings.

Though lack of warmth may slow sprouting, it is nonetheless good to get the seed into the soil just as early as possible. The seed will pass through initial sprouting stages and be ready for full response when warm weather does finally come.

So, for establishing a new lawn or sprucing up an old one, choose seed of high quality, and sow it as soon as it is possible to prepare the seedbed. Listed below are the germination periods for the better-known grass varieties:

Kentucky bluegrass	20–28 days
Merion Kentucky bluegrass	20–28 days
Park Kentucky bluegrass	14–21 days
Bentgrasses	7–12 days
Redtop	8–10 days
Meadow fescue	7–14 days
Chewing's fescue	10–21 days

Creeping red fescue	10–21 days
Perennial ryegrass	7–14 days
Common ryegrass	7–14 days

Sodding

The use of sod in establishment of turfgrass areas has become a common practice. There are many situations where sodding is to be preferred, such as on sloping areas and places where seedlings do not become well established because of traffic conditions, or when an immediate turf is desired. Certain precautions are suggested in order to insure good sod establishment. Many of the practices are similar to those required for establishing turf from seed.

1. Control Weedy Perennial Grasses—Weedy perennial grasses such as quackgrass, tall fescue, or bentgrass should be controlled prior to sodding. Sod can be laid in 4 to 5 weeks if the soil is thoroughly tilled.

2. Provide for Drainage—If tile drains are to be used, the soil should be allowed to settle over the trench areas prior to sodding. Special care will probably be needed to pack the soil in the trenches in order to prevent subsequent settling and repair. For small turfgrass areas, a gentle slope (½-1 per cent) away from the building should provide adequate surface drainage in most cases.

3. Lay the Sod—Do not allow the sod to heat while piled previous to laying. Sod should not be

[105]

laid on dry soil. A soil that is moist but not saturated to a depth of 6 inches or more allows the
new roots to become established rapidly. Stagger-
ing the ends of the pieces of sod will prevent lines
across the turf caused by slow establishment at the
edges of the sod pieces. Make sure that the edges

Sodding is often desirable when you seek the immediate establishment
of turf, especially in areas that need mid-season repair.

of the sod are in good contact with each other but not overlapping. Once the sod is laid, roll to insure sod contact with the soil. Roots will dry out rapidly if air pockets are left between the sod and the soil. If sod is laid on a slope, it may be necessary to peg the sod strips to prevent slippage.

4. *Water Properly*—A thorough watering immediately after the sod has been rolled is an *essential* step. As a general rule, watering will be necessary every day at noon in order to keep the sod moist until the roots have grown into the soil and to avoid atmospheric drought. Once the sod is established, watering can be reduced to once a week or less, depending on when the grass wilts.

After the sod is established, good management practices will be necessary to maintain a high quality turf.

SPOT SODDING

Spot sodding is planting small plugs or blocks of sod at measured intervals. Generally, the plugs are set 1 foot apart, but they may be set closer together if more rapid coverage is desired. Fit the plugs tightly into prepared holes and tamp them firmly into place.

STRIP SODDING

Strip sodding is planting strips of sod end to end in rows that are 1 foot apart. The sod strips

[107]

should be 2 to 4 inches wide. Firm contact with surrounding soil is necessary.

In laying the sod, press it firmly into the soil bed and roll it after the sod is laid. This will insure adequate contact and keep the roots from drying out.

Sprigging

Sprigging is the planting of individual plants, runners, cuttings or stolons at spaced intervals. Sprigs or runners are obtained by tearing apart or shredding solid pieces of established sod.

Sprigs are planted in rows from 6 to 12 inches apart and about 2 inches deep. The sprigs may be placed end to end in the rows rather than at spaced intervals. Thoroughly cover all of the root system, but leave some of the leaf surface exposed. The planting material is used more efficiently this way so it is the least expensive method but quite laborious.

Seed for many grasses is not available or does not produce plants that are true to type. Such grasses must be planted by vegetative methods such as spot (or plug) sodding, strip sodding, sprigging or stolonizing. Grasses planted by vegetative methods include zoysia, improved strains of Bermudagrass, St. Augustinegrass, centipedegrass, creeping bentgrass and velvet bentgrass.

Whether plugged, strip sodded, sprigged or stolonized, the planted material must be kept moist until well established. During the first year, light

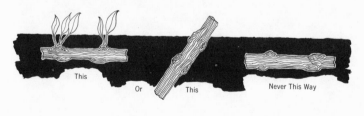

This   Or   This   Never This Way

applications of a nitrogenous fertilizer every 2 to 4 weeks during the growing season will help speed the spread of the plants.

Stolonizing

Stolonizing is practicable only when large amounts of planting material are available for planting large areas or highly specialized areas such as golf course putting greens. Shredded stolons are spread over the area with mechanized equipment. The spreading is followed by disking or rolling and top-dressing.

Large Bermudagrass areas may be established by spreading shredded stolons with a manure spreader and disking lightly to firm them into the soil. This method requires 90 to 120 bushels of stolons per acre. Creeping bentgrass and velvet bentgrass can be stolonized by spreading shredded stolons at a rate of 10 bushels per 1,000 square feet, top-dressing with topsoil to a depth of ¼ inch and rolling to firm the stolons into the top-dressing.

Sods, plugs and stolons may be purchased from local nurserymen. But, if the soil building program for your lawn is expected to take a year or more and space for a grass nursery is available, an economy may be effected if you raise your own sod for plug planting. Treat the grass nursery exactly as described above for lawn culture, giving it, if anything, more fertilizer and a more mellow growing soil, to encourage rapid growth. A plugging device which cuts the sod may be purchased and may be used to cut your own home grown plugs when your topsoil is ready to receive them.

Plug Planting

A relatively simple new device and a revolutionary grass planting method makes it possible today to spelling finis for crabgrass, one of the lawnmakers' most woeful foes.

Recent adaptation of practices long employed by golf courses to repair injured turf has proven remarkably effective in starting vigorous grasses in the home lawn or in other sods. Using a special plug-lifting tool to take choice plugs of sod from nurseries or other sources, the turf-planter then transfers these to the lawn where the same tool enables exact fitting openings to be made for the new clumps.

Development of this magazine type plug-planting tool, which raises a cylindrical tuft of desirable sod and implants it where needed, represents a significant advance for homeowners who want to establish smoother, hardier, weed-eliminating grasses in their lawns. For, repeated field experiments and numerous home-ground tests have determined not only the workability of the practice, but also the definite ultimate economy it affords.

With the aid of this plug-planting tool the aspiring lawnmaker or lawn improver, can plant his entire lawn at a cost no greater than the purchase of ready-made nursery sod adapted to his locality

Although the plug planting tool works well in establishing a new lawn, it may also be used to repair injured turf. Here a homeowner takes plugs of his old lawn prior to replacing them with high quality grass turf.

[112]

and pocketbook, plus his own time and effort in giving it a good start. Overruling the idea that this method is more expensive and involves greater labor than the customary system of planting grass seed is the fact that the newer practice has shown less than 10 per cent lawn mortality under all usual conditions, while other methods may really mean much more work and expense if the job needs to be done over several times. Furthermore, this type of planting is least dependent on season or climate. It can be done at any time the soil is not actually frozen—even in mid-winter.

By lifting plugs of crabgrass and implanting strong sod in their place, the gardener strikes a telling blow against that perennial nemesis since the crabgrass gets thoroughly smothered by the vigorous new growth of superior grasses. Add to this advantage the fact that any lawnkeeper can thus turn smilingly from the objectionable purchase, handling and endlessly repeated use of chemical weed-killers and other such assorted toxic garden nostrums and another reason for the gaining popularity of plug planting becomes apparent.

The lawnmaker may choose to devote a small area to raising his own preferred sod for plug planting. By choosing high quality grass seed best suited to his locality and requirements, and by giving this source planting a bit of careful tending, he can provide a lasting inexpensive supply of choice turf for all plug planting needs.

As to grass strains proving most successful, the

sod plugs can be of any creeping or spreading variety from the world over. Among these are Bermuda, St. Augustine, zoysia, creeping bentgrass, red fescue, centipede, and bluegrass. At the breeding nursery and trial grounds of Pennsylvania State College, under the direction of Professor H. Burton Musser, all important species and strains have been grown for comparison and experimental purposes. By its careful use with the plug planting technique, Meyer (Z-52) zoysia, a comparatively recent combined grass strain, has been found to result in firm, solid, weed-free turf within two seasons.

CHAPTER VI

Watering

GRASS, like people, must have water to live. Newly planted areas need water in a way different from old established areas. During drought, grass will go off color, lose vigor and in general be unhealthy. Grass will respond quickly to irrigation, so water to keep grass pretty and healthy.

A few facts and figures will help you develop an understanding of watering lawns. A turf area, be it lawn, golf green or football field, will use about 0.2 to 0.3 inch of water each day. This is equal to 180 gallons of water per day, or 1,260 gallons per week for each 1,000 square feet of grass.

The storage capacity of soil varies according to the texture. In general, sands will hold about ¾ inch of water per foot of depth, loams 1½ inches and clays 2½ inches.

Using this information, let's do an example. If you have a lawn with roots growing 2 feet deep in a sandy soil, the grass will deplete the available water in 6 to 7 days. If this lawn is not watered, or if it does not rain, the grass will become weakened and injured.

Using a conventional lawn sprinkler, it requires about *8 hours* of constant sprinkling to wet a clay soil to a depth of 1 foot. Sands will require less time. Irrigating for a short time with inadequate sprinklers does not really water the grass.

Principles of Lawn Watering

FREQUENCY OF IRRIGATION

The frequency of irrigation is dependent on the type of grass, the soil physical properties, and the climatic condition — especially rainfall, humidity, temperature, and wind movement.

It is often said that many turfgrass problems may be attributed to improper watering. Perhaps one of the most important factors contributing to improper watering is frequent irrigation — watering too often. In general, it is an excellent idea to let the condition of the grass determine when to apply moisture. On most general turfgrass areas the time to apply moisture is just as the plants begin to wilt. As a matter of fact, with one possible exception, this could become a rule of thumb for

[116]

watering turfgrass. The exception is on newly seeded areas which must be kept moist during the period the seed is germinating and seedlings are becoming established.

Frequent, shallow watering tends to keep the upper layers of soil near a point of saturation most of the time. This encourages shallow rooting and promotes weak turf which is susceptible to disease and insect attack as well as damage from traffic. The practice of watering deeply only when plants show signs of wilting is for most turfgrass areas a practical approach to a sound watering program and it is a big step forward in the development of healthy, vigorous turfgrass. Far too many of our turf areas are watered too frequently and for too short a time.

WATERING NEWLY SEEDED LAWNS

On newly seeded lawns a series of sprinklings will hasten germination during rainless periods. It is important to apply water in the form of a fine spray. Water applied in this manner allows the soil to absorb the water slowly which reduces the danger of erosion. There is also less chance that a hard surface crust will develop when water is applied as a fine spray.

On a newly seeded lawn, never allow the upper 2 inches of soil to dry out. To maintain this moisture level, you may need to apply water for short periods of time during the day. This will be deter-

[117]

mined by the temperature, wind velocity, rainfall and amount of sunshine occurring each day during this critical period. Follow this schedule of watering until the grass reaches mowing height and then reduce watering to once daily until the grass is well established.

WATERING ESTABLISHED LAWNS

For established lawns on fairly loamy soils, you do not need to provide water except during prolonged dry periods. If water use is restricted at this time better not use any. Periodic, light sprinklings can do more harm than good. Such applications of water usually result in a very shallow rooted turf that is easily injured by drought and heat.

On established lawns when water is needed, add enough at one time to thoroughly wet the soil to a minimum depth of 6 inches. On most heavier soils, you can achieve the depth of wetting by applying from 1 to 1½ inches of water per 1,000 square feet. The amount of water will vary, depending upon how dry the soil is at the start. Sandy soils may require 2 or more inches of water to show the same depth of wetting.

There is a popular fallacy that water should not be applied during the middle of the day when the sun is brightest because the grass will be "scalded." Watering during the brightest part of the day is

[118]

not very efficient, since the water evaporates rapidly. This is especially true for light waterings.

Water tends to cool rather than burn. The time of day for watering is not important, but early morning or late afternoon is preferable to late evening. A late evening watering leaves the grass foliage wet throughout the night and wet turf is susceptible to fungus disease.

Unfortunately, some lawn owners reason if a little is good, a lot is better, and tend to overwater the lawn. Waterlogging of the soil may induce shallow rooting of the grass, so it is really in distress if for any reason showering must cease (as during vacation time). It also encourages water-loving weeds, such as *Poa annua*. It may drown out trees if continuously practiced. Quite probably it will encourage disease, since the therapeutic effects of drying out are lessened. It accelerates crabgrass growth and the sprouting of weed seeds which might otherwise lie dormant.

MANNER OF APPLYING WATER

Water should never be applied at a rate faster than it can be absorbed by the soil. The ability of a soil to absorb moisture at a given rate depends upon a number of factors, most of which are directly or indirectly associated with certain physical soil problems. Soil properties that govern water infiltration (movement of water into the soil) are texture, structure, and the degree of compaction.

[119]

Texture (size of soil particles) and structure (arrangement of soil particles) influence not only the infiltration of water, but also govern water-holding ability and drainage of soils.

Likewise soils that exhibit good aggregation (a measure of structure) permit more rapid infiltration of water than soils that display poor structural properties. Compaction refers to a condition in which aggregation is reduced or absent; hence, the soil is dense. The degree of compaction at or near the surface is of special importance insofar as infiltration of water is concerned. It has been shown experimentally that a very thin layer of compacted soil will substantially reduce the rate of infiltration.

Another very important factor that influences the ability of a soil to absorb moisture is the rate at which the water is applied. Sprinklers that do not adequately disperse moisture, as well as sprinklers that deliver a large volume of water within a concentrated area, tend to cause surface runoff. Whenever water is applied at a rate faster than it may be absorbed by a given soil, the water is being wasted.

AMOUNT OF WATER TO APPLY

The amount of water to apply at any one time will depend upon the water-holding capacity of the soil, the amount of moisture present when irrigation is started, and drainage.

The water-holding capacity of the soil will, to a

large extent, determine how much water will be needed at any one time. Loams and clay loams are generally considered to have desirable water-holding capacity, whereas sands display very little water-holding capacity. A sufficient amount of moisture should be applied to insure that the entire root zone will be wetted. Once the soil has been wet throughout the root zones or after contact with subsoil moisture has occurred, any additional water applied will merely fill the large pores and, hence, be considered "excess."

Because water from any source is expensive, proper distribution without waste is imperative. Water will cost from thirty-five to fifty cents per thousand gallons from city water supplies. It requires 27,143 gallons to irrigate one acre, one inch, or from $9.50 to $13.50. Irrigation will increase the maintenance cost of a first class lawn 15 cents per thousand square feet when one-half inch is applied per week during periods of drought. That is a small price to pay for a good turf.

Sprinklers

There are a variety of sprinklers available for home use and they vary from the immovable kind that you jab into your lawn to the kind that "walks" all over your lawn, watering as it goes. Also available are hose-type sprinklers with pin holes that allow water to be distributed over whatever area the hose covers.

[121]

The most common types of sprinklers:

1. The impulse or "machine gun" type. This kind shoots out rapidly the fine jets of water and moves around in a circle to cover a wide area.

2. A slowly revolving type with a horizontal bow arm which moves around to deliver water all over a square area.

3. The fixed, round head which throws a circle of misty spray.

4. The traveling sprinkler, operated by an internal water-driven motor, which winds up a tethered tape as it creeps along. Most models have a rapidly whirling spray arm.

5. The long plastic hose or tube in which water sprays through many fine holes.

All of these sprinklers do an adequate job, but they all have the same disadvantage—they must constantly move to insure even watering of all lawn sections. More often than not, some portions of the lawn never get that needed drink.

UNDERGROUND SPRINKLERS

One way to change that is to install an underground watering system. They're practical and will do a better job of watering than old systems, because they're a lot more convenient and easy to use. And they're not hard to install *if* you know the right way to do it.

All underground sprinkling systems are alike in only one respect—they all use flexible plastic or rubber pipe. The pipe itself is of good quality in all systems, and we are sure that it will give many years of service underground. Underground pipe should last considerably longer than ordinary garden hose, because it is not walked on, bent or subjected to the harmful rays of the sun.

Forgetting about pipe for a moment, there are many differences between systems now being sold. The biggest difference is that some kits come completely assembled and others come in loose form, to be put together by the user. The assembled systems have heads already installed on the pipe at ten foot intervals. The Noma system, which was the first one on the market, comes all in one piece with heads already in place. The companies which have since entered the market have practically all used the "do-it-yourself" idea. Some of the do-it-yourself systems are very easy to put together—others require tools and a little plumbing know-how.

Which type system you choose depends mainly on your inclinations. The pre-assembled systems can be made to conform to almost any layout, but the do-it-yourself ones can be set up to supply more water to some areas than to others.

Most sprinkler systems use heads that spread water in all directions evenly. These heads are set in the middle of the lawn and spray water toward the edges. Other systems, supply additional heads that spray water in certain directions only. These heads are installed along the edges of the lawn

[123]

and spray water toward the center. This type of system costs more and requires the installation of more heads, but the finished job is beautiful to see and the water is distributed evenly even in windy weather.

When you plan the layout of your system, the first thing to do is find out your water pressure. Most kits give instructions for spacing of heads based on local water pressures. An average installation will have heads spaced about 15 feet apart.

Here are some general hints that may help you:

Keep heads far enough away from your house and walks.

Try to avoid planning a system that will necessitate running under a walk. It is not easy to poke a hole under a sidewalk.

Try to have the spray patterns of the heads overlap, to avoid dry spots.

Always set up the system before you dig it in and let it run for about an hour to check the spray pattern. "Running in" also softens the soil and makes slitting easier.

A sprinkler system can be put in any time that the soil is not frozen. Freezing will not harm the pipe or the fittings.

[124]

Mulching

Mulching with a light covering of weed-free straw or hay will help hold moisture and prevent washing of the seed during watering or rainfall. One 60- to 80-pound bale of hay or straw mulch will cover 1,000 square feet adequately. Mulches applied evenly and lightly need not be removed. Peat moss and uncomposted sawdust are not satisfactory mulches.

The straw mulch remains until the seedling grasses are in vigorous growth. The mulch serves the purpose of expediting rapid germination and growth, halts evaporation, and protects the new growth from bad weather.

With the grass now showing through the straw mulch, a "nurse mulch" is added. It consists simply of the same rich humus that was originally used in preparing the soil. If good compost is available, we give it preference. Spread the humus about an inch deep over the straw mulch. This added inch will nourish the grass and shade the shallow rhizomes. It maintains a uniform moistness even on the most sunny and windy days. This added inch literally "nurses" the new grass into sturdy maturity. Grown by our nurse-mulch method, the lawn seldom needs watering, except during long dry spells when deep soaking at 10-day intervals would be indicated.

Once established, a bluegrass-fescue turf is

[125]

given extra applications of nurse-mulch in the spring and fall. The fall application is fortified with bone meal for long-term, slow release of nourishment.

On terraced areas or on sloping banks, cheese-cloth, open-mesh sacking or commercial mulching cloth will help hold the moisture and seeds in place. Grass will grow through the mulching material, which may be left to rot.

New seedings must be kept moist until well established. The soil surface must never be allowed to dry out until the grasses are 2 inches tall, even though this means watering several times each day every day over a period of a month. Once the seeds have begun to germinate, they must not dry out or they will die. Avoid saturating the soil, however. Excessive moisture is favorable for the development of damping-off, a fungus disease.

Sawdust may be used instead of straw on a newly seeded lawn. It is less likely to be blown around by the wind and will not contain weed seeds as is usually the case with straw. It helps to prevent crusting of the soil and thus allows the young grass seedlings to easily break through the surface.

Use a very thin layer of sawdust, only about one-eighth inch thick. You should be able to see the soil through the sawdust. A thicker layer may tend to crust over and prevent the growth of the small grass seedlings. Do not use shavings or wood chips on a newly seeded lawn.

There is no particular advantage in using saw-dust on an established lawn. It will not work down into the soil and make it lighter as might be desired. The best way to improve the soil of the lawn is by applying liberal amounts of fertilizer. This promotes vigorous growth of the grass which results in a larger and deeper root system and thus improves the structure and organic matter content of the soil.

CHAPTER VII

Mowing

MOWING will take up most of the time you spend on the aftercare and tending of your lawn. But the best mower in the world won't give you a handsome and healthy lawn unless you follow these 3 sound mowing practices:

1. Mow high, even as high as 3 inches or more, if your mower will permit.

2. Mow regularly, as often as grass growth requires.

3. Never cut more than one-third of the total length of the grass blade at one cutting.

There are two good reasons for following the above rules. ONE—grass cut high keeps weeds and crabgrass out by robbing them of sunlight and air. Look at the shady parts of your lawn, under the trees. You'll seldom see crabgrass there because there's very little sunlight. Remember that when you set your cutting height on the mower. TWO — the health and rate of growth of your grass depend on the food manufactured in the blade — not in the roots. Also, the depth and vigor of your grass roots are determined by the extent of your top growth of blades.

How Grass Grows

Most ambitious lawn-makers are not sufficiently aware that grass, like all green plants, lives and grows principally on food manufactured in its leaves or blades. The great bulk of plant food is not drawn up from the roots as so many people believe, but is made in the blades.

The grass blade, just like the leaf on a tree, gets its raw materials to make plant food both from the soil and the air. Since the food "factory" is above ground, not below, production comes to a halt after excessive cutting or mowing.

That is why you are advised not to cut more than one-third of the blade's length at one time — you're slowing down food production too much and endangering the vitality and even the life of the plant.

Minerals which are essential to healthy growth and development do come from the soil and are absorbed by the roots to be carried through the stems to the blades. Those minerals, however, make up only 5 per cent of the solid material in the grass plant. The balance — 95 per cent — is carbon, hydrogen and oxygen which are taken from the air by the leaves or blades.

A grass plant "manufactures" food in the following way: The blades take in carbon dioxide from the air through tiny pores. In the process of photosynthesis, the blades take energy from the sunlight to recombine the carbon with the oxygen and hydrogen to make sugars, starches, and fiber. The sugars then combine with the soil minerals to make proteins, plant oils, and fats.

The grass plant uses these foods to grow and reproduce — literally to make your lawn. What is left over after the season's main growth is stored in the roots. This vital reserve provides food during the dormant stage and is drawn on to make the first growth of the new season.

This growth and recovery should not be taken for granted. Instead, its mechanics should be clearly understood and given every encouragement through proper lawn practice. All too frequently the homeowner is deceived into believing he can mow his lawn as close as he wants without injuring the innumerable individual plants.

But hard experience has shown that close cutting reduces the food "factories" in the blades, which forces the plant to draw on its food reserves in the roots. The diminished plant continues to draw on these reserves until they are exhausted and the plant then dies, literally mowed to death by an overeager lawn-maker.

It must also be stressed that repeated close mowing causes a corresponding reduction in the extent and depth of the roots, because a small top growth cannot sustain a large and vigorous root system. Conversely, a stunted root system will not successfully withstand a severe drought or put forth a healthy blade growth.

Set the Mower High

So, set the cutting bar high if you want your lawn to stay green through the summer's dry spell and keep out the weeds and crabgrass. You'll also find that high mowing will not spoil the appear-

Mowing is an important process for cultivating a good turf. By setting your mower high, often as high as 3 inches, you'll keep your grass plants healthy and allow them to crowd out their old nemesis, crabgrass.

[131]

ance of your lawn. A well-mowed lawn, 3 or more inches high, will make just as fine and handsome a carpet as the closely shaved turf of the putting green. It's the evenness of the surface that creates the beauty of a lawn, *not the closeness of cut!*

For optimum beauty your cutting blades must be sharp enough to cut cleanly without tearing or ripping the grass. In the case of the reel mower, the bedknife and reel blades must be sharp and the blade set firmly against the bedknife. It is easier to sharpen the blade of the rotary mower which can be removed or sharpened with a file right on the mower. But be sure to disconnect your spark plug before you handle the blade.

When to Mow

EARLY . . .

There is an easy way to green up your lawn two or three weeks earlier each year. You accomplish this by giving the lawn an extra early mowing just as soon as the ground is free of frost. A lawn would turn green much sooner if it were not for the dormant top-half inch of the grass and the dead leaves and other debris which serve to shut off sunlight and water. The latter prevent the chlorophyll-producing action of the turf which in turn causes the lawn to become green in color.

For this extra early mowing the height of cut of your lawn mower should be adjusted to trim off a half inch of the brown grass. Once that is re-

[132]

moved, you will discover the sunlight will be able to get to the turf and materially speed up the production of chlorophyll.

It's always a good plan to take your lawn mower in for maintenance and sharpening in February or March so you will be sure of avoiding the early spring rush. It might be a good idea to get the maintenance man to set the lawn mower at the right height for this early spring mowing.

. . . AND LATE

Opinion varies about how much mowing a lawn needs in autumn, and how short the grass should be clipped going into winter. Although it's seldom a "make or break" matter, there are good reasons for treating different lawns differently.

If your lawn is bentgrass, one of the most luxuriant turfs, it should always be clipped short — between ½ and 1 inch, even with lawn varieties such as Highland. Going into winter, there would be no change from the regular routine of frequent mowing and sweeping, so long as the grass still grows.

On the other hand, with the Kentucky bluegrasses and fine fescues, the usual combination for good lawns that can receive only average care, there is more latitude. For one thing, Kentucky bluegrass grows low naturally in autumn (in response to shorter days) and needs little mowing.

With a bluegrass lawn, try for balance between

[133]

ample green leafage and avoidance of floppiness. The more green leaf left on the plant, the more food the grass stores up, and the deeper its roots grow. We do not suggest mowing in autumn any lower than the customary height. On the other hand, with no mowing at all in autumn, grass leaves may tangle and deteriorate. Leaf loss of itself should not be harmful, for persistent sub-freezing weather scorches leaf blades brown in any event, unless they are protected by snow. But a soppy mat of old leaves may encourage disease.

A thick layer of old leaves may even "smother" new shoots beneath, causing "winter scald." Better some openness and air circulation. Moreover, these old, bleached leaves insulate the sod from springtime's sun, and may delay greening of the lawn because the soil remains cold longer.

So, with a Kentucky bluegrass-fine fescue lawn, a middle approach is probably best. Don't scalp the lawn before winter, but do keep it mowed about its customary height. If the grass leaves are not protected by snow, and become thoroughly frosted before spring, a scalping in late winter (say early March) will remove dead and useless leafage without injuring the grass. In fact, bright new shoots poking from hidden crowns will show more quickly.

Mowing Hints

1. Merion bluegrass can be cut slightly lower and less frequently than the other bluegrasses.

2. Mowing dichondra ground cover is a matter of taste. Some advise mowing occasionally during the summer, when growth is greatest, at ¾ inch. This will make finer leaves of a greater density, thereby helping to reduce the possibility of weed invasion. However, some people prefer the softer appearance of unmowed dichondra.

3. Grass mixtures should be mowed to favor the predominant or most desirable grass.

4. A higher cut during the spring and summer will help reduce crabgrass by allowing the tall permanent grasses to shade out the crabgrass seedlings. Care should be exercised not to lower the height of cut on the cool-season grasses unless temperatures are also dropping.

5. When a grass is allowed to go for a long period between cuttings, it is better for the appearance and vigor of the turf if the excess growth is cut off gradually in successive mowings to the recommended height, rather than all at once.

6. Grass in shady areas should be mowed less frequently and at a greater height than recommended for other areas. The reduced amount of light available to shaded grasses makes it more difficult for the plant to produce enough food for health growth. Higher and less frequent mowing will permit grass to survive in many areas where it would die if cut more heavily.

7. Beware of wet grass. It will mash under the mower, stick to the blades, ball up and clog the mower, slide beneath the blades, and leave an unsatisfactory appearance.

[135]

8. Turfgrass areas regularly cut with reel-type power mowers sometimes develop a series of wave-like ridges running at right angles to the direction of mowing. This washboard effect may be prevented by regularly changing the direction of mowing (diagonal or right angles).

Selecting a Lawn Mower

Today's mowers have taken much of the nuisance out of keeping a trim, happy lawn. The engines, with their recoil starters, really start and keep going. They thrive on any kind of gas; you don't have to feed them the white, unleaded kind. Oiling has been simplified and the lubrication points made easier to reach. The collective wisdom and experience of generations of users has been built into today's mowers. They are better designed, easier to clean and maintain and, if you will follow instructions faithfully and intelligently, quite dependable.

There are 3 main types: reel, rotary, and sickle bar. There are further subdivisions: the mowers you push, those that pull you after them and those on which you ride. It's up to you to pick the one you need and that will do the best job for your home grounds.

THE REEL MOWER

This is the classic mower of grandfather's day. It is still available as a hand pusher and may be seen doing a competent job in many a suburban side and back yard. Its up-to-date cousin, the engine-powered reel is very popular where the terrain is very level and close-cropped turf is desired.

In fact, the reel mower will have some trouble with grass more than two inches high and causes it to "blow down" when set for greater heights. And, as stated, a close-cropped lawn is not the hardiest and healthiest and cannot be expected to cope with drought and weeds.

THE ROTARY MOWER

The popularity of the rotary mower is a comparatively recent development and is the direct result of the vast upsurge in homestead living. The rotary is a more flexible garden tool than the reel mower, can rough it better in the wide-open spaces and can also do a fine-tooled job of mowing in competent hands.

The rotary depends on a gasoline engine to whirl its cutting blade at speeds up to 15 feet per second which means—look out, don't touch! Power through a belt or gearing may be taken from the same engine to run the wheels, giving you a power-propelled machine. Clutches for both or either function are usually available with a wide variety of hand controls as extra accessories.

The fully powered rotary with clutches controlling both blade and wheel action is a very flexible machine designed to do a topnotch job on the larger homestead. Cutting height can be adjusted

[137]

by raising or lowering the wheels or the cutting blade in a very few minutes. A clutch between the blade and the engine also means less shock and damage to the entire machine and the motor when a stone or large obstacle is struck.

The hand-propelled rotary is just as satisfactory a garden tool. It is generally lighter and smaller than the power-driven job, which means it is more maneuverable in tight corners, along borders and over rough ground. With thoughtful application, the hand-propelled rotary gives excellent service and does a fine mowing job on the average-size home grounds.

THE SICKLE BAR AND ACCESSORY MOWERS

A third category of mower, very recent in development and steadily increasing in popularity, is the mower which is part of a line of accessories. The basic power unit comprises, the engine, frame and controls, including a clutch and power take-off.

Tool attachments which may be hooked onto this unit include tillers, shredders, trimmers, digging tools and mowers. The sickle bar mower, which handles the biggest and toughest jobs, is part of the line, as well as the rotary mower and the power reel.

The basic power unit, with its variety of garden tool accessories, can be a real help to the evening and weekend gardener. It may be just the garden equipment he needs and can use to advantage if he is doing a little of everything — tilling, shredding, mowing.

But a word of caution should be inserted here. While the power mower is here to stay and is doing a better job than mowers ever did before, great care should be taken in choosing the one you — and your place — really need.

Exactly what type of mower should you use? Robert W. Miller, Extension turf specialist at The Ohio State University, says properly adjusted reel type mowers should cut cleaner with less damage to turf than the rotaries. A reel mower follows the contour more exactly, giving a uniform height of cut. Since rotaries ride on four wheels, they tend to cut higher in depressions and scalp ridges. Rotary blades travel at high speeds and are a potential danger to the operator or anyone near enough to be hit by flying debris.

However, rotary mowers have certain advantages. They are constructed simply, require less maintenance, cost less initially, trim closer, mow weeds easier, and can be adjusted easier than reel mowers.

But for quality mowing, the reel mower consistently measured higher in an Ohio State University study comparing Merion and Delta Kentucky bluegrass turf cut at one- and two-inch heights. Quality advantages were noted especially at the closer mowing height.

When you choose yard and garden equipment, do not skimp on buying a mower. You will find little pleasure in using an undersized, underpowered machine that needs constant servicing and frequent replacement. Buy a mower that is large enough to mow the lawn easily and rapidly. Choose a reel-type for the most even cut and a rotary for faster, more general service.

If you chose the power mower, here are some essential tips for using it with minimum risk to yourself, your family and neighbors:

1. Read the owner's manual and completely master the controls.

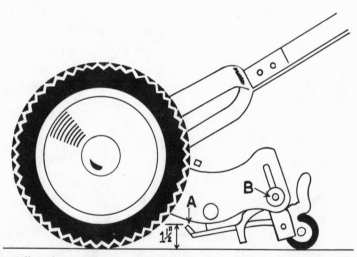

Adjust the reel mower so it will cut at the proper height: (1) Place the mower in cutting position on a sidewalk, floor, or other smooth surface; (2) measure the height of cut from solid surface to the top of the bedknife (A); (3) loosen the brackets that hold the roller (B) and lower the roller until the bedknife is 1½ inches above the solid surface; (4) tighten the roller brackets; and (5) check to see that the bedknife is the same height at both ends. Readjust the roller if necessary.

2. Clearing the children and pets from the area to be mowed is an obvious precaution.

3. The discharge chute picking up small objects from the grass may hurl them at a dangerous speed. Remove all loose "ammunitions" from the area.

4. A mowing blade whirls 2,500 times a minute. So avoid any contact and keep away from the mower's discharge.

5. Always push, never pull a mower. Your aim is to cut the grass, not your toes.

6. Never leave the engine running even briefly while you step aside or you'll tempt a child into investigating the apparatus.

7. Mow slopes sideways, not up and down. If you mow downward, the device may run away from you. Mow upward and it can back down on you.

8. Wear close fitting jeans or slacks that can't get caught in the machine. Don full leather shoes, or safety shoes.

Anytime your mower needs adjustment or fuel, cut the power and let the engine cool. A "blast" is a wonderful idea, socially speaking, but don't have one with your mower.

Once the season is over, mower care is the order of the day. All too often, this important piece of equipment is put away with gas still in the tank, sticky with mud and grass clippings and with bearings dry. A few days before the lawn is ready for its first cutting, a frantic call to mower repair shops elicits the information that work is stacked up for two months ahead. As a result, either the lawn is neglected or the mower is put back in service in a condititon which causes nothing but dissatisfaction. Is it any wonder that many home owners look on lawn and garden work as nothing but a headache?

Garden centers can be of service to homeowners by recommending proper storage care, and by urging that mowers be sent in for servicing as soon as growth for the year has definitely come to a halt. With normal use on anything less than a two acre lawn, a mower should not need sharpening every year. Every other year will keep it cutting well and should remove any minor knicks that occur.

Home lubrication at regular intervals and careful cleaning before storing are certainly not shop operations that need to be done commercially. The only other routine care should be to see that the carburetor and gas tank are clean and empty. The best way to do this at home is to run the motor until the tank is dry. Then add a pint of lacquer thinner to the tank and after allowing it to stand an hour, run until the tank is again dry. This will burn out all gum.

Mow-How

Here is a simple "mow-how" code for users of motor mowers which, if followed carefully, will protect you from possible injury.

BEFORE YOU MOW

1. Get to know your machine thoroughly by studying the manufacturer's instructions.

2. Always put the top on the fuel tank before you start the motor. It is dangerous to do it the other way round.

3. Before you start the motor, make sure that your family and pets are out of harm's way.

4. Take a walk around the lawn and clear it of stones and other objects that could get caught in the blades and be thrown out. Such objects are ejected at great speed by the blades and can cause serious injury—even to your next-door neighbor.

5. Never use a mower when the grass is wet or slippery.

6. Before starting a mower, ensure that both you and the machine are in a stable position, and that there is no chance of it toppling or running away as you adjust the speed of the motor.

WHEN MOWING

1. Always push a mower ahead of you, never pull it towards you.

2. Keep your feet clear at all times.

3. Never "aim" the clippings at pets or people, you never know what else might come out.

4. Always stop the motor and disengage the clutch before taking the machine across paths or objects that project above the surface of your garden.

[143]

5. Keep an eye open for holes or depressions. If a wheel drops down a hole, one of the blades will almost certainly hit the ground, with unfortunate consequences.

6. If your lawn has a slope in it, always mow up and down the slope—never across it.

7. Never try to unclog a mower when the motor is running.

8. Do not allow children to "have a go." The machine could easily run away from them.

9. When you leave a mower, always stop the engine.

10. Never tip a machine for inspection without first stopping the engine and removing the sparking plug. While the plug remains in the machine, it could always fire once more.

When a mower throws grass to the left, mowing

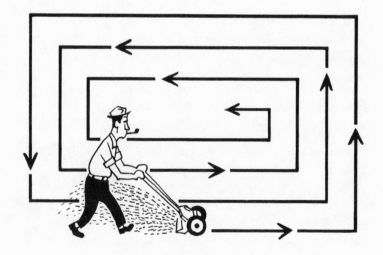

counter clockwise around the lawn will keep the clippings on the turf. Mowing with the right side next to the sidewalk will keep the clippings off the sidewalk.

A Rotary Mower Makes Fast Compost

Speed composting can now be done by a few million more gardeners, as proven by research at the Organic Experimental Gardens in Emmaus, Pa. Anyone who has a rotary lawn mower or a garden tiller with a mower attachment can make compost in as little time as 14 days. We ourselves were quite surprised to find out that leaves, weeds, straw, spoiled hay, and garden wastes of almost all kinds turned into finished compost that quickly *after being shredded* by a rotary lawn mower.

The technique of shredding is simple, safe, and fast. All that is necessary is to place the material on the ground and run over it with the mower or mower attachment. The composting materials are cut into short lengths and split open. Such shredded material creates an ideal atmosphere for decay in a compost heap. It absorbs moisture much faster than unshredded material and is wide open for bacterial action.

Rotary mowers with side exit ports for cut material create a neat pile of shredded material after only a few minutes of operation. We used a large cardboard carton as a backstop to pile up the material. A side of a building or some cloth draped over a fence would also serve the same purpose.

Almost every gardener has large amounts of these materials available at some time during the year. By running over the material with a mower, there need no longer be a lapse of several months until the organic matter decays in a compost heap. And it takes very little time to do the shredding.

For example, it required only a few minutes to shred up two bales of hay. That will give you a good idea of how quickly you can cut up a large pile of garden waste materials.

When shredding compost with a rotary mower, it is best for two people to work together. One moves the mower back and forth over a given spot, while the other feeds material in front of it. If the mower does not have an efficient exhaust chute, it will be necessary to work the shredded material by hand from the cutting area. In a small garden area, it is helpful to set up a backstop to catch the cuttings as they are ejected from the mower. That way, they will not spread all over your garden.

Meanwhile, Back at the Scythe

Scratch the surface of any traditional farmer, and you'll find a man who knows the art of mowing with a scythe. But it's fast becoming a lost art. A sickle is a weak sister and no fit substitute for jobs that a scythe should do. And power mowers cannot serve in some nooks and crannies, or on very rough stretches of land.

Doris S. Axtell gives this account of her experiences:

"Last June a heavy growth of weeds practically buried my chicken house, and no tractor or power mower could wedge in to do a cutting job. Another mowing problem was a stretch of over 110 rods of orchard grass in full blow that ran along a weaving low wall of very old stone that guarded our property on all sides. I hadn't been able to get close to the wall with the lawn mower because of root growth and the irregularity of the wall itself.

"After talking it over with my neighbor, I purchased a standard, though ominous-looking, scythe. Then I hurried home and went right to work.

"I'll tell you what I accomplished in the first hour. As I looked back, I saw ragged crescents of weeds and grass. They stood there, tall, haughty, and uncut. I had dragged up earth with the grass and I felt I was making the meadow bleed. I had struggled vainly, sometimes sweeping the blade up into the air wildly with nothing to resist my stroke. Several times I dug the point of the scythe hard into the ground, after twisting the blade in my frantic swinging. The blade must have been dulled and blunted, and it's a wonder I didn't chip it. By this time one point was clear — I was not a natural-born hand mower.

"Here's what my neighbor, the old master of

[147]

scythe swinging, told me to remember: 1. The blade must always be sharpened before using, even when it's new, and it must be dry when sharpened. That's why you see men rub the scythe with grass before they whet it. The whetstone must also be dry, and it's a good idea to lay it on your coat while you're mowing. Stand the scythe upright, with the blade pointing away from you. Put your left hand firmly on the back of the blade. Grasping it, you pass the whetstone first down one side of the edge, and then down the other, beginning near the handle and going on to the point, working quickly and hard. (It can be dangerous, but you soon get the knack.) To tell when the scythe is sharp enough you use your ear. 'First the stone clangs and grinds against the iron harshly; then it rings musically to one note;' then when it's really sharp, it purrs as though the iron and the whetstone were happy with each other. 2. Mowing well and mowing badly are separated by very little, and no new style, no matter how ingenious, has ever bettered the traditional method. The mower should think of the sycthe as a pendulum that swings, not as a knife that cuts. A good mower puts no more strength into his stroke than into his lifting. He stands up to his work, goes forward very steadily, his scythe blade just barely missing the ground. The swish and rhythm of his mowing are always the same. The bad mower leans forward in his eagerness and pain and tries to force the scythe through the grass. While standing as

[148]

nearly straight as the shape of the scythe will let him, the good mower follows up every stroke closely, moving his left foot forward.

"One thing appealing about a scythe—it's built right to lean on at the end of a long row. You should re-sharpen your scythe at the end of each long row, then carry it on your shoulder back to your beginning point and start again.

"When the art is mastered, and skill with the scythe is yours, every grass and weed will fall, and the swaths will lie in parallel order. The air will be filled with an aromatic splendor which is grass's own, and you will feel the reward that comes when a good task is accomplished."

CHAPTER VIII

Grass Clippings

Should You Let Them Fall Where They May?

IF YOUR GRASS is cut once a week, it is sound practice to leave the clippings right on the lawn so that they may become natural humus as they would under field conditions; but sometimes, the growth is so heavy or rain prevents the regular cutting, and leaving a heavy crop of clippings would lead to wads of yellow hay covering parts of the lawn. Plant pathologists argue that clippings encourage disease if they accumulate rapidly and decay slowly. In that case, the material had better be raked up and added to the compost heap as part of the green matter. By the time the lawn is cut and the grass is raked, it is sufficiently wilted and will soon start heating.

Grass clippings are not different from hay except in the matter of curing; after all, hay is nothing but dried or cured grass clippings, possibly mixed with herbs and legumes. The quality of the soil and the maturity of the growth have much to do with the nutritive content of the residues. A fertile soil, rich in nitrogen and phosphorus, produces a grass richer in nitrogen than a poor light soil; and grass cut before blooming is richer in nutrients than grass that has grown long stalks with flower heads, or, worse still, that has set seeds and turned into straw.

Comparing dried green grass and hay, the main distinction is this: green grass has a higher phosphorus and potash content than hay if the latter has been weathered long; otherwise there is no difference. Kentucky Bluegrass hay analyzes, for example, 1.2 per cent nitrogen, .3 per cent phosphoric acid, and 2.0 per cent potash. Timothy is a bit lower, perennial ryegrass often noticeably higher. Redtop analyses show a relatively high percentage of phosphorus. A mixed lawn, composed of several grasses should therefore mean over a pound of nitrogen and two pounds of potash for every hundred pounds of clippings in the dry state.

Uses for Clippings

Grass clippings can play an important role in soil-improving. First of all, a good lawn doesn't

[151]

need as much enrichment, added organic matter or mulching as do the more heavily cropped plots. As such a rich source of nitrogen, these clippings can most often be better used elsewhere. They can be a valuable fertilizer in the vegetable garden, a helpful addition in all mulches, and a major aid in converting leaves and other low-nitrogen wastes into best-quality compost.

Then, too, collecting grass clippings is one way to curtail unwanted weed growth in the lawn, since doing this helps to remove the weed seeds. Also, periodic collection of the clippings promotes better appearance, aids in keeping a neater lawn.

But don't remove all grass clippings. Some can and should be left as occasional replenishment for

Grass clippings, a good rich source of nitrogen, can be used to enrich the soil in your vegetable garden or flower plot.

the lawn itself. In fact, you're probably wrong if you *always* do the same thing about collecting grass clippings.

Grass clippings, freshly cut, contain a very large percentage of nitrogen. That is why grass is such a good soil builder. Perhaps too few lawn owners are aware of this fact. As proof of that statement, if cut grass is allowed to remain undisturbed on a pile for two days, extreme heat will build up within the very center of the heap. If not moved, the grass will soon turn into a slushy, brown muck. This heat and reaction are caused by the rapid release of nitrogen as the grass decays.

Because green grass clippings are such a wonderful source of nitrogen, they should be utilized to the utmost. There are three excellent ways in which they can be put to work in the garden and flower beds: They may be used as a mulch; they may be turned in as green manure; and they may be used in the compost heap to create the necessary heat for good decomposition.

MULCHING

As a mulch, lawn clippings surpass most others. They are easy to handle; will remain in place nicely; will fit in the smallest spaces with no trouble, and when dried, will give your rows and beds a very neat appearance. Of course you will not have enough mulch for your entire garden from the first cutting, but mulch as much as you can each week. In a short time, all of your rows will be mulched. It is a good idea to mulch first those vegetables that mature early, then work on the others.

Because it is so finely chopped, these clippings disappear completely into the soil by fall. The mulch may be replenished in late summer, but it is not necessary. For some reason, grass does not like to grow in areas covered with decayed clippings.

Green mulch, such as this, may temporarily rob the soil of available nitrogen, including both ammonia and nitrates. But this condition is so short-lived that it can, in no way, stunt the rapid growth of the plants.

GREEN MANURE

Later in the season, you may have a surplus of grass clippings on your hands. The garden has all been mulched. What to do with them now? Don't throw them away, by any means, or add to other mulch where it is not necessary. If you have a garden, scatter a few inches of the green clippings over the entire area. Turn these in immediately as green manure along with the mulch previously applied. Work a small plot at a time, depending upon the amount of excess clippings on hand. Later, you may remulch the entire area and allow it to remain thus until the following spring.

[154]

When green vegetation is mixed with the soil under favorable conditions of temperature and moisture, decomposition immediately begins. This rapid decomposition is brought about by many species of bacteria and fungi found in the earth. These microorganisms require a source of energy such as nitrogen, which green grass supplies in abundance. Because of this large amount of nitrogen in grass, these hungry bacteria and fungi will tend to draw from it, instead of robbing the soil of its necessary supply. In no time, the grass is digested into humus, and the soil made many times richer for plant growth. The nitrogen in the earth has also been stepped up, which will cause plants to become stronger and greener.

If you care to turn in green grass clippings as green manure before planting a second crop in a vacant plot, you may do so. Give the section a week or ten days to return to normal, then plant as before. Many times, if the plot has thus been treated, the second crop surpasses the first.

When used as green manure, grass clippings greatly improve the physical condition of heavy-textured soils. But to all, they give the much-needed humus and nitrogen. If acidity is a factor, a small amount of limestone may be applied with the clippings.

The third use of grass clippings is incorporating them into the compost heap to create the necessary heat for proper decomposition. The best principle to follow here is to use two-thirds grass clippings and one-third stable manure or other high-nitrogen material. — *Betty Brinhart.*

Thatch

Grass clipping may foster the development of thatch, and cause a host of problems from smothering to the harboring of insects and disease. Thatch may be defined as a tightly intermingled layer of partially decomposed leaves, stems, and roots of grasses which develops beneath the actively growing green vegetation at the soil surface.

WHY WORRY ABOUT THATCH?

Thatch accumulations are undesirable in many respects. Thatch decreases the vigor of turfgrasses by restricting the movement of water, air, plant nutrients, and pesticides into the soil. During wet periods, the thatch material may act as a sponge and hold excessive amounts of water, which materially reduces the oxygen supply available to the roots. On the other hand, if the thatch becomes dry, it is extremely difficult to rewet. Many turfgrass disease organisms may be harbored in thatch accumulations. Insects, not necessarily turf damaging insects, may live and multiply in the thatch layer.

Thatch often causes abnormal development of

[156]

the grass plants. If grass must grow through a thatched layer, it tends to develop unusually long stems with leaves forming at the top. Because of this change in the normal growing habit, plants are often weakened and may be more susceptible to disease, insects, and mechanical injury. Root development is often restricted, increasing the danger of drought damage.

Height of cut can be affected by thatch. As the thatch material builds up, the mower tends to ride on the thatch and does not cut at the desired height. If the cutting height is lowered in an attempt to overcome that problem, a mass of brown stems may result because of the unusual growth habit that has developed.

There is increased evidence that rapid thatch decomposition during periods of hot, moist weather may generate sufficient heat and decomposition products to injure or kill turfgrasses. Heat generation also dries the soil quickly, resulting in possible drought injury.

BUILD-UP OF THATCH

The rate of thatch build-up is dependent on several factors. Certain grasses tend to thatch much faster than others—some due to their vigorous growth, others because of the resistance of their leaves and stems to decomposition. All turfgrasses will thatch if given the opportunity. Bentgrass, because of its vigorous growth and habit of growth, builds up thatch quite rapidly. Merion Kentucky bluegrass is probably the most notorious thatch developer of the general lawn grasses because of its rapid growth and the resistance to decomposition of the clippings. Red fescue is a slow grower, but its leaves and stems are extremely resistant to decomposition. Red fescue requires a longer period of time to accumulate thatch than does Merion Kentucky bluegrass. Because red fescue recovers slowly after injury, the mechanical thatching operation must be less severe than with other grasses.

Management practices also plan an important role in thatch build-up. Over-fertilizing and over-watering result in excessive and unnecessary growth. Clippings left on the lawn may be a major cause of thatch development. Failure to keep an adequate pH for favorable bacterial growth decreases the rate of decomposition of the thatch material.

THATCH CONTROL

Always remember that thatch build-up occurs over a period of time, although the more vigorous bentgrasses and bluegrasses may thatch in just a few growing seasons. It seems logical that a thatch removal program should remove the thatch in the same manner as it was built up, rather than attempt to take it all out in one treatment.

Thatch control should be considered from two

viewpoints: preventive control to avoid excessive build-up, and curative control where a serious thatch problem already exists. Unfortunately, control is usually left until the latter situation develops.

From a preventive standpoint, liming, fertilizing, mechanical thatching, aerating, and clipping removal should be given consideration. Even though the soil pH is in the preferred range of 6.5 to 7.0, the pH of the organic thatch layer on the soil surface may be quite acid. Light annual applications of ground limestone at a rate of 20 to 25 pounds per 1,000 square feet will stimulate bacterial action at the soil surface and in the thatch layer.

Fertilization should be adequate for good growth, but it should not be so excessive that succulent growth is obtained. Over-succulent rank growth not only increases the thatch problem but also makes the turf much more susceptible to damage from diseases, insects, and mechanical injury.

Periodic mechanical thatching carried out in a preventive program need not be as drastic as in a curative program. Normally, this job can be done with much less expensive equipment, than that needed for a curative program. One or two treatments per season, usually in the spring and fall, should be sufficient.

Aeration benefits a thatch control preventive program, primarily through the indirect effects which stimulate bacterial activity and promote development of strong, healthy grass plants. The amount of aeration is determined more by soil conditions than by the thatch condition.

Clipping removal materially reduces the rate of thatch build-up, especially where Merion Kentucky bluegrass or red fescue dominates the grass population. Clippings can be removed with a grass catcher on the mower or by following the mowing operation with a vacuum or rotating brush sweeper.

In a curative program, the question is how much thatch can be removed in one treatment without permanent damage to the desirable grass. This must be determined by the general vigor of the plant, the root system, the climatic conditions, and the amount of thatch present. Turfgrasses that have a relatively good root system and are growing vigorously can tolerate more abuse in the thatch removal operation than can unhealthy turf.

Climatic conditions, primarily temperature and moisture, are extremely important. If temperatures are ideal for growth, and adequate moisture is available, the treatment can be much more drastic than under hot and/or low moisture conditions. Where large amounts of thatch have accumulated, it is unwise to attempt to remove all of the thatch in one treatment. Mechanical removal of thatch should be attempted only when growth conditions are adequate for rapid recovery of the grass.

[160]

THATCH REMOVAL EQUIPMENT

Machines for mechanically removing thatch accumulations fall into three basic groups: those machines having revolving swinging knives, those having revolving stationary knives, and those having revolving spring tines. Whereas a rotary mower has its blade moving in a plane that is horizontal to the ground surface, the mechanical thatcher knives or tines revolve in a plane that is vertical to the ground surface. For this reason, these machines are sometimes referred to as vertical mowers. No two machines on the market today do exactly the same job. They vary in width between blades or tines, in depth of penetration, in power, and in the amount of tearing of the existing turf. Consequently, they also vary in the quantity of thatch removed and the extent of damage done to the desirable grasses. Where thatch removal is followed on a preventive basis and there is no excessive build-up of material, adequate results can be obtained with the spring-tine-type machine with little or no damage to the desirable grasses. However, if considerable thatch accumulation has occurred and deep penetration is required for removal, a machine having solid or swinging knives should be used.

CHAPTER IX

Edging, Raking and Rolling

Keep Your Lawn on Edge

WHEN GAY BLADES of grass start overlapping into the flower beds, crowding up against the trees and shrubs, or promenading onto the driveway, the walks, etc. — it's more than time to do something about it.

The solution: put in *lawn edging* wherever it's needed. The result: better-looking flower beds, tree and bush plantings, paths, drives — *and* lawns. Also, far less work or trouble in maintaining the better looks and the finer turf.

TWO TYPES

There are two basic types of edging — the seen and the unseen. Where landscaping is planned with an uninterrupted smoothness in mind, and especially around trees, close to foundations, etc., the invisible style is a good idea. This means using one of the edging materials that serve as an underground "fence" to keep the grass in place. Among these are galvanized steel, aluminum, and plastic. All come in rippled sheets or rolls, are easily laid out, cut and driven down to the soil level.

Once in place, these barriers provide long-lasting, very neat and hidden borders that lend a trim appearance and easier care. (They may also be used for holding raised beds in place, leaving as much above the lower soil line as needed to retain the upper-level tier.) Fast installation and economy are an added pair of advantages.

The other type—visible edging—includes a wide range of potential materials, plus opportunity galore for imaginative design by the gardener. Where a raised edge or border is desirable, it can be planned as a pleasant accent, a line or circle of color and texture contrast.

Here, a number of natural substances readily fit the role—everything from bright, rich California redwood to odd-shaped flagstone set in an irregular pattern. Just a note of caution: if you choose wood of any kind, make sure that it is not a rapidly rotting one, or be sure to treat it with a fence-post preservative to prevent your edging from spoiling from the ground up.

One of the more popular and simple sorts of do-it-yourself lawn edging is made from bricks. These can be any of the various shades of red, white, etc. What's more they may be set vertically, horizontally, at angles, alternated—just about anyway that suits your purpose and eye. The same is true of concrete or cinder blocks, squares of adobe, corrugated metal, palings, flagstone or other rocks laid in interesting patterns. Still another styling may feature a trim line of low, narrow cement.

Important things to keep in mind when planning and putting in any lawn edge include the level and drainage of the soil plot, the actual height needed to keep back the grass sector, and the over-all effect on your garden or grounds.

Used carefully and with an outdoor decorative flair, edgings—both visible and invisible—can be extremely helpful and attractive adjuncts to any garden.

Go Easy on the Raking

After a long hard winter there is a natural tendency to want to get out in the garden the first warm spring day that comes along. For many persons, especially the ladies, this takes the form of running to the tool shed, grabbing a heavy, sharp-toothed steel rake and giving the lawn a thorough combing. This is done in the mistaken belief that such a procedure will help the lawn. Nothing could be further from the truth. All they succeed in doing is to rake into piles the valuable layer of mulch built up from last year's grass plants and clippings. If these were left on the lawn, they would eventually be returned to the top inch or so of soil as a valuable form of humus. The only reason for raking a lawn in the early spring is to remove any sticks, stones, pieces of wood, and other debris that might damage your lawn mower or give the lawn an unsightly appearance. Such raking should be done with one of the lightweight aluminum, bamboo or metal rakes that are shaped like a fan.

A READER ON RAKING

"I have kept my lawn in such condition that it has been admired by all who passed our place. I have built up wasted lawns and made them worthwhile. And How! Never rake the lawn after mowing it, but cut the grass every week or oftener in wet weather. This not only saves the labor of raking, but returns to the soil that which it needs. Thus is returned to the soil what the grass has taken from it as well as what it has taken from the atmosphere. On a lawn 50' x 100' you will add in this manner at least ten bushels of compost during the summer instead of removing this amount from it."

Guy C. Gregg, West Pittston, Pa.

Rolling

Recently, one homeowner was discussing his springtime lawn management. "I roll my lawn every spring with a heavy roller." Then after pausing for some seconds, he added as an afterthought, "but I don't exactly know why!"

If other lawn keepers follow the same mechanical management practices, they could be doing their lawn more harm than good. In fact, blind adherence to traditional lawn practices has long ago been discarded by the most astute organic lawn owners. It's best to have a good idea of exactly what the rolling procedure is supposed to do.

Here are some of the arguments, pro and con, for rolling your lawn:

Pro: Grass roots, like the roots of all perennials, can be heaved from the ground with the alternate freezing and thawing that takes place in late fall and early spring. But unlike other perennials, grass cannot be mulched to prevent heaving. Cover over grass in the wintertime invites mold, may smother the plants and causes more harm than good. If your lawn presents an unduly rough appearance in spring, inspect the grass roots. If you find some of them pushed above the surface, rolling with a half-filled water roller may help to push them back into contact with the soil before they dry out and die. A light top-dressing of compost or enriched topsoil applied before rolling may further protect the exposed roots. Roll first in one direction, then again at right angles to the first route.

Con: Rolling a bumpy lawn may do more harm than good if the soil is wet. This is especially true where the soil is heavy and clayey. Such soil, if it is flattened by a heavy roller, may have all the air forced out of it and may be hopelessly compacted as a result. Wet soil should never be rolled, even if the roots of the grass are heaved. Clay soil should probably never be rolled. The safest rule seems to be to roll only when the soil is fairly firm and then only if it contains enough organic matter to prevent packing.

To test whether a soil is too wet for rolling, press the foot firmly into the grass. If you squeeze water out, then do not roll. Rolling will not correct surface irregularities due to faulty grading at a time of planting.

CHAPTER X

Aerification

AN *average soil* is made up of about 25 per cent of air. As this is a considerable portion of the soil total, it must be evident that air is an important part of the soil's makeup. For the best functioning of the roots of grass the soil must be well ventilated. Fertility depends upon it.

Air is needed in the soil for proper working of the bacteria and fungi. It aids in the breakdown of organic matter. Air aids in the oxidation of mineral matter. In an air-poor soil not much of the minerals would be available for plant sustenance. The presence of sufficient air acts as a regulator of the supply of carbon dioxide, too much of which is detrimental to grass.

In the process of soil respiration, oxygen is fed to the roots. Better aeration provides a bigger root system and higher yields. In the process of plant growth, leaves absorb carbon dioxide from the atmosphere and give off oxygen. The reverse takes place in the roots, which take in oxygen and give off carbon dioxide. In the decay of organic matter, carbon dioxide is given off.

The composition of soil air differs somewhat from that of the atmosphere above ground. In the first place, much of the air in soil is dissolved in the soil water, but as such it is available to the needs of plants. The humidity is greater in the soil —a condition necessary for the optimum well-being of soil organisms. The carbon dioxide content is much higher in soil air and therefore, the percentage of oxygen and nitrogen is less. In the soil there may be hundreds of times more carbon dioxide than in the air above it. Too much of this gas is detrimental, but enough is needed to maintain biochemical activities, the processes similar to human digestion, which in plant functioning begin to take place before nutrients enter the roots.

DEVICES FOR BETTER AERATION

Among the methods used for increasing the air supply in soils are the addition of organic matter, the application of rock powders, soil drainage, subsoiling, cultivation, mixed cropping, earthing up, etc. By far the most important of all of them is to see that the soil is supplied with sufficient organic matter. It is axiomatic in agricultural literature that the more humus present in the soil, the better will be the aeration, the more pore spaces it will contain. There seems to be a direct relation between the amount of humus and the volume of pore space. The more of the former—the more of the latter.

CHEMICAL FERTILIZERS

What is often overlooked is that some chemical fertilizers harden the soil and reduce the pore spaces. Nitrate of soda is a typical offender. In the yearly application of this fertilizer, the plant uses up much of the nitrate, but little of the soda, which keeps piling up in the soil. This soda combines with carbon, which is always present in the soil, forming the compound *carbonate of soda,* which is washing soda. Where large amounts of nitrate of soda are used, the soil becomes so hard that it can be cultivated only after a rain.

ROCK POWDERS

Part of the organic method of farming is the liberal use of rock powders rather than chemical fertilizers. In his book *An Agricultural Testament* (Oxford University Press), Sir Albert Howard describes how the continued use of basic slag, which has a rock powder-like makeup, produced humus in a soil by its ability to aerate it. It stands to reason that the application of rock powder to a heavy soil is bound to improve its aeration. Wherever a tiny particle of rock finds itself, there it will be completely surrounded by air. It creates billions of new pore spaces where none existed before.

It is helpful to understand that these rock powders may be roughly divided into two classes. One group consists of limestone, phosphate, and the potash rocks. Another class of rock which has been neglected—the basalts, traprocks, sandstones, etc. —may be called the bland rocks. These are well supplied with minerals but do not contain enough potash, phosphate or calcium to give trouble if overused. They are cheaper, and can be used much more liberally, thus greatly improving the aeration of a soil.

SOIL NUTRIENTS AND EARTHWORMS

The presence of sufficient air in the soil is necessary for the transformation of minerals to forms usable by plants. In an experiment it was found that forced aeration increased the amount of potassium taken in by plants. All textbooks state that nitrate formation in soils can take place only in the presence of a liberal supply of oxygen. Many of the processes in the soil are oxidations—sulfur transformed to sulfur dioxide, carbon to carbon dioxide, ammonia to nitrate in these processes.

One of the greatest aids to soil aeration, the earthworm will burrow down 6 feet and more, leaving his passageways as means for the entry of

[171]

air. Russell in his book *Soil Conditions and Plant Growth* (Longmans, Green and Co.), suggests that earthworm eggs be planted in farm soils to increase aeration where it is poor. But applications of organic matter would be better, because not only does the humus itself bring about better aeration, but the effect of the presence of organic matter automatically multiplies the earthworm population.

CURING HARDPAN

The hardpan that forms from lack of organic matter and use of chemical fertilizers, impedes the aeration of the soil below it, but the earthworm, if present in sufficient numbers can destroy it. In well-run organic soils, there should be millions of earthworms per acre.

In helping to increase the soil's aeration, the earthworm serves a valuable purpose in one respect. There are many disease-producing bacteria that can thrive only under anaerobic conditions, that is, where there is a lack of oxygen. With a teeming earthworm population the conditions are kept aerobic.

We must not forget also the effect of other burrowing insects in maintaining soil aeration. Termites make tunnels which roots sometimes use, and a device which measures the population of insects per cubic inch of soil shows that in good soil, plentifully supplied with organic matter, there are many more of these little beneficial soil creatures. They consist of springtails, mites, worms, centipedes, etc.

Heavy application of chemical fertilizers kills off many of the earthworms and beneficial insects, thus depriving the soil of a valuable aerating device.

Air is an urgent need of many beneficial soil organisms that aid in transforming soil nutrients for plant use and that take part in the various oxidation processes, including the oxidation of humus. Oxygen gives the bacteria part of their energy. If it were not for the aerobic bacteria, no organic matter would decompose in the soil. These valuable organisms manufacture protein from these organic residues.

Aeration aids the formation of mycorrhiza on the roots of many plants. The mycorrhiza is a fungus organism that acts in partnership with the roots of plants to feed it valuable nutrients.

CARBON DIOXIDE CONTROLS AND WATER

If the soil air contains too much carbon dioxide, given off by the roots, there will be a depression in growth. Various methods of ridding the soil of an oversupply of this gas include changes in soil temperature, and rain water, the latter bringing oxygen into the soil. In the practice of the organic method, the soil is more porous because of its organic-matter content and will absorb more rain water.

When manure decays, much carbon dioxide is

produced, but the effect of the application of manure is to increase the pore spaces in the soil, which increases the rate of diffusion of this gas into the atmosphere. Sir E. John Russell has shown that green manuring, particularly if the crop is fairly succulent, will also put up the carbon dioxide content of the soil air. If seeds are sown too soon afterwards, the carbon dioxide may inhibit germination or harm the very young root systems' seedlings.

Rain carries oxygen and brings it into the soil—down to subsoil levels. In regions where there is plenty of rainfall there is much better soil aeration than in arid regions. In areas of little rainfall the soil becomes silt. It lacks porosity and forms crusts. I have seen soils low in organic matter where crusts formed during dry spells. On our farm 23 years ago—before it was farmed by the organic method—crusts used to form. But not today. Some soils that are low in organic matter even lose their permeability during heavy rains. Then waterlogging occurs easily. Percolation stops, and asphyxiation sets in. The root growth of crops is seriously affected. —*J. I. Rodale*

MECHANICAL AERATION

Mechanical aeration provides an excellent means of correcting or alleviating soil compaction which may be quite serious on many lawn areas. Compaction occurs primarily in the surface area of the lawn. A compacted layer as thin as ¼ to ½ inch can greatly impede water infiltration, nutrient penetration, and gaseous exchange between the soil and the atmosphere. Compaction of this type in the surface layer of soil can be corrected or reduced by the use of suitable aerating equipment.

Aerating machines remove plugs of soil from the turf area, thereby creating an artificial system of large or noncapillary pores by which moisture and plant nutrients can be taken into the soil. They also provide a breathing system through which caron dioxide can escape from the soil and oxygen can enter the soil. A rapid intake in movement of water and air is recognized as a prime

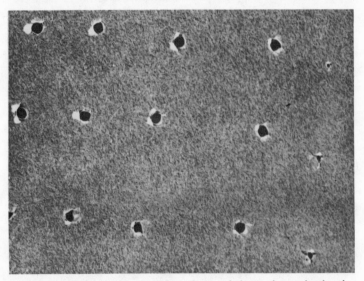

This unusual photograph, enlarged several times, shows clearly what one kind of mechanical aerator can do to the turf.

[175]

necessity in correcting damages to the turf caused by compacted soils.

Spring and early fall are the best times to aerate. Summer aeration of cool-season grasses, such as bluegrass, bentgrass, and fescue, is not generally recommended because these grasses are in a semi-dormant condition, whereas crabgrass is quite active. A safe general rule for time of aeration is to aerate only when the desirable grasses are growing vigorously. The type of equipment recommended will depend upon the size and use of the area. Equipment varies in size, from the small, hand, tubular-tined forks to large, tractor-drawn units capable of aerating large areas in relatively short time. Power-driven, homeowner size units are available. Many lawn and garden supply houses have aerating equipment available on a rental basis, and many landscape agencies will do the job on a custom basis.

If the soil to be aerated covers only a small area, the job may be done with a tubular-tined fork. Thrust the fork into the soil in rows 6 inches apart, removing cores of soil with each thrust. If

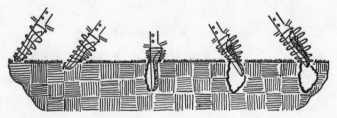

By removing plugs of soil from the turf, mechanical aerators enhance the exchange of air and water.

[176]

the soil is very close, remove the cores; if not, leave them to wash back into the sod. Holes made in this fashion must be at least 4 or 5 inches deep. The small spikes attached to hand rollers do not penetrate deep enough to do any good.

Until only recently, aerating was not a simple job for the homeowner with a lawn consisting of a few hundred square feet. No power tools were available in small sizes for the medium-sized garden area; the tools on the market were hand-operated and presented a strenuous job to the average gardener.

But that is no longer the case. Manufacturers of garden tillers have come up with an attachment that makes possible a perfect program for home lawn aeration. An attachment consisting of aerating disks, which can be attached to the tiller unit, is now available.

Aerating is best done in the late fall and early spring. The disks themselves may be spaced at any desired distance, although most gardeners prefer using 3 disks spaced about 4 inches apart. By using the machine in a north and south direction and then perpendicularly in an east and west direction, it is possible to slice the entire lawn area up into 4-inch squares of sod.

While the slices are open, it is an excellent idea to apply a thick covering of finely ground-up compost, leaf mold, peat moss or other organic fertilizers over the entire surface of the lawn. By using the rotary mower attachment, the fertilizer can be blown into these crevices. This material prevents heavy clay soil from completely reuniting and provides the roots with moisture and nu-

A close look at the action part of a garden tiller shows how the aerating disks have been added to cut and slice the lawn, thereby reducing fungus and insect infestation and thinning dense root zone thatch.

[178]

trients. (You'll be amazed how quickly color can come back to a lawn that had previously looked worn-out.)

Aerating disks can slice the soil to a depth of 3 inches. This "slicing" does not injure the lawn as some persons may at first think. Actually, it is beneficial from a propagation standpoint, since new grass shoots begin to take root at the joint of the older grass plants. If aeration is done early enough in the spring, the entire area will meld into one smooth surface in about a month.

Equipment having solid tines or spikes should not be mistaken for aerating equipment. Aerators always remove a soil core, whereas solid tine spikers do not. Spikers actually increase soil compaction because the movement of the soil by the penetration of the tine forces the soil into a denser mass. —*John C. Harper, II*

CHAPTER XI

Fertilizing

What's wrong with Chemical Fertilizers?

IN THE 1930's, an Englishman named Sir Albert
Howard saw what only the most advanced conservation scientists and thinkers of today realize—that
the cycle of life which is vital to the health of all
the inhabitants of this planet can be disrupted by
chemicals in the environment. An artificial substance or practice that is introduced into the routine of farming can't be considered successful just
because it increases yields for a few seasons, Sir
Albert reasoned. If it disrupts the normal cycles of
nature, ultimately there will be horrible penalties
to pay. He saw many ways that chemical fertilizers
upset the balance which is characteristic of nature,
and J. I. Rodale clearly and forcefully amplified

[180]

those points to Americans through the pages of *Organic Gardening and Farming* magazine. In the early days of the organic movement—particularly in the 1940's and 50's—we were thought odd for even suggesting that a fertilizer could have an effect beyond the field on which it was applied. Now the tragedies of technology have rudely shocked many scientists into taking a questioning attitude toward all new chemical substances. The polluting foam of the "hard" synthetic detergents was one of those tragedies.

CHEMICAL FERTILIZER MENACE
READILY OBSERVABLE TO ALL

It isn't necessary to look at the probability of ultimate broad harm to the world's environment to see the dangers of chemical fertilizers. Their weaknesses are apparent to anyone who looks carefully at the soil to which they are applied. Artificial fertilizers are strong substances, which flood the soil with larger amounts of plant foods than it can accept without disturbing its balance. After an application of chemical fertilizer, almost every living element in the soil gets jazzed up beyond its normal rhythm of life—for a short time. In that frantic period, the humus stores of the soil are depleted, because humus is the one thing that helps balance out the insult to the soil from outside chemicals. As a result, soil structure and texture is degraded, causing rain to have difficulty entering

[181]

the soil. Hardpans build up, accentuated by the soluble chemicals that are reaching down through the soil. The proper balance of all food elements is lost, because no man can figure out how much of each soluble nutrient plants will need in any given season. Nature's intention is for plants to select their nutrients moderately from the soil's reserves of food which are held mainly in insoluble form, and which are gradually released by the action of the weather, bacteria, earthworms, and a multitude of other forms of soil life. The chemical way pushes those life processes to a sidelines role. The soil is thought of not as a throbbing center of life, but primarily as something firm to hold up plants while their roots are bathed in various chemical solutions.

NOT EVEN NECESSARY FOR PRODUCTIVE LAWNS

All those points—and more have been emphasized for years by organic lawn owners. And we have proved not only that chemical fertilizers have hazards, but that they aren't really necessary for lawn growth. There are many good natural fertilizer materials available, ranging from phosphate rock and limestone to the wide variety of organic materials made from composted municipal and industrial wastes. Much larger amounts of such natural materials could be made available to farmers and gardeners, and at lower prices, if more people would be willing to forego the easy promises of the chemical people. Artificial fertilizers do have the advantages of being more concentrated and therefore quicker to apply, but can farmers and gardeners justify degrading their soil and even poisoning other people for such a reason?

The quick and easy way to try to solve insect problems is to go the chemical route, having little regard for the merits of the natural systems of balance which kept this old world spinning and thriving for millions of years before we came along.

The organic school does not accept the use of artificial fertilizers for many reasons. Chemical fertilizers are quick-acting, short-term plant "boosters," and are responsible for: (1) deterioration of soil friability, creating hardpan soil, (2) destruction of beneficial soil life, including earthworms, (3) altering vitamin and protein contents of certain crops, (4) making certain crops more vulnerable to disease, and (5) preventing plants from absorbing some needed minerals.

The soil must be regarded as a living organism. An acid fertilizer, because of its acids, dissolves the cementing material, made from the dead bodies of soil organisms, which holds the rock particles together to form soil crumbs. It spoils the friability of the soil. On the surface of the soil such cement-free particles settle to form a compact, more or less water-impervious layer. This compact surface layer of rock particles encourages rainwater to run off rather than to enter the soil.

[183]

For example: A highly soluble fertilizer, such as 5-10-5, goes into solution in the soil water rapidly so that much of it may be washed away without benefiting the plants at all. But the sodium in the fertilizer like sodium nitrate tends to accumulate in the soil where it combines with carbonic acid to form washing soda, sodium carbonate. This chemical causes the soil to assume a cement-like hardness. Other minerals, when present in large concentrations, percolate into the subsoil where they interact with the clay to form impervious layers of precipitates called hardpans.

Hardpans seal the topsoil off from the subsoil. Water cannot pass downward into the subsoil, and water from the water table cannot rise to the topsoil in which the plants are growing. Many plants cannot live when their roots are kept too wet. Then too, the subsoil below the hardpans is anaerobic and rapidly becomes acid. In such anaerobic acid soils, the soil organism population changes radically and in ways which are unfavorable to crop plants.

Such highly soluble chemicals as chlorides and sulphates are poisonous to the beneficial soil organisms, but in small amounts act as stimulants. These chemicals stimulate the beneficial soil bacteria to such increased growth and reproduction that they use up the organic matter in the soil as food faster than it can be returned by present agricultural practices. When chemical residues accumulate in the soil, the microorganisms may be killed off by hydrolysis (water-removing). The high salt concentration in the soil water will pull water from the bacterial or fungal cells, causing them to collapse and die.

ARTIFICIAL FERTILIZERS CHANGE THE SOIL ORGANISM POPULATION:

Many artificial fertilizers contain acids, as sulphuric acid and hydrochloric acid, which will increase the acidity of the soil. Changes in the soil acidity (pH) are accompanied by changes in the kinds of organisms which can live in the soil. Such changes often are sufficient to interfere greatly with the profitable growth of grass. For this reason, the artificial fertilizer people tell their customers to increase the organic matter content of the soil, thus offsetting the deleterious effects of these acids; also to use lime.

NITROGEN-CONTAINING FERTILIZERS, LIKE SODIUM NITRATE AND CYANAMID, AFFECT THE NITROGEN-FIXING SOIL BACTERIA:

About 78 per cent of the atmosphere is made up of gaseous nitrogen. Living soil contains enough nitrogen-fixing bacteria to fix enough atmospheric nitrogen to supply abundantly the needs of crop plants. In the presence of soluble nitrates, these bacteria use the nitrogen which man has provided in his artificial fertilizers and fix absolutely none from the atmosphere.

ARTIFICIAL FERTILIZERS ARE RESPONSIBLE FOR POOR AERATION OF THE SOIL:

There are several ways by which artificial fertilizers will reduce aeration of soils. Earthworms, whose numerous burrowing make the soil more porous, are killed. The acid fertilizers will also destroy the cementing materials which bind rock particles together to form crumbs. Lastly, hardpans result which seal off the lower soil levels, keeping them more or less completely anaerobic.

THE USE OF ARTIFICIAL FERTILIZERS CAN MAKE GRASS MORE SUSCEPTIBLE TO DISEASE:

Chemical fertilizers rob grass of some natural immunity by killing off the policemen microorganisms in the soil. Many plant diseases have already been considerably checked when antibiotic-producing bacteria or fungi thrived around the roots.

When grass is supplied with much nitrogen and only a medium amount of phosphate, it will most easily contract mosaic infections also. Most resistance is obtained if there is a small supply of nitrogen and plenty of phosphate. Fungus and bacterial diseases have then been related to high nitrogen fertilization, as well as to a lack of trace elements.

[186]

GRASS GROWN ON LAND CONTINUALLY DOPED WITH
ARTIFICIAL FERTILIZERS OFTEN ARE DEFICIENT
IN TRACE ELEMENTS:

To explain this principle will mean delving into a little physics and chemistry, but you will then easily see the unbalanced nutrition created in artificially-fertilized grass. The colloidal humus particles are the convoys that transfer most of the minerals from the soil solution to the root hairs. Each humus particle is negatively charged and will of course attract the positive elements such as potassium, sodium, calcium, magnesium, manganese, aluminum, boron, iron, copper, and other metals. When sodium nitrate, for instance, is dumped into the soil year after year in large doses, a radical change takes place on the humus particles. The very numerous sodium ions (atomic particles) will eventually crowd out the other ions, making them practically unavailable for plant use. The humus becomes coated with sodium, glutting the root hairs with the excess. Finally the grass is unable to pick up some of the minerals that it really needs.

Beware of fast-acting fertilizers. Repeated tests by organic gardeners have shown that they are short-term feeders and that they can't build up soil to virgin goodness. Only 10 to 15 per cent of their nutrients are used by plants. The rest is washed out or locked up chemically in the soil.

Extremely few fertilizers are complete plant foods—despite what you read in advertisements for chemicals. No man yet knows all the nutrients that a plant needs. The only way to be sure of putting into your soil a complete plant food is to duplicate the way soil was built originally. Add the natural rocks and silt that supply minerals, plus compost, manure or other organic matter. They will supply, in a shotgun manner, the humus that is the key to soil balance.

BUGS ATTACK CHEMICAL-FED LAWN GRASSES

Researchers at the University of Florida's Agricultural Experiment Station have discovered that artificial forms of nitrogen commonly used in lawn fertilizer mixtures may result in increased chinch bug damage. Actually, extensive tests showed where chinch bugs apparently had crawled over organically-fertilized grass to reach plots fertilized with inorganic nitrogen. The pattern was the same in 3 replicated plots. Dr. G. C. Horn and Dr. W. L. Pritchett, who tested many lawn grasses being used in the U.S., found that both the source and rate of nitrogen had a tremendous effect on the susceptibility of St. Augustinegrass to chinch bug injury. The organic nitrogen they used, a processed tankage from industrial waste, resulted in the least chinch bug damage, whereas a high rate of inorganic nitrogen (ammonium nitrate) resulted in the greatest damage. The Florida studies also revealed that lawn fertilizer mixtures commonly used contain much more phosphorus and potash than grasses need.

ORGANIC VS. INORGANIC FERTILIZER

When the word "organic" is used on the fertilizer label, it usually refers to that part of the nitrogen that is derived from natural or synthetic organic materials. The balance of the nitrogen, phosphoric acid and potash are derived from mineral sources. In most so-called organic fertilizers, mineral sources make up from one-half to three-quarters of their total composition.

There is also a difference of nitrogen availability between the organic and mineral types of fertilizer. The nitrogen of inorganic fertilizers is readily available soon after application, giving the grass one dramatic clout over the head with an abundance of nitrogen. The nitrogen of organic ferti-

A fertilizer rich in organic nutrients gives your lawn nitrogen in a readily available form and does not leave any unpleasant residue, but it should be prepared according to your lawn's individual needs. Here a gardener is ready to apply lime, rock phosphate and sifted compost.

[189]

lizer is less readily available, since it has to be broken down by soil bacteria to become available for
plant use. This requires favorable soil temperature, adequate moisture and time. Thus, organic
nitrogen is released more slowly and evenly to
plants. Because the organic nitrogen is released
over a longer period of time, there is less need for
frequent applications.

Another important difference between these two
types of fertilizers is the degree of turf injury that
may be caused by their use.

Less danger of "burning" turf occurs with a fertilizer whose nitrogen is mostly in the organic
form. Finally, there is the danger of combining
inorganic commercial fertilizers with chemicals
for insect and weed control.

Solving the Soil's Nutrition Problems

One of the best ways to gain an understanding
of the major nutrient problems of soil is to have it
tested — either with your own soil test kit or sent
out to your state experiment station or commercial
laboratory. Generally a test of this kind will answer
whether or not your soil has a sufficient amount of
the major nutrients — nitrogen (N), phosphorus (P),
potassium (K). A test of this kind will also tell you
whether your soil is acid or alkaline.

When fertilizing, always remember that the objective of the organic method is to feed the soil,

not necessarily the grass. Therefore the major objective is to increase the over-all fertility of this soil and not just supply the minimum amount of nutrients to produce a single crop in one season.

The chemical fertilizer user has long made use of special proportions of fertilizers, such as 5-10-5, 4-8-4, etc. Such a fertilizer formula is merely a simple way to show the amount of nitrogen, phosphorus, and potash in the mixture of fertilizer. For example in the combination 2-4-2, 2 per cent is nitrogen, 4 per cent is phosphorus and 2 per cent is potash.

The Importance of Nitrogen: Nitrogen is a major element in grass nutrition. It is responsible for producing leaf growth and greener leaves. Deficiency causes yellow leaves and stunted growths.

If you believe your soil is deficient in nitrogen, you can correct it by adding compost, manure or other nitrogen-rich organic fertilizers such as dried blood, tankage, cottonseed meal, cocoa bean and peanut shells, bone meal or sewage sludge. Returning weeds, grass clippings and other garden wastes to the soil will add to its humus content and improve its nitrogen content at the same time.

Organic versus Chemical Nitrogen: Organic forms of nitrogen are more stable in the soil and become available for grass plant growth more gradually than nitrogen from chemical fertilizers. When concentrated chemical nitrogen is applied to the soil, it produces a shot-in-the-arm effect to plant

[191]

growth. The plants are subjected to too much nitrogen at one time. Then, if a sudden heavy rain storm drenches the field, the chemical form of nitrogen is to a large extent washed out, and the plants can become starved for lack of the element.

The Value of Phosphorus: All growing grass needs phosphorus. It is important for a strong root system and for good growth. If plants are unusually small and thin, it may be an indication of a phosphorus deficiency in the soil. Phosphorus is also said to hasten maturity, increase seed yield, increase resistance to winter kill and diseases, while a deficiency causes stunted growth and sterile seed.

Sources of Phosphorus: You can best add phosphorus to your soil with rock phosphate which is a natural rock product containing from 30 to 50 per cent phosphorus. When the rock is finely ground, the phosphate is available to the plant as it needs it. Rock phosphate is especially effective in soils which have organic matter.

Besides rock phosphate, other phosphorus sources are basic slag, bone meal, dried blood, cottonseed meal and activated sludge.

The Value of Potassium: Potassium is the third major nutrient and is very important to the strength of the plant. It carries carbohydrates through the plant system, helps form strong stems, and helps to fight diseases which may attack. If plants are slow-growing and stunted, with browning leaves there is probably a potassium deficiency. Potassium is said to accomplish the following: decreases water requirement of plant; makes plants more resistant to diseases; reduces winter kill; promotes color; is essential for cell division and growth; aids plants to utilize nitrogen; balances effect of excess nitrogen or calcium; reduces boron requirements.

Deficiencies can cause firing of the edges of leaves which later turn brown and die. This affects lower leaves first, causing shrivelled, sterile seeds.

Potash Sources: Natural mineral fertilizers supply insoluble potash which the grass plant can only take up as it needs it. That's why rock potash and other rock powders rich in potash are recommended. It has been found that the more soluble potash there is in the soil, the more of it plants will take up. And this "potash feast" will actually prevent the plant from taking up other elements it needs. Since the natural mineral fertilizers are insoluble, there is no worry about this occurring.

There are three main sources of potassium used by organic gardeners and lawn owners:

1. Plant residues
2. Manures and compost
3. Natural mineral sources, like granite dust, greensand and basalt rock

Included in these categories are wood ashes (6 to 10 per cent), hay (1.2 to 2.3 per cent), and leaves (0.4 to 0.7 per cent). The best plan is to use both organic and mineral potash fertilizer—organic for short term potash release and mineral for the longer period.

[193]

Other plant foods needed by crops include calcium, magnesium, sulfur, iron, zinc, molybdenum, tin, and iodine. These are called trace or minor elements.

These trace elements are very important to proper growth of plants even though they are only needed in small amounts. Some in fact have been found to serve as partial substitutes for other nutrients and also have been found to increase plant resistance to disease.

ORGANIC FERTILIZER MIXTURES

If a fertilizer formula contains raw organic matter, try to turn it under at least several weeks before planting. Even more time may be needed if the bacterial population of the soil is low from past use of chemical fertilizers. If you can grind up organic matter such as leaves, alfalfa, or straw, they will decay much quicker.

Don't worry about getting exactly the correct proportion when mixing organic fertilizers. Do not hesitate to substitute cottonseed meal for blood meal. One reason that the organic method of fertilizing has so many staunch supporters is that it is almost impossible to go wrong.

Fertilizing your soil organically is a simple procedure. For example, when manure is not available, don't worry. Your local hardware or garden supply store most likely has bone meal. If

[194]

you mix dried blood with it, you'll have an effective balanced fertilizer.

Since ordinary compost is much too lumpy for use on lawns, it should be thoroughly ground up. You can use a shredder or a rotary mower for this. If you do not have access to this equipment, place the compost on a wide board and work it back and forth with a hoe until it is shredded very fine. Then work it through a sieve (about ½-inch mesh), the coarser residue being applied to the vegetable patch, or being worked through the sieve again.

HOW LONG DOES IT TAKE TO CONVERT A
CHEMICAL LAWN INTO AN ORGANIC ONE?

The answer depends mostly on the homeowner, but the switch can be made in as little time as it takes to collect organic materials and apply them to the soft soil. The main job at the start is to round up as much organic fertilizer material as possible. Some of these such as commercial compost mixtures, dried manures, etc., can be worked directly into your soil to increase its humus content. Another portion of these materials, such as hay, sawdust, cocoa hulls, etc., should be set aside for later use as mulches.

Plan on immediately setting up a small composting area with the remainder of the materials you've collected. In less than a month's time, you can have a high-grade organic compost that will be the real start of your organic lawn.

[195]

Commercial organic fertilizers are available at just about any garden supply store, so there's no reason for the organic convert-to-be to postpone converting to the organic method. These materials will help a sick-looking lawn and you'll be pleased with the noticeable improvement in your soil brought about by organic methods.

LIME FOR LAWNS

Do all lawns need regular applications of lime? No, they don't. Lime requirements depend on several factors: where you live, the type of soil under your lawn, the sort of fertilizing program you practice. Where soils are naturally alkaline, they should receive no lime, of course. Where organic matter and humus content is high, it acts as a pH (acidity-alkalinity) buffer and makes liming less frequently needed.

Many homeowners damage their lawns by "feeding" them lime. Lime applications can improve growth and appearance of lawn grasses, but when not needed they can cause trouble.

Ground limestone is the most widely used liming material for turfgrass areas. It can be purchased at garden supply centers, hardware stores, farm supply stores, and at some supermarkets. It consists of limestone rock which has been ground to a very fine particle size.

There are other liming materials such as hydrated or slaked lime and burned or quicklime. These materials are not recommended for general use on turfgrass areas.

Liming creates a favorable soil environment for plant growth. When soil becomes strongly acid, toxic amounts of iron, aluminum and manganese restrict root growth. Liming chemically inactivates or removes these elements from the soil.

Although limestone can be applied any month of the year, spreading in September through November would be preferred.

Both hydrated lime and burned lime are generally unsatisfactory for use on turfgrass. Both can burn turf. They readily stick to feet and can be "tracked" through the house. Also, they may cake or plate on the turf thus decreasing their effectiveness.

When establishing new lawns be sure to do a thorough job of mixing limestone with the soil. This is extremely important. Work the limestone into the seedbed to a depth of 6 inches.

Don't lime unless a soil test shows that limestone is needed.

Don't apply fertilizer to an acid soil.

Keep limestone away from acid loving plants such as azaleas and rhododendrons.

ORGANIC LAWN FOODS

Bone Meal: A stockyard by-product particularly

rich in nitrogen, phosphoric acid and calcium. It is excellent for preparing land for a new lawn or for top-dressing old turf. The coarser ground meal is slower-acting while the finer grinds are quick to act, often producing greener grass when spread on turf within two weeks. A mixture of coarse and fine is recommended for all-around performance.

Castor Pomace: The ground remains of castor beans after oil has been squeezed out. An excellent and slow-acting plant food, castor pomace should be used in combination with other organic soil nutrients.

Cottonseed Meal: The squeezed fibrous residue of the seeds of the cotton plant is, like castor pomace, slow-acting but an excellent source of nitrogen. Like it, cottonseed meal should be applied with other foods.

Cattle Manure: Cleanings from cattle pens, good to work into soil a season before planting if fresh or should be weathered before being applied as a fertilizer. Dehydrated manures can be applied directly to the soil.

Sheep Manure, Pulverized: Suitable for mixing as top-dressing with other foods. The drying process destroys most weed seeds which tends to keep down the amount of weed growth on lawns top-dressed with this manure.

Tobacco Scrap: Stem and leaf fragments from tobacco factories. Excellent, long-acting source of potash and other nutrients because stems and veins decay slowly. Also ward off many insects which dislike tobacco.

DON'T FORGET TOP-DRESSING

Every lawn should be top-dressed at least once each year. Twice a year, spring and fall, is even better.

If the lawn is being aerated, top-dressing should be applied immediately after opening the soil and raked or brushed into the holes. If it is not aerated, the dressing must be brushed into the sod thoroughly with a street-sweeper's or a barn broom. In the former case, use as much top-dressing as you can force into the openings. But if there are no openings, do not apply the dressing more than 3/8 of an inch thick.

Material for the top-dressing may be sifted compost, rotted sawdust mixed with a nitrogenous fertilizer or equal parts of topsoil and leaf mold, peat moss or old manure. In addition, a complete lawn fertilizer constructed out of good organic materials to correct your lawn's deficiencies should be mixed into the dressing.

Organic fertilizers most recommended for top-dressing an established lawn are listed below. The amounts given represent the amount to be applied to a lawn after the program has been in progress for more than one year. Because many of the organic compounds break down slowly in the soil, the amounts should be doubled for the first year's application. It is also advisable to increase them for grasses which demand rich feedings.

Fertilizer	Nitrogen	Percentage of Phosphoric Acid	Potash	Apply, per 1,000 sq. ft.
Cottonseed meal	6.5	3	2	50 lb.
Castor pomace	5	2	1	50 lb.
Dried cow manure	1.8	1	2	100 lb.
Dried sheep manure	1.9	1.5	2	100 lb.
Raw bone meal	4	22	0	50 lb.
Blood meal	12 to 15	3	0	25 lb.
Wood ashes	0	1.5	7	30 lb.
Tankage	6	8	0	50 lb.
Granite dust	0	0	8	30 lb.
Phosphate rock	0	30	0	30 lb.

MIXING THE TOP-DRESSING

Organic materials should be spread over the lawn in a thin layer, mixed with the fertilizers and possibly also some topsoil. Usually, the organic material — compost, sawdust, dried manure, peat — is too lumpy to make a fine layer. It should be ground up first to make it very fine and put through a ½-inch mesh sieve. If you have a shredder, put your organic materials through it before attempting to mix and sift them. If you have no shredder, a rotary mower may be run over the pile of materials several times or it may be broken up with a hoe. Mix all the materials, after sifting, until the dressing is a homogeneous mass. Spread it with a fertilizer spreader or broadcast it by hand, going over the area twice in directions at right angles to each other.

WHEN SHOULD YOU FERTILIZE?

When's the best time to fertilize your grass? That depends on the type of grass you grow. Cool-season grasses should not be fed when they are going into their semi-dormant summer period. Nitrogen supplied in late spring will benefit the weeds, not the grass. Warm-season grasses, on the other hand, should have their heaviest feeding at that time. When the new shoots of Bermudagrass or zoysias appear, a good top-dressing with a nitrogenous fertilizer will help them to recover from the winter.

Bermudagrass that was overseeded with a winter grass is especially in need of summer feeding. The soil around its roots is doubly depleted, by its own growth of the last season and again by the grasses which grew over it through the winter.

Some Bermudagrasses are heavy feeders and require 4 to 6 feedings during a season, whereas St. Augustinegrass or zoysia will do better on lesser amounts.

Where grass roots and tree roots compete for available moisture and fertilizer, fertilize once a month starting in early spring through early fall. Sandy soil should receive more frequent applications of nitrogen due to leaching.

For the cool season turfgrasses Kentucky bluegrass and fine-leaved fescue, apply a minimum of 2 applications of fertilizer uniformly in either late March or early April. Make a second application in late August or early September.

For a high quality turf, you should use 4 applications, spaced about 6 to 8 weeks apart. Make these applications in March, May, August and October.

For Merion Kentucky bluegrass lawns, apply fertilizer at 4 to 6 week intervals throughout the growing season.

HOW MUCH FERTILIZER?

Any grass for simple maintenance (not for a stimulating build-up job) requires two pounds of pure nitrogen over each 1,000 square feet of lawn during the year. Double that amount improves turf. Nitrogen is relatively unstable, and if it is not entirely used by the grass itself, it will be used by the soil organisms that are at work breaking down grass clippings or modifying the soil. It must be replenished annually. If it is supplied in organic fertilizers, it will break down more slowly to feed the soil throughout the year. But even in organic meals, it is best to apply it in two doses, two-thirds at one time and one-third at the other.

If clippings are left on the lawn, little phosphorus or potash are needed in the annual feeding. But when these substances are supplied, they should be administered in the form of rock fertilizers which will break down slowly.

Turfgrass authorities do not generally recommend the use of fresh animal manures on established grass. Moist or wet materials carry very little plant food for their bulk, and an application

GUIDE TO NITROGEN FERTILIZER OF TURF
(Based On One Pound Of Actual Nitrogen Per Application)

Total Lbs. N per Season	Monthly Application Pounds of Nitrogen per 1,000 Square Feet								NOTES
	Mar.	Apr.	May	June	July	Aug.	Sept.	Oct.	
6	1	1	½	½	½	½	1	1	Nitrogen level for quality turf—mainly Merion Kentucky Bluegrass.
		3					3		
4	1		1			1		1	Recommended nitrogen level for most lawns.
		2					2		
3			1			1		1	Late spring application of nitrogen helps reduce spring flush of growth.
2		1					1		Minimum nitrogen level recommended. Primarily for areas of low maintenance.

From *Lawns*
Agricultural Extension Service
The University of Connecticut

large enough to supply the needs of a lawn would mar its appearance and might smother the grass. Manures worked into the soil before the lawn is planted are valuable, for the large amount of humus they supply. But after the grass is established a finer-textured and more concentrated form of fertilizer is better.

Sludge for the Lawn

The use of sewage sludge by lawn owners throughout the United States has been climbing upward in recent years. In cities where sludge has been sold, such as Boise, Chicago, Wichita, Grand Rapids, Duluth, Omaha, Santa Fe, Schenectady, Houston, Roanoke, and Milwaukee, superintendents of sewage treatment plants report that demand for sludge has been increasing.

Most cities and towns don't sell their sludge, but make it available to local residents free at the plant site. In Illinois, for example, according to Sanitary Engineer Carl Gross, "virtually every city and sanitary district which operates a sewage treatment works makes the digested and air-dried sludge available at the treatment works to anyone. In a few instances, there is a nominal charge but in general, the sludge is available at no cost."

ACTIVATED OR DIGESTED

The fertilizer value of the sludge produced

[204]

depends largely on which processing method is used.

Activated Sludge: This kind is produced when the sewage is agitated by air rapidly bubbling through it. Certain types of very active bacteria coagulate the organic matter, which settles out, leaving a clear liquid that can be discharged into streams and rivers with a minimum amount of pollution.

Generally, activated sludge is heat-treated before being made available to gardeners and farmers; its nitrogen content is between 5 and 6 per cent, phosphorus from 3 to 6 per cent. Its plant food value is similar to cottonseed meal—a highly recommended organic fertilizer.

Digested Sludge: This type of residue is formed when the sewage is allowed to settle (and liquid to drain off) by gravity without being agitated by air. The conventional anaerobic digestion system takes about 10 to fourteen days from the time the sewage reaches the sedimentation tank until the digested solids are pumped into filter beds, often sand and gravel, for drying. The final step is removal of the dry material, either to be incinerated or used for soil improvement.

A few medium-sized cities located in agricultural areas dispose of a part of their short-time activated and subsequently digested sludge in liquid form. This is delivered to farmers within a radius of about ten miles and is used for direct application to land.

Digested sludge has about the same fertilizer value as barnyard manure. Nitrogen varies from two to three per cent phosphorus averaging about two per cent. It often has an offensive odor that persists for some time after application to a soil surface during cool weather. "This odor differs greatly in character, however, from that of raw sludge," Dr. Myron Anderson, senior chemist for the Agricultural Research Service at Beltsville, Maryland, states, "since drastic changes have taken place during digestion. The odor from digested sludges may be eliminated by storage in a heap during warm weather."

AMOUNTS TO USE

The city of Marion, Indiana, has printed an excellent little pamphlet which includes the following suggestions for using sludge as a fertilizer and soil builder:

1. For starting new lawns — prepare the seed bed by mixing the sludge with the soil. A minimum dosage of one part sludge to two parts soil may be used if the soil is of a heavy clay texture. Spade the ground to a depth of at least 6 inches, making sure the sludge is thoroughly intermixed with the soil. Never have layers of sludge and layers of soil in the seed bed.

2. For feeding well-established lawns — the sludge should be applied in the winter and early spring months when the ground is frozen. The lawn may be covered with a layer of sludge one-half inch deep during the cold months of Decem-

ber, January and February. This cover will provide an insulation to protect the grass roots from
the harmful effects of freezing and thawing during this time of the year. In addition, ample plant
food will be made available for a luxuriant growth
of grass in the spring.

3. For reconditioning old lawns—on yards or
portions of yards where the soil has been too poor
to support an average growth of grass, it is recommended that the procedure under (1) above be
followed. It should be remembered that grass
roots grow into the soil to a depth of 6 or 7 inches
only when the ground is of such a composition
that will permit this growth. To top-dress and
seed a section of ground that has not been properly prepared is a waste of time and money.

Heat-dried activated sludge is generally acid, its
pH averaging 5.0 to 6.0. Air-dried digested sludge
after a short period of storage will normally show
a drop in pH to about 6.0. Experience shows that
the continued use of any type of sludge, unless
previously conditioned with lime, requires the periodic addition of lime to the soil to prevent harmful acidity.

SLUDGE IS SAFE

In the U.S. Department of Agriculture report on
sludge, Dr. Anderson writes:

"Activated sludges need heat-treatment before
use as fertilizer. Such treatment is normally

[207]

provided for material to be marketed. The heat used for drying normally, accomplishes the destruction of dangerous organisms. This means that properly heat-dried activated sludges may be used with confidence regarding their safety from a sanitary standpoint. . . .

"It seems that states have generally accepted the conclusions of the Committee on Sewage Disposal of the American Public Health Association that heat-dried activated sludges are satisfactory from a sanitary standpoint, and that digested sludges are satisfactory except where vegetables are grown to be eaten raw. All danger is thought to be removed by action in the soil after a period of about three months during a growing season."

EXCELLENT FOR LAWNS

What kind of results can you expect when you add sludge to the soil? LeRoy Van Kleek, Principal Sanitary Engineer of Connecticut's Department of Health and an experienced gardener, answers that question quite conclusively in his report, "Digested Sewage Sludge as a Soil Conditioner and Fertilizer."

". . . Sludge is particularly adapted to lawns. Sludge deepens the green color of grass and stimulates a luxurious growth. Its benefits seem noticeable for several years. It should be applied late in March and again if desired early in September. . . .

[208]

". . . The value of sludge should not be judged solely by comparison of chemical analyses with artificial fertilizers, but by the results it produces in plant growth. Dependence exclusively upon commercial fertilizers without consideration for the maintenance of humus content and good soil structure is an unsound practice."

GUARD AGAINST AN APRIL-GREEN LAWN

Don't let your lawn turf pull an April fool on you. It can. It may start fast and rich-looking only to peter out some hot summer afternoon or bitter winter night.

During the spring season, there is a drastic reduction in the soluble carbohydrates in roots and basal portions of plant tissue because of the fast top growth and potentially rapid root growth. It appears that photosynthesis for food fixation is not fast enough for rapid top and root growth under very liberal nitrogen fertilization during the spring season. The tops have first access to fixed sugars, so roots are restricted. Liberal nitrogen during the spring is also harmful because this encourages certain diseases, such as leaf spot of common Kentucky bluegrass.

During the warm summer season, warm to high temperatures slow up photosynthesis much more than top growth; thus, liberal nitrogen fertilization stimulates top growth which causes low soluble carbohydrates in the basal part of plants which hinders root growth. In other words, high sum-

[209]

mer temperatures cause the cool-season grasses to burn up their sugar-like food reserves and food fixation is not rapid enough to compensate for this depletion. This will weaken the plants and thin out stands which will lead to weed encroachment.

It is best not to fertilize any more than is absolutely necessary during the summer months for the cool-season grasses because weedy plants, such as crabgrass, are better adapted to high temperatures than the cool turfgrasses. Liberal nitrogen during the summer months stimulates these weedy growths. Note that late summer-winter fertilizer programs encourage dense sods so that weedy annuals, such as crabgrass, have less chance to encroach the next spring.

The persistence of cool-season turfgrasses can be encouraged by using fertilizer practices that control the growth processes of the cool-season grasses and discourage the encroachment of weedy grasses.

The mowing management should also be adjusted to the growth conditions. It is desirable to mow cool-season grasses, such as bluegrass, closer in the late summer-early spring than during the summer. Closer mowing during the late summer-autumn season will encourage the development of young, new tillers which will remain more vigorous during the winter and subsequent season than the older tillers. Mowing higher after the spring flush growth will shade out germinating weedy encroachers, also reduce soil temperatures;

[210]

tall sod residues insulate the soil against temperature increases.

GREEN GRASS IN WINTER

You can have a green lawn, even in winter by beginning organic fertilizer programs for all cool-season grasses with late summer applications.

New shoots and roots are initiated during the cool autumn-winter season; thus, the nutrients supplied by phosphorus, potassium, and nitrogen should be available for growth by late summer.

Nitrogen and potassium are apt to be lowest in the autumn season because the season's growth has "drained" the soil of these nutrients. On new turf areas where phosphorus and potassium are apt to be low, it is desirable to apply 1 to 1½ lb. N along with 2 or 3 lbs. phosphorus and potash per 1,000 sq. ft. in September. Another pound of N may be applied in late October and June for common Kentucky bluegrass lawns. Green leaves and a pleasing green color of turf for fine and coarse fescues, bluegrass, and bentgrasses have been maintained all winter long by fertilizing with nitrogen during the late summer-winter months.

Fall and winter nitrogen fertilization does not kill cool-season grasses. There is a common idea that heavy late summer and fall nitrogen fertilization will cause lush, succulent grass that will cause winter kill. Research at an altitude of more than 2,000 ft. during the last three years, where winter temperatures dropped to 0° F. or lower, shows no winter killing. Nitrogen fertilization stimulates photosynthesis; that is, more carbon dioxide is fixed into sugarlike plant foods. The late summer-autumn and winter temperatures are too low for the tops to make much growth; thus, more food is fixed than is utilized. The cool nights that inhibit growth apparently stimulate the rate with which food is fixed the subsequent day. Because low and freezing temperatures restrict top growth much more than photosynthesis, sugary materials in the stubble, roots, stolons, rhizomes, and leaves accumulate during the fall and winter season. Actually light and frequent rates of nitrogen during the autumn and winter stimulate food fixation by leaves even though there is no visible growth; root growth and basal shoots are also stimulated during the fall-winter season by nitrogen fertilizer. Thus, late summer-winter nitrogen fertilization along with adequate phosphorus and potassium will improve the denseness of the turf, the amount and depth of the root system.

CHAPTER XII

New Life for an Old Lawn

Do You Need a New Lawn?

A LAWN that has become thin and weedy may need complete remaking. But before you decide to do that job, be sure that the lawn has degenerated to the point where it will not respond to organic fertilizing, weed control and mowing. If the lawn will not respond to such care and renovation, remaking is the only alternative, but give some thought to why the operation is necessary.

Insufficient and improper use of lime and fertilizer, cheap and improper lawn grass mixtures, mowing too close, and light watering or over-watering usually account for sparse, thin lawns.

In some situations, a dense layer of undecomposed organic matter, called thatch or mat, accumulates at the soil surface. This layer interferes with the movement of air, water and nutrients which restricts healthy root development. The situation generally develops with the bentgrasses but also can occur with other grasses.

It is important to consider reasons for failure. If they are not corrected, a renovation job will be short lived and of little value. If you need more information on renovation, ask your county agricultural agent.

FEEDING THE TURF

The more you fertilize, the more vigorously your grass will grow. The more it grows, the more often you must mow to keep it in prime condition. On the other hand, starving your grass will not solve your maintenance problems. On the contrary, a starved lawn is full of weeds and diseases, is sparse, unpleasant to play or relax on, and a bad advertisement for your skill as an organic lawn owner.

There is one principle that is imperative to good lawn maintenance—testing the soil. Remember that when you fertilize, you feed the soil, not the grass. Most of the troubles that arise from improper fertilizing could have been eliminated by a simple soil test. Just as a doctor does not treat a patient without first discovering a remedy, so should you discover the deficiencies of your lawn before you attempt to treat them.

[214]

A New Soil Test?

If you are any kind of a homeowner, chances are you had a soil test taken before you ever planted your lawn. But the needs of your lawn may well have changed since your last test, for many reasons. 1. Perhaps you've been offsetting the deficiencies you discovered earlier by periodic applications of organic fertilizer. 2. Maybe you've allowed the grass clippings in your lawn to build up over a period of time. When you do, they often decompose and send their nutrients into the soil, thus changing its composition. 3. Many times a lawn that is grown extensively in shade competes with the surrounding trees for nutrition. Because the trees rob the soil of nutrients, the lawn often suffers.

For these and other reasons, one of the first steps to revitalizing your lawn should be a new soil test. If you have had the foresight to obtain a good soil testing kit, you can test the soil yourself. If not, your state agricultural service is usually happy to analyze samples they receive. Before you take that step, consult your local agricultural agent for the best way to gather and send samples.

A soil test should determine if fertility is out of balance, and what amounts of organic fertilizer, if any, are needed for the best planned growth. The best time to correct soil fertility is during the late fall or early spring.

[215]

WHAT'S LACKING IN YOUR LAWN?

Occasionally you can tell what nutritional deficiencies exist in your lawn by careful observation. Nitrogen deficiency causes stunted growth of the entire grass plant. Leaves are relatively small, thin, yellowish-green to yellow. Careful examination shows yellow to brown color at the tip of the leaf and down to the midrib. Roots may be stunted, but usually less so than the tops. Nitrogen deficiency is often confused with lack of moisture. A moisture deficiency differs in the wilting of the plant and curling of the leaves.

Phosphorus deficiency results in slow growth of the entire plant. Leaves are an unhealthy dark green and often, irregularly distributed brown patches occur. Roots are stunted, but again, less than the tops.

Potassium deficiency also causes stunting of the entire plant. Eventually, it will dry up and take on a brownish color. Leaves appear dull green, sometimes yellow and edges turn brown. Bronze-colored spots often develop and tips are scorched. The older leaves are affected first.

Calcium deficiency also causes stunted growth, this time accompanied by leaves that become hard and stiff, with mottled or brown spots. Roots are stubby, profusely branched and the growing tips usually die.

A lack of iron also shows in pale, bleached leaves, a phenomenon known as chlorosis. This symptom appears in lawns where the pH is too high. Iron can become available to plants only in soil which is slightly acid. Some grasses are more sensitive to this deficiency than others and require a lower pH, but for most grasses, a pH of 6.0 to 6.5 is about right.

Reseeding

Why not seedings from time to time, merely to keep things spruced up? When you fertilize or practice weed control, the results are accepted as rather temporary. Yet, somehow, seeding becomes regarded as a once-only proposition. Thereafter all efforts are bent toward perfecting and taking care of the original planting. This may cost more than would occasional reseedings!

Of course the only good-looking grasses you would want in your front lawn are the fine-textured kinds—Kentucky bluegrass, the fine fescues, bentgrasses of the Highland type, and a few others. Kentucky bluegrass and the fine fescues are renowned as perennials, persisting indefinitely and spreading to fill in the lawn. It is quite true that a single initial seeding with these grasses could last a lifetime. But almost every lawn has difficult sites as well as favorable ones. These may be under trees, where shade and tree root competition prevails. Or areas receiving lots of use, or places where the soil is thin and poor. Might it not

1. Seeding doesn't have to be a once-and-done proposition. Keep your lawn in constant repair by reworking a weakened area with an extra dose of compost and topsoil.

2. Rake the area so the ground is even and the seed is not washed away.

be economical to regularly bolster such areas with additional seed, the same as with fertilizing, watering, and so on? The cost of reseeding will probably be less than trying to maintain good grass persistently in locations where a lot of attention would be required.

THE "THIN" LAWN

If the lawn is simply thin, do not waste grass seed on reseeding it. The reason for a thin turf, if it was once well seeded, is either lack of food or improper mowing practice. Fertilizer and intelligent cutting will thicken it in a single season, but seed will not. Do not reseed unless there are bare areas of at least a foot in diameter.

3. Roll it gently to press the seed down and encourage fast germination.

[219]

A good way to plant seed in small bare spots is this:

1. Place a bushel of soil on a sidewalk or driveway.

2. Add 5 pounds of complete organic fertilizer.

3. Add one pound of mixed grass seed or seed of a desired grass.

4. Mix these thoroughly with a shovel.

5. Then two people work together as follows: One person throws a handful of the mixture into the thin spot. The other person immediately vigorously scuffs the grass and soil surface with a garden rake, leaving the loosened dead grass on the surface as a mulch.

6. Keep the soil damp for 3 weeks.

If the bare spots are larger than a foot in diameter, spots such as may occur where the wrong seed was planted, in the shade, where the dog's kennel stood last summer or where traffic was unduly heavy, a more thorough preparation for reseeding may be necessary. First, before you waste the time and effort, make sure that the same causes will not make a new bare spot over the old one after you have repaired it. If traffic is the problem, perhaps you should put in either flagstones or a fence to stop the traffic. If the wrong seed was used for shade, add the right seed.

After you have eliminated the cause of the spot, dig up the bare spot to a depth of 4 to 5 inches, adding fertilizer or compost as in the soil used for small spots. Break up clods and remove all weeds and debris. Rake the soil until it is fine and smooth on top. Now, sprinkle the proper seed evenly over the area. If you seeded the lawn previously with a seed that was satisfactory, use the same seed or seed mixture for that spot. If the seed used previously was wrong for that particular situation, correct it now. A good device for spreading seed evenly in a small space is an ordinary household flour sifter.

After seeding, rake the area lightly and then firm the soil with the back of the spade. Firming in that way will not compact the soil, but will press the new seed down in contact with it. Unless you are lucky enough to complete the job just before a shower, sprinkle the newly seeded spots with a nozzle set for fine mist spray. Keep the soil moist for at least 3 weeks. As in any other seeding, this repair job is best done either in fall or very early spring in the North, or in late spring when the summer grasses are starting into growth in the South.

If you have a lawn of one of the grasses best started with sprigs or sod, plant the bare patches with sods from the thickest part of your turf. Carefully dig up two-inch plugs from a turfy spot and fill the hole with rich topsoil. The runners from the surrounding sod will make short work of filling the gap. Plant the sprigs or sods, keeping them moist until they are established and weed the area at regular intervals until the stolons cover the bare soil.

[221]

WHAT IS MEANT BY OVERSEEDING?

We usually refer to overseeding as the sowing of seed on established lawn grasses. As an example, you might sow Italian rye on Bermuda. This brings up the question of the desirability of such a practice.

As you know, Bermudagrass becomes dormant and turns brown as soon as cold weather sets in. Remember, too, that Italian rye is a cool season annual and will gradually die as the weather warms up in the spring. However, you have a choice.

If you are satisfied with just a little green during the winter, a light seeding will do it; but if you want a pretty green lawn and seed heavily, then you are faced with a problem.

A light overseeding of rye does not seriously interfere with the growth of Bermuda when the temperature rises in the spring; but, a heavy seeding will die and form a mat which does seriously interfere.

About one and one-half pounds of ryegrass per 1,000 square feet of lawn area is considered as light and three pounds for the same area as heavy.

A LAWN WITH LOW SPOTS

In a lawn with low spots where the soil has settled, raise the hollows to the level of the general contour. Small dips and basins collect water after a heavy rain where grass roots may smother before the excess drains away. It is not necessary to remove the grass from the low spots, but if you wish, you may take it up carefully as sods, to be replaced later. If you do that, cut the sod as thin as possible. An inch of soil and root is better than two inches — it will make contact and grow into the soil below more quickly. Shade the sods as you lift them and cover them with wet burlap to prevent drying out of the roots.

Fill the hollow with enriched topsoil and roll it enough to firm it. Use enough organic matter in the fill to prevent compaction. If you have applied fill over the original sod, roll the soil until it fills in among the grasses and the turf below, seed, rake and roll again. If you removed the sod, less firming will be needed until after the sod is returned. Fit the squares of sod tightly together and spread an inch of enriched topsoil over them. Brush and rake it in until it fills all cracks between the sods. Water thoroughly and keep the spot moist until the new grass is throughly established.

Resodding

Bare spots or weak areas on your lawn from heavy traffic or extensive use can only be quickly repaired by resodding. That is the process of planting a strip of grass previously grown into the bare spot. The sod may come from a nursery or may be re-transplanted from another area of your own lawn. Normally sod that is obtained commercially is extremely expensive and beyond the budget of the casual lawn lover.

If you've decided to resod areas of your land and intend to use sod you obtain yourself, you have got to be extremely skillful. Rarely can the homeowner remove sod with a shovel and lay it in another spot smoothly and uniformly. In fact, for more extensive jobs, sod-cutting machines are available which can cut the strips at standard depths and widths. The big job in sod laying is to remove the sod from the soil. Re-transplanting it is a simple matter. Prepare the soil as you would an area to be reseeded. Be sure to add the necessary limestone and organic fertilizer. Water the area well before the sod is placed. Apply at least one inch of water late in the afternoon of the day before the sod is to be laid. That will settle the area and give the soil a chance to drain. Should a gap of an area exist between the established lawn and the newly laid sod, fill it in with finely screened soil. Then water the newly laid area thoroughly. As soon as it is dry enough to walk on, roll or tamp the sod to give good contact with the soil beneath. Then continue watering every two or three days to insure secure rooting. Continue watering for two weeks.

CHAPTER XIII

Zoysia:
The Lawn You Plug In

ZOYSIA is short for a remarkably different kind of lawn that may be just what your yard ordered!

If you're looking out on a sad substitute for what you'd like your lawn to be right now, this news is for you. If your grass has turned an unbecoming brown in the midst of a summer's heat and dry spells . . . if it seems to be waging a losing battle with weeds, crabgrass, insects or lawn disease . . . and if normal summer use and traffic have left it a lot the worse for wear, you could easily have licked every one of these vexing riddles by planting zoysia last spring—and you can find out how today.

Here's a surprising sort of lawngrass that helpfully reverses all such troublesome turf tendencies. It turns greenest in mid-summer, actually thrives on heat and sunshine, and completely ignores drought. Furthermore, it grows so thick and sturdy it squelches crabgrass, never gives any other common weeds a chance to get started, and beats the bugs and grass ailments with a healthy, verdant smile. To top it off, the zoysia can really take it. While retaining its looks and spongy feel, this lawn stands all the jumping youngsters, trudging visitors and heavy-footed in-laws it needs to.

Oh, yes—I might well add right here—it's a lot less work to take care of, needs mowing just about one-third as much as most other lawngrasses. And so, there'd be an unhesitating vote for zoysia from the guy who usually gets the cutting chore.

Here's what the University of Maryland Extension Service says about zoysia as a grass for home lawns:

Zoysias have been used for turfgrasses for many years, primarily because of their durability during the summer. Zoysias grow best during the hot summer months and therefore retain their green color when many of the cool-season grasses, such as bluegrasses and fescues, have become dormant and turned brown. And, depending upon the variety, zoysias are quite resistant to droughts, diseases and insects.

Used primarily in home lawns, they are also good for special areas such as lawns around summer homes, beach homes, swimming pools, and around tennis courts. During the summer growing season, they produce a dense, dark green turf but

[226]

Small plugs of sod are often used in planting zoysia since it does not produce seed true to type. Generally plugs are set one foot apart, but they may be set closer for more rapid coverage. When zoysia is established in your lawn, you can use it as a "nursery" by removing plugs from the old sod and transplanting them elsewhere.

[227]

lose their color after the first heavy frost in fall and remain straw-colored during the winter and early spring months.

Zoysias are usually sold as plugs, sprigs or sod, though a small amount of seed is available. Meyer, Emerald and Midwest are the most common varieties. To be sure of getting the right variety, always buy planting material that has been certified.

PLUGS, SPRIGS, OR SOD?

Most suppliers of zoysia planting material offer a choice of plugs, sprigs or sod. Zoysia seed is not produced commercially in the United States, but some seed is imported from the Orient. Seedlings produced from seed are weak and have difficulty competing with weeds and other grasses which germinate faster and are more vigorous. Plants from seed are also quite variable and not as desirable as those produced vegatatively. Improved selections of zoysia are grown only from vegetative planting material.

Plugs are very easy to plant and are usually large enough to assure survival of some zoysia plants in each plug even under the most adverse growth conditions. Plugging is the most popular method of planting zoysia in Maryland.

Sprigs — sod which has been separated into individual runners or stolons — are more economical than plugs or sod. They are not as easy to plant as plugs, however, and can be used only in new lawns or in other areas with a prepared seedbed.

Sodding is the fastest way of producing a zoysia lawn, but it is also the most expensive.

Zoysia producers often sell planting material at reduced prices during the "off-season." These "off-season" plants are acceptable if the producer guarantees their survival.

ESTABLISHING A ZOYSIA TURF

To establish a new lawn, plant sprigs or plugs on 6-, 8-, or 12-inch centers. Such plantings usually require 6 to 18 months to produce a complete cover, and, with good management, they may spread 6 to 8 inches in one summer.

Plugging is done with a simple tool (plugger) which makes a hole 1, 2, or 3 inches in diameter in the soil or sod. A plug 2-inches in diameter and 1 to 2 inches deep is the most common size.

To plant sprigs, open a slot or row in the soil with a spade, hatchet, ax or similar tool; then place the sprig in the slot as shown in the diagram. One end of the sprig should be at least 2 inches below the soil surface with the other end, preferably a joint with some leaves above the surface. A bushel of sprigs is roughly equivalent to 1 square yard of sod, but will plant a much larger area. In new lawns, a minimum of 2 to 4 bushels of sprigs should be planted in each 1,000 square feet. The greater the amount of sprigs planted in an area, however, the faster a complete coverage will be produced.

Sod should be used only in establishing a new lawn. *Never place sod on top of existing turf.* Place sod only on a firm, well-prepared seedbed that has had fertilizer and lime thoroughly mixed with the soil *before* sodding.

If you want to establish zoysia in your old lawn, plugs are best. First remove a plug of old sod the same size as the one to be planted; next, put a small amount (¼ teaspoon or less) of organic fertilizer, then, insert the zoysia plug.

Plugs planted in existing turf may require 2 to 5 years or more to produce a complete cover. Mowing and fertilizing are the most important factors in determining the rate of spread. Close mowing (¾ to 1¼ inches high) and summer fertilization favor the zoysia whereas high mowing (1½ to 2½ inches) and fall fertilization favor the bluegrasses and fescues.

Once you have a zoysia area established in your lawn, you can use it as a "nursery." Zoysia plugs can be removed from this area and transplanted into other areas. After the zoysia has been planted, plugs from the old sod can be turned upside-down and inserted into the hole from which the zoysia plug was removed. In a short time, these spaces in the "nursery" will be completely covered over by the zoysia.

WHEN SHOULD YOU PLANT?

Plant plugs and sprigs between May 1 and August 1. This allows the new planting to take maximum advantage of favorable summer growing conditions. Plantings made in the fall often do not become established well enough to withstand the first winter. In addition, the plants may be pushed out of the soil by the freezing and thawing (heaving) motion of the ground.

You can plant sod later into the fall with less chance of winter killing. Plantings of dormant sod are safer than plantings of dormant plugs or sprigs, but late spring or early summer plantings of any type of material are better than plantings in any other season.

TAKING CARE OF NEWLY PLANTED LAWNS

Keep newly planted zoysia moist until new growth is observed. Apply water immediately after planting and as often as needed thereafter to keep the soil from drying out. Do not keep the soil *saturated*, but *moist*.

Because most weeds will not tolerate close mowing, frequent and close clipping, especially with a rotary mower, helps to control weeds until the zoysia is established.

LIMING AND FERTILIZING

Have your soil tested *before* planting and periodically after establishment to determine the exact fertilizer and lime needs of your lawn. Your

[231]

county extension agent has complete details on how to take soil samples and where to send them.

Zoysia grows best in a soil with a pH of about 6.5. If your soil pH is lower than this, use lime to reduce the acidity. Lime not only controls soil acidity but also makes other nutrient elements more available to the plants. As a general rule, about 50 pounds of finely ground (pulverized) limestone or its equivalent per 1,000 square feet every 3 years is sufficient.

Apply fertilizer when the zoysia is making its most active growth — May through early September. Ten pounds of 10-5-5 fertilizer or its equivalent per 1,000 square feet each month during this period will hasten the rate of spread.

Thereafter, apply fertilizer according to soil tests. You can maintain zoysia very easily with 3 or 4 applications of a complete fertilizer such as 10-5-5, which has a high nitrogen content in relation to its phosphorus and potash content. You can use organic nitrogen fertilizers during the summer, but you should use a complete fertilizer for the last application in late summer.

MOWING

Mowing is another important factor in the rate of spread. Mow zoysias at a lower height than bluegrass and fescues — a height of 3/4 to 1 1/4 inches is best for all varieties. Maintain this height throughout the growing season. You may raise the mowing height about ¼ inch during the late fall until the grass is dormant, but reduce it again the following spring.

THATCH CONTROL

Thatch—the accumulation of leaves, clippings, roots, etc. above the soil surface—is one of the most common problems with zoysias. You can remove thatch very easily with a vertical mowing device or power raking machine. Remove thatch as often as needed—usually every 1 to 2 years, depending on how much the grass is fertilized and whether clippings have been removed. Clipping removal helps reduce this problem but will not eliminate it.

Some homeowners have burned their zoysia with fire in early spring to eliminate thatch. This practice is *not* recommended because of the fire hazard to trees, shrubs, and buildings. Mechanical control is much better even in areas where fire hazards are low.

DYEING THE LAWN

Zoysias, which turn brown in the fall with the first heavy frost, can now be colored green for the winter months. Several pigment-type materials similar to paint are available commercially for dyeing brown lawns. A single application of dye after the zoysia is completely dormant will usually

[233]

last all winter. If you would like to know more about these dyes, contact your county extension agent.

DISEASES AND INSECTS

As a group, zoysias are quite resistant to diseases and insects. Only the Meyer variety has problems of any significance. A rust disease has been reported on Meyer zoysia lawns but this problem has not been widespread.

Varieties

Meyer zoysia, sometimes called Meyer Z-52, is the most widely-used variety. It adapts to a wide range of climates but should be planted only in sunny locations. Meyer has dark green leaves that closely resemble Merion Kentucky bluegrass in color and texture. A dense turf of Meyer is quite resistant to wear and to weed invasion.

This variety of zoysia can be used on almost any soil type from clays to sands. It has been used widely on sandy soils where drought conditions may damage bluegrasses and red fescues during the summer months. Meyer tolerates mowing heights as low as ½ inch but does its best when clipped regularly at a height of 1 inch. The first killing frost in the fall causes Meyer to turn a light straw-color brown, and it keeps this color until it resumes growth the following spring—usually between April 15 and May 1.

Emerald zoysia is a hybrid that has fine leaves and produces a dense dark green cover. Once established, the turf is highly resistant to weed invasion. Like other zoysias, Emerald stays brown from the first hard freeze until spring, but when properly managed, this variety may remain green a few days longer in the fall and may green-up earlier in the spring.

Thatch accumulation is a problem with Emerald because it produces such a dense turf (See Thatch Control section). Reel type mowers should be used on Emerald, and should be set to cut the grass at 1 to 1¼ inches high.

No serious insect or disease pests have been found on this grass. However, Emerald has not been one of the most widely-used lawngrasses to date.

Midwest is a vigorous, dark green, coarse-leaved variety of zoysia. It has an open growth habit and spreads most rapidly of all the zoysias when planted in a clean seedbed.

Midwest is best adapted for athletic fields, playgrounds, golf course fairways and other areas where summer use is heavy. Because of its coarse, open growth, it can be overseeded with cool-season grasses in the fall, thus providing green color throughout the year.

Zoysia matrella (Manilagrass) is another selection of zoysia. Like the other zoysias, it spreads by sto-

[235]

lons (above-ground creeping stems) and forms a dense carpet-like turf that resists wear and weed invasion. It grows best on fertile soils and is quite sensitive to acid soils. It is not widely used, however, because it spreads slowly and is not as winter-hardy as the other zoysias.

Authorities Comment

The U.S. Department of Agriculture has had this to say on the subject:

Meyer zoysia is considered to be best adapted in those areas where the ordinary cool season grasses (bluegrass, fescue, bentgrass) do poorly in the summer. This condition is typical in an area of the United States having Philadelphia, Pennsylvania; Omaha, Nebraska; St. Louis, Missouri, and Richmond, Virginia, as its corner points."

Grass expert Dr. Fred V. Grau, who was director of the USGA Green Section when this strain was developed and who picked Z-52 out of the 50-odd selections principally because of the advantages already mentioned, adds the following with respect to its range of adaptation:

"I like to think of Meyer zoysia serving best in the 'twilight zone' between the cool season grasses and the warm season grasses. This belt may be 200 miles wide, stretching from Philadelphia and Richmond through Washington to Cincinnati, Louisville, Memphis, on to Kansas City and St. Louis, up to Omaha and down through the Southwest.

Where bluegrass does poorly because of high summer temperatures, and where Bermuda-grasses tend to suffer because of low winter temperature, zoysia performs relatively better."

Even beyond these areas, testing has shown promise of further adaptability. During the past few years, extensive experimentation on Meyer zoysia has been performed by Dr. S. A. DeFrance and S. W. Hart at the Rhode Island Agricultural Experiment Station, Kingston, R.I. They have expressed the view that Z-52 appears to be winter hardy in Southern New England, and that it may be of value in this area around summer homes situated on or near the seashore where winter color is not a factor, but where summer color, drought resistance, adaption to poor soil, and infrequent mowing would be to its advantage.

A HOMEOWNER'S EXPERIENCE WITH ZOYSIA

We were more than a bit wary when we bought our first zoysia 4 years ago. Most zoysia cannot be produced from seed, but must be planted vegetatively either by plugs — usually two inches square — or by root runners obtained by tearing pieces of established sod. We started by buying 200 plugs, although you can start with as few as 100 plugs for less than $7 and propagate your own runners. If you plant the plugs one foot apart as recommended, they will fill an area 10 by 10 feet, growing in to yield up to 3,600 two-by-two-inch plugs, or an unlimited number of transplants. Zoysia generally needs two seasons to become thoroughly established, and unless sprigs or plugs are thickly planted they may take two to three years to cover.

Underfoot zoysia feels like a plush carpet, a feature we especially appreciate. It also provides a wonderful play surface for the children and has withstood tricycle riding and every other surface torture they have invented.

We originally planted our plugs in an existing lawn, but have since found that for really rapid spread the old grass should be scalped or dug out. The plugs planted in our lawn took two to three seasons to cover and choke out the old grass, but when we have planted zoysia in an area where no grass had been, it filled in well during one growing season. It just depends on whether you are in a hurry or are willing to wait.

It will take you longer to plant a zoysia lawn as each plug is individually set in the ground one foot apart, but once it is established you can truly forget about your lawn. We used a bulb plugger for planting the initial plugs, but now I usually dig up a square foot of the sod and break it into runners which are easily planted with a trowel. Zoysia responds to the same fertilizing program you use for other grasses, producing a really thick turf.

Once the plugs or runners are planted, they should be kept well watered for the first week or two.

Zoysia turns straw-colored in winter after the

first killing frost. While I have heard people protest they don't want a brown lawn all winter, such turf does not bother me because it is still smoothly dense.

Zoysia will grow nicely—once it's successfully started. Many people originally got it for seashore homes with sandy soil. It is wonderful on slopes and problem banks where ordinary grasses fail. The only place it will not thrive is in deep shade because it should have 3 or 4 hours of sun each day. We handled this by seeding red fescue in the shady spots.

Although zoysia roots spread rapidly, top growth is quite slow so there is much less mowing. While our other grasses require mowing at least once a week in summer, we mow the zoysia only once a month. It should be cut very close—about one-half inch—for the best appearance, since zoysia when allowed to get tall has a fluffy, thatched look.

So, weigh the pros and cons carefully when you decide if zoysia is the lawn for you. It certainly has been for us. —*June Kilmarx*

OTHER EXPERIENCES

Some time ago, we contacted a number of readers who had ordered Meyer zoysia plugs last summer. In general, they report decidedly satisfactory starts. Some said it was too soon to offer a full appraisal; others replied that the plugs had

[239]

taken hold promptly, started spreading even during late summer and early autumn, and showed strong growth plus good appearance — happy evidence that a preferred turf was well under way.

Several who answered our query about zoysia suggested that others interested in trying it follow planting and watering directions carefully, and urged that all existing grass be cleared before setting out the new plugs. This, they felt, would encourage a faster start, prevent any rank growth from impeding root spread of the zoysia. Although this recommendation is not usually made (many have combined zoysia with bluegrass, bents, etc., and had excellent combined lawns, longer color result); it is worth considering.

Mr. R. G. Howes of Fort Thomas, Kentucky, writes: "The zoysia lawn has worked exceptionally well. I do not have any crabgrass or other weeds, and it is a beautiful lawn, looking something like Kentucky bluegrass. It would be my suggestion that anyone who uses zoysia take all the grass off their yard before putting it out, and then be sure to water it well for 10 to 15 days. My zoysia grass is very pretty."

From St. Louis, Missouri, Mr. Chester Gawrych notes: "As of this day we are well satisfied with the plugs. Every one has taken and it is starting to spread." And at Carlsbad, New Mexico, Mr. Kenneth Nelson reports: "The zoysia planting has worked very well. I am not a gardener. That's why I planted zoysia so that someday I would have a green lawn with minimum watering and mowing."

At nearby Allentown, Pa., a trial planting of 1,000 Meyer zoysia plugs was made late last summer on the new home grounds of Jack Kushner. His soil, for the most part hardpacked builder's clay left after grading, wasn't very favorable for any sort of grass planting. Still, Mr. Kushner reports that his zoysia lawn has worked out satisfactorily to date, although it hasn't spread too rapidly in the poorly prepared soil. He advises anyone with similar conditions to improve their topsoil first. "I'm very pleased," he concludes, "and I'm eager to start taking second-year plugs to extend zoysia to the rest of my lawn."

PROS AND CONS OF ZOYSIA

According to the University of California Agricultural Extension Service, here are the advantages and disadvantages of a zoysia lawn.

Advantages

1. Zoysia grass lawns are permanent, lasting many years.

2. Zoysia grasses make a tough, wear-resistant, cushiony turf.

3. They grow slowly . . . The average homeowner may be satisfied with the appearance maintained by mowing 10 days to 2 weeks apart, about half as often as for Bermudagrass.

4. Zoysias thrive on high temperatures of summer.

[241]

5. They grow on a wide range of soils, from sandy to heavy loams, if there is good subsoil drainage.

6. They make reasonable growth and cover with little fertilizer, but will have a better color if well fertilized.

7. The density of a mature turf will crowd out weeds.

8. Zoysias are practically free from disease and insect pests.

9. They grow well in moderate shade or full sun.

10. Zoysias are salt and chlorine tolerant. They may be used around swimming pools.

Disadvantages

1. Zoysia grasses will lose some green color in winter. Color loss may be slight in coastal areas, but nearly complete in the desert. The length of this off-color period will vary from a few days to a month or more, depending on location and weather.

2. Ten to 15 months are required to produce sod in the various climatic areas of California. Weeds must be controlled during this time.

3. Zoysias must be planted by sprigs or plugs of turf, because seed is unreliable, slow to germinate, and variable.

4. A power mower is required for easy cutting.

5. The density of a mature turf prevents successful use of cool-season companion grasses for winter turf in cold areas where off-color period is long.

Comparing Zoysia with Common Lawn Grasses

	ZOYSIAS	IMPROVED BERMUDA GRASSES	KENTUCKY BLUEGRASS
Length of turf life-subtropical regions	Many years	Many years	1–4 years
Color Hot weather Cool weather Frost and cold	Excellent Good Poor	Excellent Good Poor	Poor Excellent Fair
Leaf width and texture	1/16"–1/8"	1/32"–1/8" depending upon variety	1/8"–5/16"
Thatch	Moderate to heavy—not exposed by mowing	Heavy—may be exposed by mowing	Slight to moderate
Mowing frequency and height	10–14 days at 1/2"–1"	5–7 days at 1/4"–1/2"	7 days at 1 1/2"–2"
Planting	Sprigs or plugs	Sprigs or plugs; common bermuda by seed	Seed
Time to cover	10–15 months	2–4 months	2–3 months
Amount of water and irrigation frequency	1–2 inches every 1–3 weeks	1–2 inches every 1–2 weeks	1/2–1 inch every 5–10 days
Fertilization	Every 2 months	Monthly	Monthly except during hot weather

[243]

CHAPTER XIV

Organic Control of Lawn Insects

Ants

ANTS build nests in the ground and usually form mounds around the openings. The anthills may smother the grass under them as well as destroy the grass roots in the immediate area of the anthill. Although anthills annoy many people, especially in lawns where the grass is kept short, actually, your lawns could not do better than to contain large numbers of these natural aerators. If the hills and castings are unsightly, allow the grass to grow a little longer, so that they will be hidden.

Do not use cyanogas or other chemicals for exterminating ants, as this will impair your soil. If ants are a problem, try sand, bone meal, or powdered charcoal. Once your land becomes rich organically, you will find that the ant problem will take care of itself. Organic matter in the soil increases the moisture content and makes conditions less favorable for the ants.

Asiatic Garden Beetle

The Asiatic garden beetle is most commonly found along the Atlantic seaboard. A close cousin of the Japanese beetle, the pest is a uniform cinnamon brown and comes out to feed only at night. Asters are its first choice as a food, although it feeds on more than 100 different plants including many vegetables, ornamentals and fruits. Its favorite area of attack is the foliage near the ground, often stripping it clean. In lawns, the beetle causes brown patches, often feeding on the roots of the grass. In the grub stage, it is grayish with a light brown head.

Control of the Asiatic garden beetle is very similar to that of the Japanese beetle. It has been successfully halted by the use of the milky spore disease. See Japanese beetle for complete control techniques. Because it is a night feeder and easily attracted to porch and car lights, the homeowner may achieve satisfactory control through the use of a light trap.

Billbug

Billbugs or snout beetles are often found in grassy areas throughout the country. They may be particularly destructive in the eastern two-thirds of the country. Billbugs often cause serious losses to corn by tunneling and feeding inside the stalk. In the grub stage they feed on small grains, rice, peanuts and, of course, on grass.

Normally smaller than an inch, the pests have a curved snout that often causes them to be mistaken for curculios. Although their hard body walls and wing covers make them somewhat durable, they have a tendency to play possum when they are discovered. In the grub stage they are chunky and whitish with a hard brown or yellow head. They are normally found at the grass roots and can be rather troublesome.

Control of the billbug is best achieved by digging down to the roots and destroying him. It's a good idea to undertake a fall program of cleanup by checking for infestation in nearby lots or grassy areas. When discovered, spading or plowing is the best way to upset the life cycle of the pest. It may be wise to conduct a general cleanup of your own backyard, eliminating all the likely hiding places and areas of infestation.

Centipede

Your lawn may be victimized by the centipede, the common name for the symphlid. This active white little pest travels through the tiny cracks in the soil and feeds on many garden plants. The little annoyers are rarely seen above the surface, as they have a strong dislike for light, but their presence in the lawn is revealed by the stunting effect that they impose on grass whose root systems they weaken.

Control of the centipede is difficult, and experiments are being conducted to determine an effective way of eliminating the pest. Homeowners may want to take advantage of the fact that this soil denizen is repelled by light. That suggests eliminating rocks or trash that the centipede may use as a hiding place. It is best to take these precautions early, as the centipede is most troublesome in spring. Digging up the soil around the border of your lawn may also disturb the home of the centipede and cause him to look further for a more compatible environment.

Chinch Bugs

Hairy chinch bugs are serious pests of lawns. They are likely to be more serious in lawns containing bentgrass; however, bluegrass is also attacked. Damage to lawns by chinch bugs is caused by the young bugs or nymphs, which are about ¼ inch long, black with a white spot on their back between their wings.

Chinch bug infested lawns may have many large irregular dead patches. The bugs will be found within a circle of grass which has turned yellow around these dead spots. There are often two yearly generations of chinch bugs with nymphs being present in the lawn the last half of June for

[247]

the first generation and again the last half of August for the second generation.

To control this pest, seed lawn in soil made up of ⅓ sharp builder's sand, ⅓ crushed rock and ⅓ compost. Soybeans grown as a companion crop with corn, shade the bases of the corn plants, thus making them unattractive to the shade-hating chinch bug. Shade trees planted on the lawn may discourage the insect also.

These insects have been found to prefer hot, sunny lawns such as football or baseball fields. It may be helpful to shade your lawn with trees or shrubs if possible. At any rate, experiments conducted at the University of Missouri have shown that well-fed lawns will give better chinch bug control than those starved of nutrients. Tests showed that when the insect is fed on plants grown in nitrogen-poor soil, it not only lives longer, but lays more eggs.

To test for chinch bugs, select a sunny spot along the border of a yellowed area of lawn. Cut out both ends of a large tin can. Push one end of the can into the soil about 2 inches and fill it with water. If chinch bugs are present, they will float to the surface of the water in less than 5 minutes.

Cicada-Killer Wasp

The cicada-killer wasp or digger wasp can make a mess of your lawn in mid or late summer. Normally a rather large wasp (up to 1½ inches) the pest is normally black with a yellow banded abdomen.

You'll know if you have a wasp infestation if you see tunnels going far underground. The openings are marked with little mounds of earth. Not only is the pest a nuisance, but it can also be frightening to those who get too close.

The key to the control of the cicada-killer wasp is to rid the area of cicada insects. The wasp will go to great lengths to find a cicada in a nearby tree. When it does, it will sting the cicada, paralizing it and glide or crawl with it back to its burrow. When the dead cicada is safely home, the wasp lays an egg in it and seals off the hole. When the egg hatches, it feeds on the cicada for about 2 weeks and then makes a cocoon and rests in it until the next season when it pupates and produces an adult.

Hand control may be one of the most effective methods of control. Literally swatting or squashing the wasps is one of the best ways to be sure they don't infest your lawn. As mentioned, cicadas are an important part of the life span of the wasp, and eliminating them from the yard and nearby surroundings seems important. Look for twigs or small branches that have turned brown but are still hanging on before breaking off and falling to the ground. Cut off and destroy those injured twigs as soon as possible.

[249]

Clover Mite

The clover mite may host on various plants around the home grounds, including apple, apricot, almond, cherry, peach, pear, prune, raspberry, and many trees and shrubs. Lawns are one of their favorites. In southern states the mite winters on various clovers and malva, but in the north it winters as small red eggs on bark and around garden buds. The mites come out to do battle in the early spring, and feed on the foliage, causing it to yellow and lose vigor. Heavily infested lawns may dry up and die.

There are several species of these minute creatures, and, although they are red or green, they are seldom seen because they are barely visible to the naked eye.

These pests thrive in stagnant, very humid air, so to prevent them, keep your plants where good air circulation is maintained, and where the air is not excessively humid. Contrary as this may seem, the appearance of mites is also favored by air that is hot and dry, so avoid this, too. If mites have shown their faces on your lawn, give them a rude welcome by spraying them forcibly with plain water. This procedure is effective if it is repeated every 3 or 4 days for two weeks. The mites often die after being knocked around by the water spray; if they live, they often do not return for more. A three per cent oil spray has also been found effective.

When feeding, mites puncture the leaf tissue

with their mouthparts and extract the plant juices. Loss of chlorophyll and other cell contents produces a characteristic blotching or stippling of the grass, causing it to become grayish or brownish in color.

One interesting control method that protects orchards from the mite and can be applied to lawns was developed by Dr. G. Edward Marshall of Purdue University. Dr. Marshall decided to try some materials that could be used to cover the leaf surface of the trees, preventing the tiny spiders from damaging the leaves. The most effective material proved to be a mixture of 20 pounds of cheap wheat flour and 2 quarts of buttermilk. The flour was mixed to a fairly thick slurry by the use of a high pressure gun, and the 2 quarts of buttermilk were added as the slurry was almost complete. This combination was added to 100 gallons of water for application.

As you might guess, the flour and buttermilk make a very sticky "gravy," and that's just the quality Dr. Marshall was after. Unlike an oil cover which would form too continuous a film and reduce transpiration, the flour-buttermilk spray works perfectly as it destroys the mites by sticking them to the leaf's surface. Many of them are enveloped in the solution on the foliage and suffocate. In simple terms, the mites try to burrow through the leaves; their mouths become stuck in the glue-like mixture; and they suffocate with their hind ends up in the air. Some of the sprayed mites appear to have exploded after the spray dried. Organic growers may use their own versions of the flour and buttermilk formula. Rock phosphate or ground limestone may be substituted and mixed with a liquid that will help it to adhere to the grass. (That's what the buttermilk does, binding the flour into a paste.)

Use the spray mixture after the grass has had a chance to become mature and as soon as the mite population is up. Thorough application is needed. Probably at least two sprays will be needed where mites have been a problem, but in his second year of this research, he found that some orchard plots didn't need any sprays. Apparently natural controls like ladybugs, lacewing flies and predacious mites did the job there.

Cutworm

There are several species of cutworms which cause lawn injury. Most species are smooth, greenish, brownish or dirty white grubs with or without striping on the body.

Presence of the feeding larvae may be suspected if adult moths have been seen in the area. The moths are of medium size with a wing spread of from one to two inches. They are usually multicolored of dull hues such as brown, blackish, gray or dirty white.

Cutworms are among the earliest insects to begin feeding in the spring. Most species have but one generation a year, although occasionally there are two. Generations usually overlap so that moths appear throughout the summer.

Cutworms injure grass by cutting off the blades at the base leaving small, elongated or irregular closely cropped brown spots in the turf. In general the larvae remain concealed just below the surface of the ground or in clumps of grass during the day, coming out at night to feed.

Cutworm control on a small scale has been successfully accomplished by flooding the lawn with water until it is puddled. This treatment brings the cutworms to the surface where they may be collected and destroyed.

C. Lester Osborne of Oakfield, Tennessee, has developed a control of his own for cutworms. He found that by taking the stems of wild onions and tying them around his vegetables, the cutworms won't touch them. The same methods met equal success when used with flowers and could probably be adapted for the home lawn. Perhaps the strong odor of the onion repels the cutworms from the area and causes him to seek a less pungent prey.

As an added protection make a bait of the following:

Hardwood sawdust 27%
Wheat bran 25%
Molasses .... 2 quarts
Water .... enough to saturate

Pine sawdust should never be used, as it repels the worms. Scatter a handful of this mixture around the lawn at dusk, or spread evenly along each field row of corn. The sweet molasses will attract the worms from the plants. As the cutworms crawl around in the bait, it will cling to their bodies and harden by morning, rendering them helpless. Since they will be unable to burrow back into the ground to hide from birds, wind and sun, they will soon be destroyed. Although this bait is not 100 per cent effective, it will eliminate an amazingly large number of worms each night.

If cutworms are really a problem, then organic gardening, as evidenced by Maud R. Jacobs of South Carrollton, Kentucky, is the best solution. Here's her story:

"While in Texas recently, I was told by good gardeners in several parts of the state that plants and lawns fertilized with chicken manure are never touched by cutworms, no matter how great the infestation in adjoining parts of the same garden. If a similar thing should prove true in other parts of the country, and a testing in individual gardens is the easiest way of testing the matter, gardeners who keep poultry might well find it worth while to use fertilizer from their flocks on lawns most likely to be attacked by cutworms."

H. Hoehn of New Westminster, B. C. relates this idea in the control of cutworms:

"We discovered that cutworms are quite choosey in their diet, preferring certain kinds of weeds, so it is well not to weed too thoroughly. A wilted weed will betray the presence of a cutworm which can easily be unearthed and destroyed.

[254]

"We also discovered that the cutworms invade the lawn from the surrounding grass, from all sides. Knowing that they prefer sunflowers to any other diet, we planted several rows of sunflowers very thickly as a border, then, on spying a wilted sunflower, the guilty 'varmint' soon paid the penalty of sin. The year we did this (in Saskatchewan) was a particularly bad year as crops were reduced in many cases 50 to 75 per cent. Everyone for miles marvelled at our lawn as theirs was in many cases 75 per cent destroyed and even more, and had to be reseeded.

"As an example of how well this worked — in one typical morning in which we took a count — there were over 100! The danger period only lasts about two weeks."

Earwig

Both adult and nymph earwigs are troublesome. They are usually reddish-brown with a prominent forceps at the tail end and can grow up to 3/4 inch long. The earwig hides during the day and forages at night. It discharges a foul odor, but it seldom causes severe damage to plants. It is chiefly a health hazard.

The use of traps has been very effective in the control of earwigs. Here is a typical trap that can be used: take four pieces of bamboo a foot in length — each piece open at both ends and tie with nylon yarn into a bundle at both ends. Lightly

[255]

paint them with a green paint, and when they are dry, put them under bushes, against fences and any other place where earwigs are likely to gather. Leave them there for a few days; early one morning shake the earwigs out of the holes into a bucket of hot water or kerosene. Bantam hens have also been reported as an effective control against earwigs.

Frank C. Pull of Newark, New Jersey, reports the use of another type of trap:

"We placed a stick along side any plant attacked and inverted a flower pot stuffed with paper on the other end. The earwigs climbed up the stick and hid in the paper which was pulled out and the earwigs destroyed."

Ground Pearl

Ground pearls have small, shining bodies with an iridescent luster, and can be found loosely scattered in soil or on the grass roots. The pests are becoming more of a serious problem in the United States, and have been found to infest Bermuda, centipede and St. Augustinegrass in the Southeast. The only successful treatment seems to be ample organic fertilizer and careful watering throughout the growing season.

Japanese Beetle

The infamous Japanese beetle is a hungry and

greedy pest, rendering damage to more than 275 trees, shrubs, and plants.

Japanese beetle adults usually appear on the foliage about the third week in June. These beetles are about 1 inch long and ¼ inch wide. The head, thorax, and abdomen are metallic-green in color, while the hard outer wings are coppery-brown. There are two tufts of white hair on the abdomen just behind the wing covers and five tufts along each side of the body. Adults are mid-day fliers, their period of greatest activity being from about 9 a.m. to 4 p.m. The female beetle feeds on foliage a few days after emerging before it enters the turf to lay from one to four eggs. It then emerges again, and after feeding a few more days, returns to the soil to deposit another batch of eggs. This procedure continues until a total of from 40 to 60 eggs have been deposited. All eggs are laid about 2½ inches beneath the surface. The life time of the beetle is from 30 to 45 days.

Eggs are nearly spherical in shape, ¹⁄₁₆ to ⅛ inch in diameter, and white when first laid changing to cream color before hatching. Eggs are deposited in the soil and hatch into tiny grubs in about 10 days.

Grubs immediately begin to feed on the humus in the soil and on the roots of various plants. As the grubs increase in size, they work their way close to the soil surface where they continue to feed on the roots of grasses, causing the grass to die out in small patches. By late September, or on the approach of cold weather, the grubs, which by that time, are about one inch long and are white to grayish-white in color, gradually move downward in the soil, where they spend the winter. The depth to which they migrate undoubtedly is affected by temperature, soil type, and soil moisture, but usually it varies from 6 to 14 inches. In late March or early April of the following year, the grubs again approach the soil surface to continue their feeding. In late May, they change into the pupal stage.

Pupa is cream-colored, bobbin-shaped, and about ½ inch in length. It is from this stage that the insect transforms into the adult beetle. The life cycle of this species requires one year.

Perhaps the most widely known means of safe control for the Japanese beetle is the milky spore disease, developed in 1933. This is a bacterial organism that produces a fatal disease in the grub. Since it brings about an abnormal white coloring in the insects, this was dubbed "milky" disease. And because it was present naturally throughout the soils of Japan, this milky disease germ is the main reason that Japanese beetles are kept fully in check in their native territory.

As with scores of other destructive pests, the beetle became a problem only when brought accidentally to areas devoid of its natural enemies, areas lacking the predators, parasites and insect diseases designed by nature as an ever-present effective counter balance. Fighting them with their

[258]

own deadly ills and with hungry pest-consuming insect foes is the basis of biological control.

After several years' work, the control specialist tackling the Japanese beetle enigma came up with a method of producing the milky disease in the laboratory. When it was added to the grub infested soil in 14 states in an initial testing, the beetle killing results proved astonishing. Local and federal governments since then have started over 150,000 "colonies" of milky disease in the Northeast alone. The most significant fact, though, is that wherever the milky disease has been established, the Japanese beetle no longer rates as a serious pest.

The spore powder—a standard mixture of the germ spores, chalk and filler—is produced commercially under a process patent owned and licensed by the Department of Agriculture. Since its introduction, groups of homeowners and whole communities, along with individual gardeners, have joined forces and their efforts have been successful in eliminating the beetle in their sectors by using the spore powder.

Grubs of Japanese beetle are hatched and live in the ground—frequently in lawn turf—until they mature into adult, winged beetles. All through their lengthy grub stage, however, they are subject to attack by several of the milky diseases. The most important of these is known as type A, caused by a germ organism technically termed *Bacillus popilliae*.

As the grub feeds where this is present, it ingests some of the spindle-shaped disease spores, which are 1/4600th of an inch long — so small that billions may exist in one infected grub. The spores form slender vegetative rods in the grub's blood, and these grow and multiply, developing in a few days into the milky spore.

When the infected grubs die (as they invariably do), the spores which fill the body cavity are left in the soil. They are taken up by other grubs as they feed, and these in turn become diseased. As the cycle goes on, the number of spores in the soil increases, more and more grubs are killed, and fewer beetles emerge. Here are some important facts on the milky spore disease treatment:

It is cumulative; that is, it continues and spreads itself. Ordinarily, only a single application is required for lasting control and protection. The disease powder kills only Japanese beetles and a few of their close beetle relatives. It is totally harmless to the soil, to beneficial insects, bees, earthworms, all plants, animals, and humans. It is not affected by weather extremes, by cold, heat, rains, drought. All the homeowner does is apply a teaspoonful of the spore disease powder on his grass or sod in spots 3 to 4 feet apart and in rows the same distance apart.

It can be applied at any time except when the ground is frozen or when it is windy. Recommended for treatment are only mowed or cropped areas. A pound of the spore powder will treat about 4,000 square feet of turf for moderately good results (up to 60 per cent kill within twelve months)—and, of course, continued and increasing protection. Higher application rates bring even greater results in less time. Authorities agree that the spore disease control averages 80 to 90 per cent in overall effectiveness.

Besides the milky spore disease, there are other methods of controlling the Japanese beetle. If the lawn lover remembers that diseased and poorly nourished grass and plants are especially attractive to pests like the Japanese beetle, he can see the importance of using well nourished soil made rich by the addition of organic matter. Plants that are in proper condition and are organically fertilized will resist the onslaught of diseases and pests. Prematurely ripening or diseased fruit is very attractive to beetles. Remove this fruit from the home grounds. The odor of such fruit attracts beetles, which then attack the lawn. Carlton Barnes of Sykesville, Maryland makes this contribution to beetle badgering:

"Anyone having trouble with the Jap beetle, just plant a row of Wilson soybeans and the beetle will eat the beans and let your lawn alone. Also, if you have smart weeds let them grow—the beetles prefer them to anything else."

Perhaps the most interesting homemade remedy comes from W. J. Crawford of Vista, California, who brews his own concoction to stagger the Jap beetle. Here are his instructions:

"Take a one gallon or larger glass jug (dill or other pickle containers are fine) make a ferment in

[261]

it about half full by putting a teaspoon of sugar, a very small amount of dissolved yeast, two or three chunks of peaches, apricots, smashed grapes, anything that ferments into wine. Even add two or three ounces of cheap wine; water of course until about half full—in two or three weeks it will be the strongest alcoholic mess you ever saw and irresistible to Japanese beetles.

"Put the jar out in the yard, pile a little earth around it or anything to keep it from tipping over, lay a small stick across the top and from it hang a cloth about one inch from the top and you're in business. Every evening there will be from 5 to 20 beetles in it. They can be removed with a strainer and burned."

June Beetle

There are more than 30 species of June Beetles, *Phyllophaga spp.* The adults of the different species, which vary from light brown to nearly black in color, emerge from the soil during May and June. Adults feed at night on the foliage of such trees as oak, hickory, walnut, birch, elm, willow, and many others. They hide in the soil during the day where the females lay eggs, usually in grass areas.

Eggs of these beetles, when first laid, are pearly-white and elongated, becoming swollen and almost spherical 6 or 7 days later. They hatch into tiny grubs in about 3 or 4 weeks.

The young grubs feed on the decaying and living vegetable matter in the soil during the first summer. As cold weather approaches, they burrow deeper into the soil, remaining there until the spring of the following year when they return near the surface to continue their feeding on the roots of plants. The grubs feed ravenously and grow rapidly throughout the second summer, causing most of the damage to turf during this year. About mid-October, they again burrow into the soil to pass the second winter. In the following spring they once more come to the surface and feed for a month or two on the roots of grasses and other plants. About the middle of June they move downward in the soil and change to the pupal stage. After spending a month as pupae, they change to adults but remain in their pupal chamber throughout the fall and winter and emerge as adults the following May and June. The female beetles begin to lay eggs in the soil shortly after emerging and thus start another cycle.

For control, see white grub.

Lawn Moth

Lawn moths may seem like other moths except that they have a pronounced projection from the front of the head. The pale brown moths, about ½ to 1 inch long, often fly aimlessly about for a short distance when they are stirred from their resting place. The moths are important because

[263]

they lay eggs on the lawn surface which hatch into sod webworms. (See sod webworms.)

To control lawn moth use Bio-Guard, a safe dust made especially to kill caterpillars and leave unharmed pets or beneficial insects. Bio-Guard is a non-toxic control which kills the moths in their caterpillar form within hours after they have eaten anything treated with it.

Mole Cricket

The mole cricket is a large (1½ inches) pale brown insect which lives deep in the ground during the day and comes out at night to pulverize a garden bed. Most common injury to lawns is caused by the tunnels it makes in the upper inch or two of the soil. Often they cut off the roots of the grass, causing it to die.

One of the most successful controls for the mole cricket is the use of "Doom," a milky disease spore similar to the one used for control of the Japanese beetle. The disease is not harmful to people, pets or beneficial insects. See Japanese beetle for a complete description of control by milky spore disease.

Mole

When obnoxious ridges appear just under the surface of your lawn, you're probably getting a visit from a family of moles. Although the ridges in themselves are annoying and unsightly, the problem is compounded by mice who often use the mole tunnels.

Many homeowners have achieved successful control through the use of commercial traps set into the tunnels. Naturally these must be checked and emptied daily.

Contrary to popular belief, moles do not feed on grass roots or bulbs and other vegetable matter but are ever in search of grubs, worms, and other soil insects. The fact that partially eaten bulbs are found in mole runs, indicates that other rodents such as field mice use the runs for their convenience.

A positive precaution in setting mole traps is to sterilize them before setting to eliminate all human odor. Scorch the trap over a burning newspaper, then use gloves to set the trap. Moles do not see, but are guided by their highly sensitive nose which guides them to their prey.

Moles fan out from their main run in search of food, therefore setting a trap over one run may bring no results. To establish the main run that leads to their underground den, press down all runs with a roller or other means, then note the one used consistently.

One *Organic Gardening* reader discovered an interesting way to rid her garden of moles. Mrs. Frank Bjerstedt of Mentor, Ohio, tells this story:

"I have heard that the castor oil plant had the ability to repel moles, but since we have young children, I didn't want to chance one of them getting at the beans. So, I purchased some castor oil and prepared an emulsion of the oil and liquid detergent in a blender, two ounces oil to one of detergent, and whipped it until it became as thick as shaving cream. I then added water equal in volume to the mixture and whipped again. Taking a regular garden sprinkling can, I filled it with warm water, added about two tablespoons of the oil mixture, stirred, and immediately sprinkled it over the areas of heaviest mole infestation. Deeper soil penetration will be achieved if sprinkling can be done after a rain or good watering.

"Result—no moles, many worms, and a beautiful lush, smooth lawn. I gave two treatments two weeks apart, but I suspect one would have been enough."

Northern Masked Chafer

The Northern masked chafer is chestnut-brown in color and is covered with fine hairs. Adult beetles emerge from the soil during the latter part of June and early July. Adults are night fliers in habit and remain in the soil during the day. Unlike the Japanese beetle, they are strongly attracted to light. Careful observations have failed to find adult feeding of any kind.

Female adults begin to lay eggs in the soil within a few days after they emerge from the pupal case. Eggs of this beetle, when laid, are pearly-white and egg-shaped. Most of them are laid between 4 and 6 inches below the soil surface. The eggs hatch into tiny grubs in about 20 to 22 days.

[266]

Tiny grubs begin to feed on the roots of plants and other organic material in the soil almost immediately after hatching. As the grubs increase in size they work their way close to the surface where they continue to feed on the roots of grasses. About the middle of October, or at the onset of cold weather, grubs begin to descend in the soil, where they spend the winter at a depth of 14 to 16 inches. When this occurs, the grubs are usually about 1¼ inches long. In the following spring the grubs begin to move upward and by early May all are feeding close to the surface. In early June they again begin to move downward in the soil, but only go to a depth of about 6 inches, where they transform to the pupal stage.

The pupa when newly transformed is creamy-white in color, gradually turning to reddish-brown. It spends an average of 18 days in this stage. It is from this stage that the insect transforms into the adult beetle. The life cycle requires one year.

For control, see white grub.

Oriental Beetle

See Japanese beetle.

Rose Chafer

The rose chafer, commonly called the rose bug, is a tannish, small beetle found in the Eastern and Northern states. The beetle is fond of a long list of plants and may be found on anything from apples to strawberries.

The beetles swarm in early summer and feed first on flowers and then on fruits. The feeding period lasts about a month and then the eggs are deposited, usually in sandy soil typical of that in coastal regions. The larvae feed somewhat on grasses or small plants and then move deep into the soil to spend the winter.

Control of rose chafer can be effected by the handpicking of the insects. Some gardeners have surrounded newly planted areas with cheesecloth, for the beetles seem to be repelled by it even if access is still possible. Indications are that the use of extremely hot water may be lethal to the rose chafer. Apparently the insects do not like hot conditions, and hot water from the spigot, if it is as hot as 125 degrees, may be enough to kill the beetles. Care should be taken that the water does not cool before it is applied to the insects. A solid jet rather than a fine spray may be the best method of application.

Rootworm

See White grub.

Slug and Snail

Slugs and snails are grayish insects with worm-like legless bodies. Each snail and slug builds its own highway by secreting a slimy material which hardens into a silvery trail. This material not only smooths the way for these creatures, but it forces them to stick to the trail whether it be right side up or upside down. Slugs can even form mucous ropes for suspending themselves from supports or for going from one level to another. When snails decide to move, it takes them about 15 days to move one mile, while slugs can cover the same distance in about 8 days. Slugs differ from snails by having no shell or a mere rudiment of a shell.

These animals cannot stand dry conditions. During periods of drought, snails place a pane of "glass" over the entrance to their shell house. A film of mucous is stretched across the entrance to the shell. This quickly hardens into a transparent "windowpane." In the same way, they close their house for the winter. But in winter the door is barred with a heavy pane that is not transparent.

Mulched lawns are always so moist that snails and slugs direct their silvery highways toward them. Under the mulch they find welcome relief from the drying effects of the noonday sun. The organic gardener must use common sense and understanding in dealing with them. A thoughtless few will throw up their hands and yell for help, but not so with the student of nature.

F. C. King of Cumberland, England, an unusually observant gardener and writer suggests that the lack of earthworms and consequently of earthworm casts on the land today is giving rise to the terrible slug menace. Worm casts are alkaline and

[269]

thus inimical to slugs which seek a more acid soil for their abode. Mr. L. Ford, another Englishman, says that slugs prefer wilted weeds to growing plants. According to Mr. Ford, slugs will (1) attack seedlings mercilessly if the soil is clean cultivated and lacks humus, (2) attack seedlings on clean cultivated soil dressed with ripe compost, but (3) will not touch seedlings if there is a top-dressing of (a) unripe compost, or (b) ripe compost plus chaff, straw or wilted vegetable matter.

Snails and slugs tend to be nocturnal; i.e., they move about and feed at night but rest in a dark, cool, moist place by day. Advantage must be taken of this habit to eliminate them from the yard if they are troublesome. Place shingles or other similar material in the garden to serve as traps. Each morning destroy the individuals which have hidden away under the traps for the day.

The body of snails and slugs is soft and highly sensitive to sharp objects such as sand and slag and to such dry and slightly corrosive substances as slaked lime and wood ashes. A narrow border of sharp sand or cinders around a bed or border will serve as an effective barrier against them. A sprinkling of slaked lime or wood ashes along a row of tender plants will keep the snails and slugs away because their soft bodies are sensitive to these materials.

Winter is the time when snails and slugs feed on the roots of the perennial plants, and January is the month when they appear in the largest numbers and cause the greatest damage to the unprotected crowns of nearby plants. The defense against these creatures should be built in the fall. Eliminating them from nearby plants is a big step toward successful control in your lawn. Before the first frost stiffens the ground, remove all soil from above the crowns of the plants. Watch carefully for any slugs which may be in this and destroy them immediately. Then cover the entire top of the plant and fill the entire excavation up to the surface of the ground with coarse river sand. This rough sand is sharp and painful to the tender bodies of the slugs, and will act efficiently in keeping them away from the roots. In the spring when the plants are cultivated and humus is added to the earth, the sand will become mixed with the soil and assist with the needed drainage of the soil. — *Dr. William Eyster.*

In olden days before the advent of commercial pesticides, slugworms were eliminated by pouring a thick mixture of soap suds over the infested soil. Strong soap suds were also the "most simple, cheap and efficacious medicine that I have been able to discover for the cure of the bite of the caterpillar on our apple trees," according to a Massachusetts orchardist. Here are his exact words:

"When the washwomen have finished cleansing their clothes—which should happen by 12 at noon every Monday—take the old wash pail full of the suds—mopstick and all—apply the suds to the nest; break that open and rub the mop against it till you have given each inhabitant a wet coat, and you will have no more trouble with them. Every

[271]

individual wet with this liquor will immediately die."

Sod Webworm

The sod webworm is one of the more destructive insect pests of bluegrass. Damage to grass is caused by the feeding during the larval or worm stage. The adult moth does not cause damage.

Larvae are generally about 1 inch long when full-grown by ⅛ inch in diameter, a dirty, yellowish-white color with a light brown head and at least four parallel rows of small dark spots running from head to tail. Larvae lie in a curled position in the thatch of the grass.

Adult webworms are about ¾ inch long, cigar-shaped, and buff colored. There may be a small darker line on the top of each wing cover. Two small finger-like projections are visible at the front of the head. When at rest, the wings are wrapped around the body to form a half circle. Adult moths can usually be kicked up by persons walking through or mowing the grass. They usually fly up a short distance across the lawn in a zig-zag pattern and quickly dart back into the grass.

Sod webworms spend the winter as partially grown larvae several inches deep in the soil. At the approach of warm weather in the spring, the larvae move upward and begin feeding on the lush spring growth of grass. In the spring and summer, the sod webworm larvae live on the surface of the soil in small silken tunnels among the thatch of the grass. They chew grass blades off just above the thatch line, pull the blades into their silken tunnels, and eat them. Injury therefore appears as small brown patches of close-clipped grass about the size of a softball. When many larvae are present, the small brown patches run together and form large irregular dead patches. During June some of the larvae complete their development and change to the pupal or resting stage. By late June and early July adult moths emerge from the pupae, pair-up, mate, and soon begin laying eggs at random in the bluegrass for another generation. At least two generations, and possibly three, are produced in one year. The second generation, which appears in late July and August, may cause the most damage. When the temperature remains below 40° F. in the fall, most of the larvae have already gone down in the soil to overwinter. Where webworms are abundant, numerous small holes about the diameter of one's finger are often found randomly spaced in the dead patches. These holes generally extend down to near the soil line. The holes are made by blackbirds seeking out the larger sod webworm larvae.

Control—Since control measures are directed at the larvae, the best time to treat is when the majority of the eggs have hatched and small larvae are present, but before excessive damage occurs. Most people want to do something when they see many moths flying at night or kick many up in the daytime. When you see moths, this means that the larvae have completed their development and are leaving the lawn. The time to treat is about two weeks after a sharp decline in the number of moths seen. At this time the eggs that were laid by the flying moths should have hatched and a new batch of larvae should be in the lawn feeding. Generations of the webworm do overlap, therefore, some adults and larvae will be present nearly all summer long.

See lawn moth for more on control.

White Grub

Grubworms are the larvae of hard-shelled beetles. They are whitish, have brown heads, and usually lie in a C-shaped position in soil around the root area of grasses. In Ohio, there are three kinds of grubs which occur most commonly and cause the greatest damage. The three kinds of grubs are (1) June beetles, (2) Northern masked chafer, and (3) Japanese beetle. Damage in lawns by grubs appears as brown patches of dead grass which can be rolled back just like a carpet. In general, the damage should be noticeable from May on.

Active ground moles in a yard are a good indication that grubs are present, since moles feed on grubs. The best way to tell if you have grubs is to examine the soil from May to September by cutting a foot-square flap on three sides and rolling it back to observe the presence or absence of the C-shaped grubs. Do this in several places in the lawn.

White grubs feed most heavily in the spring when they are full grown. The adults are usually dark gray snout beetles with a light band along the side of their bodies. They grow up to a half inch long, and feed on the roots and tubers of plants. These yellowish white, curved grubs look like a worm and are somewhat fleshy. A single beetle may live 2 to 3 months and lay about 600 to 700 eggs, which may hatch in 2 weeks in warm, moist weather.

White grubs can cause serious damage if they are present in sufficient numbers. They cut off the grass roots and are the favorite food of moles, who may be attracted by them. Sod affected by grub damage can be rolled back over the spots where they have been at work. If the lawn shows brown patches and loose sod in late spring or late summer, rake off all the loose turf and turn over the soil under it. Continue to turn it up at intervals of a few days until late fall. Birds will make short work of the exposed grubs. If you have chickens or ducks to move to the area, they will make an even better job of it. Poultry is also valuable in the event of an attack of chinch bugs.

Clean cultivation can go a long way to the elimination of beetles. It is essential to fertilize the soil heavily so that grass may become strong enough to fight off the insect's attack.

Wireworm

Wireworms are slender, jointed, unusually hard-shelled worms. They are light to dark brown, clumsy in action and range in length up to 1½ inches. These chewing insects feed entirely underground, attacking germinating seeds and the roots, underground stems and tubers of growing plants. Damage is most likely to occur on poorly drained soil or on land that has been grass sod. The best control measures to use against wireworms are those that will destroy the conditions under which the insects usually develop.

Good drainage tends to reduce wireworm damage. Newly broken sod land should not be used for resodding if other soil is available. If sod land must be used, it should be thoroughly plowed or stirred once a week for 4 to 6 weeks in the early fall preceding spring planting. Stirring the soil exposes many of the insects and crushes many others. Enriching soil with humus will also improve aeration and reduce wireworm attacks.

Aeration of the soil is desirable and can be increased by breaking the hardpans in the subsoil. This is best done by increasing the organic matter in the soil so that it will contain a numerous population of earthworms, who also specialize in subsoiling and aerating.

One gardener has found that the attractiveness of the potato can lure the wireworm into a trap. Near the affected plants he places half a potato, with the eyes cut out to prevent its growing. A pointed stick is run through the middle of the potato and stuck into the ground, and the trap is covered with about an inch of soil. In a day or two, the stick and potato can be removed from the ground with any wireworms that have taken the bait. Some days as many as 15 to 20 have been found on one slice of potato.

CHAPTER XV

Prevention of Lawn Diseases

By AND LARGE, good lawn practice will prevent or limit disease attacks from the start. Disease is encouraged by: (1) poor soil drainage; (2) excess moisture; (3) poor circulation of air because of surrounding trees, shrubs or buildings; (4) incorrect mowing; (5) stimulation of grass with fertilizer during the summer; (6) strong soil acidity.

Correcting poor soil drainage and maintaining adequate soil aeration builds your lawn, because they permit stronger root and top growth. On the other hand, a soggy soil that is water-soaked makes an ideal environment for a sick lawn, because the disease organisms need an abundance of moisture for the early stage of spore development and infection of the plant.

Watering late in the evening is responsible for

more lawn disease than perhaps any other bad practice. This is because the grass remains wet through the night, thus directly encouraging mold and fungus growth.

Anything which favors the undue and prolonged presence of moisture, like a heavy mat of grass clippings, contributes to the incidence of fungus growth. So, if you leave heavy grass clippings on the lawn for their mulch value, be sure to rake them over lightly to break them up and permit circulation of air.

Close mowing of bluegrass lawns is another practice which encourages disease. Such cropping weakens the grass and helps produce more succulent or tender leaf growth which is vulnerable to fungus. Many diseases attack the lower leaves first. On lawns cut higher than 1½ inches, new leaves can be formed as fast as the lower ones are infected and no permanent damage will occur.

The bentgrasses, because of their ability to obtain moisture and nutrients from the soil due to their prostrate type of growth, can stand close cutting — down to half an inch. Given favorable conditions the bents will successfully resist heat, drought, insects, and fungus attacks.

Nevertheless, the bad effect close cutting has even on such grasses is illustrated in the following pair of experiments. In the first, bentgrass was trimmed down to one-quarter of an inch. Under this severe handicap, it produced 25 pounds of roots to each 1,000 square feet of lawn surface and had an average working depth of 4 to 5 inches.

But, when the same bentgrass was cut at one inch, it grew 40 pounds of roots to 1,000 square feet and had an average working root depth of 8 to 9 inches. There is little need to labor the point — healthy grass that will resist and throw off fungus attacks is cut high and it grows a root system that really digs into the soil and takes hold!

Applying fertilizer to speed midsummer growth is another practice that can lead to lawn trouble. The tender young leaf blades are particularly vulnerable to fungus diseases whenever temperature and moisture conditions are favorable to their enemies. But fertilizing in the early spring and fall stimulates growth during seasons when the danger of disease is greatly reduced.

It must also be stressed that proper and adequate liming is a valuable aid in the prevention of disease. Turf which is grown on strongly acid soil is much more susceptible to disease and disorders than a lawn which is raised on a slightly acid or neutral soil.

Turf areas which are completely enclosed by buildings, trees or shrubs may suffer from bad circulation of air. This means that the grass will not only remain wet for long periods, but that it will be excessively warm. These two adverse factors, excessive humidity plus warmth, not only inhibit sound lawn growth, but also favor the development of grass disease. The remedy is simple: restore adequate circulation of air by pruning or removal of some of the trees and shrubs.

The most effective way to keep turf diseases out

of your lawn is to plant a mixture of grasses. Different diseases attack different varieties; brown patch strikes the bentgrasses while leaf spot hits the bluegrasses. So, when a single grass is planted, there is little to halt the spread of a disease from leaf to leaf once it has started. But in a mixed turf, the disease organisms soon reach a species of grass that is resistant and further progress is halted. Where possible, plant disease-resistant varieties.

Algae, Green Scum

A green or blackish scum may form on bare soil or thinned turf. This is most common in low, wet, shaded, or heavily used and compacted areas. The mass of algae (small plants) dries to form a thin, black crust, which later cracks and peels.

For best control, correct the soil drainage. Aerifying the soil with a hand aerifier or tined fork will help. It may be necessary to install drain tile if water-logged soil is a problem. Reduce foot traffic on the lawn by putting the area into a walk or patio or erect a fence.

Brown Patch

Brown patch is a common turf disease found in lawns and golf greens. Typically it causes irregular spots of varying size which are first a light yellow-green, later turning to a medium brown as the grass dies. The dead grass stays erect and does not

[280]

mat down. The fungus attacks the roots, killing first the fine feeding roots and later the entire root system. In periods of wet weather or where lawns are watered frequently, the fungus may grow up on the lower stems and leaves. Heavy fertilizing and constant watering accelerate the disease.

The fungus responsible for brown patch attacks practically all species of grasses, but it is most serious on bentgrasses, fescues, Kentucky bluegrass, ryegrass, centipedegrass, and St. Augustinegrass. Brown patch is one of the most prevalent lawn grass diseases in the warm, humid regions of the United States. It occurs during warm, wet weather. Brown patch is most damaging following excessive applications of nitrogen fertilizer. This promotes a lush growth of grass that is readily attacked. The disease spreads by fungus threads, or mycelium. New infections can start from mycelium carried on shoes, mowing equipment, or grass clippings.

Excess thatch and mat, high temperatures (75° to 95° F.), high humidity, and soft, lush growth due to excess nitrogen favor brown patch. A cold weather (40° to 60° F.) form of the disease occurs infrequently. The disease is more common in warm inland areas.

To control brown patch, eliminate the heavy watering of the lawn. If watering is deemed necessary, water sparingly in the morning. Set the mower high so that the grass will not be cut back so much when it is mowed and remove excessive

[281]

clippings. Close cutting puts a strain on grass and makes it susceptible to disease. Remove the clippings after mowing. Avoid the excessive use of commercial fertilizers that are high in nitrogen. Reduce shading and improve soil aeration and water drainage.

Chlorosis

The Georgia Agricultural Experiment Station makes the following report on Chlorosis:

Chlorosis (yellowing) of turf is a symptom of iron deficiency. Iron is an essential element in the production of chlorophyll. Chlorophyll is the green pigment in plants necessary for manufacturing food which provides energy and building materials to keep the plant alive and growing. Several turf grasses display iron deficiency symptoms. Centipede, however, is the most sensitive of the turfgrasses in its requirements for iron. The three factors which most commonly contribute to iron-deficiency chlorosis (yellowing) and dying out of centipede in the spring are: 1. overfertilization, 2. extended dry periods during the previous fall, and 3. too much lime.

Overfertilization results in luxurious growth of the grass and removal of most of the iron that is in a form that can be absorbed and used by the centipedegrass. In more cases, chlorosis may develop immediately. During the latter part of the previous growing season, iron deficiency may have reduced the amount of food manufactured which

[282]

resulted in the grass entering the winter in a weakened condition. Thus, the turf is slow in reestablishing an adequate root system in the spring and shows severe chlorosis during this period. If chlorosis is not too severe, the grass may regain color and recover. However, in the more severe cases, the grass may actually starve to death as a result of failure to manufacture adequate food to maintain life.

Damage from late-fall drought often goes unnoticed because homeowners may assume that winter dormancy rather than drought is responsible for premature browning of the turf. Drought-damaged turf is badly weakened and enters the winter with a low food reserve, which is inadequate to develop a sufficient root system to absorb enough iron to supply the plant needs during the early spring.

The iron deficiency symptoms of centipede as well as other southern turfgrasses sometimes result from too much lime (high soil pH). Thus, one should have the soil tested and treated according to recommendations.

Prevention of iron deficiency chlorosis (yellowing) can usually be accomplished by maintaining centipede lawns under relatively low levels of soil fertility and the soil pH below 6.0.

Dollar Spot

Dollar spot is a disease characterized by small circular areas about 2 inches in diameter. When the disease is established, the spots turn nearly white. They may coalesce or remain separate, and generally appear over the entire lawn. The leaves are water-soaked at first and later brown. In the final stages they turn straw colored. Fine, white cobwebby fungus threads may be seen in early morning.

Susceptible grasses include bentgrasses, blue-grasses, Bermudas, ryegrasses, and fescues.

Moderate temperatures (60° to 80° F.) and excess moisture, excess mat, and thatch, favor dollar spot. Turf deficient in nitrogen tends to develop more dollar spot than turf adequately fertilized with nitrogen. For control, keep thatch at a minimum. Water only when needed to a depth of 8 to 12 inches. Apply adequate nitrogen. High mowing is a remedy.

Although this trouble may occur on the home lawn, it is more frequent on golf greens. Vigorous raking of the grass will help to eliminate the spots from the home lawn.

Fading-Out

Fading-out is caused by a complex of *Helminthosporium* and *Curvularia* species of fungi that attack bentgrasses, fescues, and Kentucky blue-grasses. It occurs in all parts of the country. The disease is most destructive during hot, humid weather from May to October. Diseased areas appear yellowed or dappled green as though the grass were suffering from iron deficiency or low fertility. When the disease becomes severe and uncontrolled, the grass "fades out," leaving dead grass in irregular reddish-brown patches 2 to 3 inches in diameter. Sometimes these spots merge to form dead areas a foot or more in diameter.

Kentucky bluegrass and common Kentucky bluegrass are susceptible varieties, but Merion and Newport are resistant. Cool (50° to 70° F.) moist conditions favor the disease which first appears on shaded plants. It is most severe on closely clipped turf.

It's a good idea to reduce shade in the yard and improve soil aeration and water drainage. Do not mow grass lower than 1¾ inches. In general, the same management practices recommended for controlling *Helminthosporium* leafspot are recommended for controlling fading-out.

Fairy Ring

Fairy rings are a common problem in many home lawns and they can rapidly disfigure valuable turf.

The fungi which cause the rings belong to the mushroom family, live in the soil and grow outward in a radial direction. When conditions are favorable, mushrooms emerge from the underlying fungi growth and form the characteristic rings or parts of circles, Dr. Dickens explains.

At certain stages, the grass is stimulated by ni-

[285]

trogen by-products from fungi activity and a circular green band of grass appears. Then, soil in the center of the ring becomes hard, compact, impervious and difficult to water. In severe cases, sod is completely infiltrated with white mold which causes stale soil, with a strong, musty odor. The mold may reach one to two feet into the soil.

Fairy rings are easily controlled if treated early. The area occupied by the ring should be aerated with a spading fork by making holes two inches apart and as deep as possible. Begin outside the ring in a safe margin of two feet and work toward the center. Do not use the spading fork in any other part of the lawn or yard without first washing it thoroughly. In small, severe cases you may have to entirely remove the soil to a depth of one foot and 18 inches on either side of the affected area. Discard the soil and replace it. Best idea before this problem occurs, is to test your soil for adequate nitrogen. If the soil is deficient, add a substance high in nitrogen, like dried blood or feathers. Fairy ring develops most frequently in soil high in undecomposed organic matter.

Fusarium Patch

Fusarium patch is caused by a fungus which probably overseasons as a network of fungus threads in grass residues. The disease is observed only in central and northern California.

[286]

When it strikes, roughly circular patches of 1 to 2 inches may enlarge to 12 inches. Leaves first become water-soaked, turn reddish brown, then bleached. Minute, white or pinkish, gelatinous spore masses occasionally are seen on dead leaves. Fungus threads, also white or pinkish, may be seen in early morning.

Susceptible grasses include bluegrasses, ryegrasses, fescues, and zoysia. It is especially common on Poa annua and creeping bentgrass varieties.

Cool (40° to 60° F.), moist conditions such as prolonged rainy periods in winter, favor the disease. It usually appears first on shaded plants. To control it, reduce shade; improve soil aeration and water drainage. Avoid excess nitrogen fertilization.

Grease Spot

When your turf is killed in small roughly circular spots (2-6 inches) which tend to run together, grease spot could be the problem. Blackened leaf blades wither rapidly and turn reddish brown. Leaf blades tend to lie flat, stick together and appear greasy. The roots may be brown.

Grease spot usually appears in low spots that are wet for long periods. Disease depends upon excess moisture. Reduce shading, improve soil aeration and water drainage to eliminate the disease. Water when needed to a depth of 8 to 12 inches.

[287]

Helminthosporium Leafspot and Foot Rot

This disease, which gets its name from the Helminthosporium fungi that cause it, is one of the most widely distributed and destructive grass diseases. Kentucky bluegrass is one of the species most severely damaged.

The principal fungus causing leafspot in Kentucky bluegrass, also causes a foot rot condition known as going-out or melting-out. The disease occurs mainly during cool, moist weather of spring and fall, but it may develop throughout the summer. Pure strands of Kentucky bluegrass favor development of the disease; mixtures of several recommended species usually retard development because most mixtures contain naturally resistant species.

Damage is most conspicuous in the leaves. However, the fungus responsible for the disease also causes a sheath rot or foot rot. The fungus produces reddish-brown to purplish-black spots on leaves and stems of Kentucky bluegrass. Leaves shrivel and the stems, crown, rhizomes, and roots discolor and rot. Leafspots and foot rots produced on other grasses by different species of Helminthosporium resemble those on Kentucky bluegrass. Dead grass in attacked areas often is attributed to drought injury. Weeds and crabgrass usually invade these areas.

The disease in Kentucky bluegrass lawns can be controlled by growing the resistant variety, Merion. Some leafspots develop on Merion, but it is more resistant than common Kentucky bluegrass and is seldom killed by the destructive foot rot stage.

Follow these management practices to reduce damage: Mow upright-growing grasses to a height of 1¾ to 2 inches rather than ½ to 1 inch. Apply enough fertilizer to keep grass healthy and thriving. Avoid overstimulation with nitrogen, particularly in the spring. Remove clippings, especially on lawns receiving heavy fertilization. It is suggested that the homeowner consider the use of Tifton turf Bermuda hybrids if it is at all possible, as they are resistant to leafspot.

Lawn Rot

Lawn rot is caused by a fungus which attacks the stems and leaves of the plant causing a soft rot of the tissue. This rotting gives a matted appearance of the affected areas unlike Brown Patch. Newly seeded grass is more likely to be affected than older established turf. On new seedings diseased areas have the appearance of having been soaked with gasoline. The causal fungus requires plenty of moisture and warm temperatures, hence is destructive only during periods of warm, wet weather or when the grass is watered frequently at night during summer weather.

To prevent an outbreak of this disease, water infrequently in the forenoon. Bentgrasses usually suffer more from this disease than other types. It is best to make every effort to avoid prolonged heavy watering of the lawn.

Leaf Blotch

When tiny, purplish to reddish spots occur on leaf blades and leaf sheaths, leaf blotch may be the culprit. Seedlings are very susceptible, but plants rapidly become resistant. Affected seedlings wither, die, and turn brown. Roots and crown may develop small lesions. Bermudagrasses are the most susceptible.

Leaf blotch damages young seedlings or adult plants weakened by factors such as excess thatch, deficient nitrogen, and unfavorable growing conditions. To control the disease, remove thatch at regular intervals, and apply adequate nitrogen.

Moss

The appearance of moss in a lawn is not necessarily an indication of acid soil. Its presence is most likely to indicate plenty of moisture and a lack of phosphorus and potash in the soil. Soil improvement followed by reseeding can be expected to get rid of the moss.

Any lawn that is properly fertilized and watered and planted with the right seed so that the grass plants flourish, should be free of moss. Moss appears most frequently in thin and shady patches where the grasses have not covered the soil for some reason. It does not necessarily mean that the soil is acid, though the pH should be checked. It is more likely a sign of low soil fertility. Apply plenty of organic fertilizer, aerate the soil and treat like any other spot which needs reseeding, either in early spring or in fall. Make every attempt to improve the soil drainage. Also, remove any organic matter such as rotten wood or decaying plant matter that may be beneath the surface.

Mushrooms

Mushrooms, commonly called toadstools, often appear in lawns during rainy spells in the summer. Mushrooms are the above-ground growth of certain fungi which grow on decaying vegetable matter in the soil. In lawns this organic matter frequently consists of buried stumps or tree roots. Mushrooms are chiefly a nuisance as they do no harm to the grass and are best removed by raking or sweeping. No material will kill the fungus without injury to the grass. When toadstools or mushrooms appear, test your soil to check its pH. Then top-dress with enough natural ground limestone— preferably dolomite, which supplies magnesium as well—to bring it up to a desired level. Pulverized oyster shells, wood ashes, and other calcium-rich wastes are also usable. Best pH for healthy lawn growth is slightly acid—about 6.5—or just under neutral (7.0). To raise a soil one full unit—say from 5.5 to 6.5—apply approximately 50 pounds

[291]

of lime per 1,000 square feet, 10 to 15 pounds less for light, sandy soils, more for heavier loams or clay types. If a large amount is needed you can apply half in early spring, the other half in fall.

Remember, too, that a lawn's total environment is important. Good fertilizing practices — with plenty of humus incorporated to buffer against acid-alkaline extremes — aeration, drainage, proper mowing and watering are the way to a handsome turf, free of toadstools and other problems.

Powdery Mildew

Powdery mildew shows as isolated wefts of fine, gray-white, cobwebby growth mainly on the upper surface of the leaf blade. The growth becomes more dense, and the leaves appear to have been dusted with flour or lime. Infected leaves usually turn yellow and wither. It is found more commonly on bluegrass (especially Merion) in the spring and the fall when nights are cool.

Mildew is caused by a fungus which grows on the surface of the leaf. Sucker-like structures grow into the outer leaf cells from which the fungus obtains its nourishment. Mildew is most severe in shaded areas or where air circulation is poor.

To control powdery mildew, keep the lawn vigorously growing by fertilizing and maintaining adequate moisture in the soil. Improve air circulation to remove humidity pockets by pruning trees and shrubs where possible. Merion bluegrass is more susceptible than common Kentucky bluegrass. Before you decide on using Kentucky bluegrass, find if Helminthosporium disease is frequent in your area, for it often attacks Kentucky bluegrass.

Pythium Diseases

Pythium diseases occur in humid areas and may be more widespread than is generally realized. The fungi are destructive at 70 degrees F. and above, especially in poorly drained soils. These diseases are most common on newly established turf, but if conditions are favorable, they occur on grass regardless of age.

Diseased areas vary from a few inches to several feet in diameter and they sometimes occur in streaks as though the fungus has spread from mowing or from water flow following heavy rains. Injury is most noticeable in early morning as a circular spot or group of spots about 2 inches in diameter surrounded by blackened grass blades, that are intertwined with the fungus threads. Diseased leaves become water soaked, mat together, and appear slimy. The darkened grass blades soon wither and become reddish-brown, particularly if the weather is sunny and windy. Grass is usually killed in 24 hours and it lies flat on the ground rather than remaining upright like grass affected by the brown patch disease. New grass does not grow back into the diseased area.

The most important management recommenda-

[293]

tion is to avoid watering methods that keep foliage and ground wet for long periods. Other suggestions: Avoid excessive watering during warm weather. Delay seeding until fall because cool, dry weather generally checks the disease.

Red Thread

Red thread fungus is caused by the *Corticium fuciforme*. It over-seasons as pinkish or red gelatinous crusts of fungus threads. Although the disease occurs commonly along the coast of northern and central California, it is rare in southern California.

The turf is killed in patches 2 to 15 inches in diameter. Pink web of fungus threads bind leaves together. Pink gelatinous, fungus crusts, ¼ to ¾ inch long, projecting from leaves, are characteristic. Bentgrasses, bluegrasses, fescues, and ryegrasses are susceptible to the fungus. Red thread usually appears on plants deficient in nitrogen, and during periods of prolonged cool, wet weather.

Control includes applying adequate nitrogen and reducing shading.

Rust

Rust fungi attack many lawn grasses, but are more serious on Merion Kentucky bluegrass than

[294]

on other grasses. Common Kentucky bluegrass is less susceptible to rust than Merion, but it is susceptible to the more destructive Helminthosporium leafspot. Rust has been reported on Merion Kentucky bluegrass from Rhode Island to California and from Canada to Oklahoma. It seems likely that rust fungi will attack Merion wherever it is grown.

Rust usually occurs in late summer. Heavy dew favors rust development. It remains until frost.

Symptoms are yellow-orange or red-brown powdery pustules that develop on leaves and stems. If a cloth is rubbed across the affected leaves, the rust-colored spores adhere to the cloth and produce a yellowish or orange stain.

Lawns containing pure stands of Merion Kentucky bluegrass are especially susceptible to attack by rust fungi. Damage is less severe if Merion Kentucky bluegrass is mixed with common Kentucky bluegrass or with red fescue. Recommended mixtures are 50 per cent Merion and 50 per cent common Kentucky bluegrass; 50 per cent Merion, 25 per cent common Kentucky bluegrass, and 25 per cent red fescue. Susceptible grasses include bluegrass and ryegrass. Moderately warm moist weather favors rust development. Moisture in the form of dew for 10 to 12 hours is sufficient for spores to infect plants. Best control is to keep plants growing rapidly by fertilization and irrigation.

A well-managed program of lawn care that includes the proper mowing, organic fertilizing and watering will go a long way in the control of rust.

Seed Rot and Damping-Off

Seed rot and damping-off are diseases caused by soil-inhabiting fungi and are troublesome during the cool, wet weather of spring. The seeds rot in the soil just after the seed coat is broken. Seedling grasses on new lawns appear water-soaked, blackened and then shrivel and turn yellow to brown, rotting off at the surface of the soil. Patches up to 4 inches in diameter are affected causing new seedlings to appear spotty in growth.

Seed rot and damping-off are favored by excess water, sowing seeds of low viability, and sowing seeds above the recommended rates, especially during periods unfavorable for seed germination and growth.

Properly graded lawns usually do not suffer from this disease. If hollows are present in your lawn, water them carefully so that the soil does not become water-soaked, or better yet, eliminate the hollows by filling them in. Do not exceed seeding rates in vulnerable areas and water only when necessary. Sow only fresh, healthy seed at recommended rates and seasons.

Slime Mold

A group of fungi known as slime molds often covers grass with a dusty, bluish-gray, black, or yellow mass. Slime molds are not parasitic on grass, but they are unsightly. They feed on dead organic matter. The most damage they do to grass plants is to shade and discolor the blades. Slime molds occur during wet weather; they disappear rapidly as soon as it becomes dry. The large masses can be readily broken up by sweeping with a broom or by spraying with a strong stream of water. During prolonged damp weather slime molds can be especially annoying. Then it's best to rake or brush the spore masses and forget about watering.

Snow Mold

The fungus of snow mold attacks the grass during the winter, either under the snow cover or during the cold winter rains. The injury shows in the spring as irregular spots of nearly white, dead grass. The disease makes no further progress with the coming of warm weather.

To avoid snow mold, eliminate the fall fertilizing with commercial nitrogen fertilizers which cause the grass to become succulent. Mow with the mower set high, and rake the grass vigorously. Keep the lawn cut to prevent a mat of grass from developing.

Stripe Smut

Stripe smut is a fungus which grows internally through the leaves and stems of grass plants. When it strikes, black sooty deposits form on leaves. They later brown and the grass dies.

Resistant varieties are the answer to the home-owner. Plant either Park Newport, K-34 or K-1.

Miscellaneous Injuries

Sunburn and drought injury are very similar in appearance but may occur independently. Sunburn sometimes occurs during very hot weather following cool, cloudy weather. Different species of grass, sunburn differently and this may cause spots in the lawn resembling brown patch. Drought causes the same brown discoloration of sunburn but over larger areas, first in the open sunny areas and later under trees if the drought is prolonged. Watering before it appears will forestall drought injury but unless one is equipped to put on several inches of water at a time, watering is of doubtful value after the grass has once turned brown. Neither sunburn nor drought will permanently injure grass and it will recover as soon as fall rains and cooler weather arrive.

Chemical fertilizers applied on wet grass may cause serious burning. Female dogs can cause burned areas on the lawn; eventually these dead spots are surrounded by a ring of heavy green growth of grass. Rugs, rubber mats, and metal dishes put on the grass in the hot sun will surely leave their mark on the grass.

Along the shore, salt spray or flooding with high

tides causes serious injury to lawns. The injury from spray is temporary, but if the area is flooded for several hours the damage is likely to be permanent. If the flooding is of short duration, flushing with fresh water immediately afterwards will minimize the injury. There is no chemical that will get rid of the salt in the soil quickly.

Here's a list summarizing the causes of injury often mistaken for disease:

1. Dog "injury."
2. Fertilizer burn.
3. Mowers in poor condition.
4. Drought injury.
5. Gas or oil spillage.
6. Soap used for washing cars.
7. Insect damage.
8. Salt (applied to ice and snow moves in solution to turf area).
9. Hydrated lime burn.
10. Soil compaction.
11. Winter killing other than snow mold.
12. Sunburn or scald.
13. Objects placed on lawns cause burning or reduce light causing yellowing of grass blades.
14. "Scalping" by close mowing.
15. Over-watering.
16. Wet leaves or an excess of grass clippings.
17. Annual bluegrass "going out."
18. Weed killer injury.
19. Unadapted grasses.

[299]

CHAPTER XVI

Weeds and What to Do About Them

HOMEOWNERS with well-kept lawns often spend three to five dollars per 1,000 square feet for lawn weed control. Additional amounts are spent every year for seed, fertilizer, insecticides and fungicides.

Weedy lawns usually indicate poor management, or a mistake in establishment. Weeds are not always the cause of poor turf. They become a problem because they are better adapted to conditions under which turf grasses perform poorly. These include low fertility, extremes of soil reaction, poor soil structure, low clipping or lawn seed mixtures.

Classifying Weeds

Most weeds belong to two principal families — broad-leaf and grass. How broad is a broad-leaf?

[300]

Gardeners and homeowners have been constantly perplexed by the distinction and classification of broad-leaf weeds. Actually, the term is quite simply understood when you realize that "broad-leaf" is a literal translation, not an exact meaning.

In fact, many of the broad-leafed weeds are quite narrow. Those of chickweed and spotted surge, for instance, are less than ¼ inch wide, but they still classify as broad-leaf weeds. The reason? Broad-leafed weeds are any weeds that are not grasses. There's no mistaking them. They look like weeds, not grasses. They often have showy flowers; the leaves have a network of small veins originating from a principal vein which divides the leaf in half; and a strong main root called a taproot is usually present. However, some broad-leaf species do have fibrous root systems. Dandelion and knotweed are typical broad-leaf species.

When it comes to grassy weeds, the classification is not as obvious. Sometimes it's hard to tell whether a strand is a grassy weed or the real stuff. Most grassy weeds destroy the texture and color of the lawn. The worst of these is crabgrass, which turns a rusty color after the first frost while the rest of the grass is still green and healthy. True grasses have jointed hollow stems; the leaf blades have parallel veins and are several times longer than they are wide; the root systems are vibrous; and most seed heads are similar to small grain. Foxtail and quackgrass are typical grasses.

There's still a third category—sedges. They are

grass-like plants with three-cornered stems which bear leaves extending in three directions. They are neither true grasses nor true broad-leaves.

Some homeowners cringe in frustration when they see weeds like this dandelion appear on their lawns. Organic weed controls can change that because they offer effective, lasting and safe protection.

ANNUALS, BIENNIALS, PERENNIALS

Several additional groupings could be made but from a control standpoint, determination of life span—annual, biennial or perennial—is most important.

An annual germinates from seed, grows, matures, and dies in less than 12 months. Crabgrass, foxtail and prostrate spurge are examples of annuals.

A winter annual starts its life cycle in the fall and completes it the next spring. Henbit and shepherd's purse are winter annuals.

Biennials take two years to complete their life cycle. They form a rosette and store food in their fleshy root the first year and flower the second year. Many thistles are biennials. From a weed control standpoint, biennials can be considered as annuals or perennials.

Perennials live more than two years. Field bindweed and white clover are typical perennials.

Cool season plants grow best during cool periods and mature or go dormant during the hottest part of the summer. Bluegrass and dandelions are cool season perennials. Winter annuals are also cool season.

Plants that remain dormant vegetatively or as seed until temperatures warm up in May and June are known as warm season plants. Crabgrass, foxtail and prostrate spurge are typical warm season

[303]

annuals. Germination of warm season annuals seldom occurs before May 10.

Weedy warm season perennial, such as nimblewill, present objectionable appearances in cool season lawns. They remain dormant and brown in the spring 45 or more days longer than bluegrass. In the fall, warm season species turn brown after the first frost; cool season grasses usually remain green an extra 30 days or more.

IDENTIFICATION AIDS

Comparison of a weed with pictures of the weed is the easiest way to identify an unknown. Note the distinctive characteristics listed for many of the species. Observe the growth habits. Does the plant grow upright or prostrate? Is the stem fleshy? Does it contain milky sap? Does it root at the joints? Does it have a square stem? Note whether a plant is annual, biennial, or perennial; cool season or warm season.

For example, a green weedy grass found in March is not crabgrass, foxtail, or nimblewill since they do not start growth that early.

Here's a list of common weeds and their classifications:

Barnyardgrass-A	Bermudagrass-P
Beardgrass–P	Bindweed–P
Bedstraw, Yellow–A	Black Medic–A
Bellflower, Creeping–P	Blue Field Madder–A

[304]

Bromegrass–P
Buttercup, Creeping–P
Buttercup, Tallfield–P
Carpetweed–A
Carrot, Wild–B
Chickweed, Common–A
Chickweed, Meadow–P
Chcikweed, Mouse-ear–P
Chicory–P
Cinquefoil–P
Cleavers–A
Clover, Bur–A
Clover, Little Hop–A
Clover, White–P
Crabgrass–A
Cranesbill, Wild–P
Dallisgrass–P
Dandelion–P
Dock, Curly–P
Egyptiangrass-A
English Daisy–P
Fescue, Tall–P
Filaree–A, B
Fleabane–A
Foxtail, Yellow–A
Garlic or Onion–P
Goosegrass–A
Gosmore–P
Ground Ivy–P
Hawkweeds–P
Heal-all–P
Henbit–A
Knawel–A
Knotweed–A
Kochia or Summer Cypress–A
Mallow, Roundleaf–A
Moneywort–P
Mullein–B

Nimblewill–P
Nutgrass–P
Nusedge, Yellow–P
Oatgrass, Wild–A
Orchardgrass-P
Oxalis–P
Ox-eye Daisy–P
Paintbrush, Yellow–P
Paspalum–P
Pennywort–P
Peppergrass–A, B
Pigweed–A
Plaintains, Broad-leaved–P
Plaintains, Buckhorn–P
Poison Ivy–P
Puncturevine–A
Purslane–A
Quackgrass–P
Rush, Bog–P
Rush, Path–P
Sandbur–A
Sedges–P
Shepherds Purse–A
Sorrel, Red–P
Sorrel, Sheep–P
Sorrel, Wood–A
Speargrass–A
Speedwell–A
Spurge, Spotted–A
Squirrel-tail-grass–B, P
Thistle–B, P
Thyme, Creeping–P
Vervain–A
Violets–P
Waterleaf–A
Witchgrass–P
Yarrow–P

A – Annual
B – Biennial
P – Perennial

[305]

Organic Ways To Control Weeds

Before you stoop to the temptation of using poisonous chemicals, sprays or powder mixtures to control weeds, give some thought to the many non-toxic controls. We don't mean to imply that it isn't easier to dump some combination of weed killer-fertilizer into a spreader and cover your lawn with it. Thousands of homeowners throughout the country are forsaking their spray bottles and poisonous mixtures in favor of a safer, albeit more involved, methods of weed eradication. They've come to value the children and pets in their neighborhood and realize that when they broadcast poisons throughout the soil they're unleashing a potential killer that doesn't discriminate between weeds and wee ones, between crabgrass and children. And that's just an obvious basis for thinking twice about commercial pesticides. For a more extended discussion, see the section on the avoidance of chemicals on the home lawn.

NON-TOXIC WAYS TO CONTROL WEEDS

1. *The Soil as a Weed Fighter.* Declining soil fertility is a prime cause of weed growth. Fertile soil, especially soil well conditioned with organic matter, is not naturally conducive to weed growth. Many types of weeds appear to thrive only on soil that is low in some minerals and has an excess of others. As many farmers have learned, declining

[306]

fertility lets such weeds as broomsedge and tickle-grass invade fields and pastures. Building up a soil organically, therefore, is one of the best ways to lick the weed problem.

Also, it is a fact that a soil rich in organic matter is more easily worked, and cultivation and tillage can be timed most advantageously. Such soil is in good shape after a rain and can be worked without causing clods to form. Spring tillage on a good organic soil can prepare a fine seedbed.

Young grass plants in organic soil grow rapidly; their root systems tend to crowd out those of weeds, and their rapid vegetative growth often makes thick shade that helps suppress weeds. Too, weed seeds lose their viability sooner in a bacteria-rich soil than in one poor in bacterial life. With organics, ordinary management operations will usually go a long way toward controlling weeds.

2. Prevent seed production in nearby fields. Weed seeds don't originate only from seed you sow. Weeds can be borne by wind, water, or even carried on clothing of people walking from nearby weed infested areas. If you have a nearby lot or field in which the weeds have run rampant, chances are good that you'll never obtain acceptable weed control in your own lawn. But you can get a head start if you have the weeds on that lot mowed at least twice a year to prevent them from maturing seed. If you live out of town you may want to fence in such an area and turn loose some sheep. They're one of the most effective weed fighters known.

[307]

3. Hand pulling. Maybe it's a bit more work, but it's one of the most effective weed preventives known. Hand pulling can be an end to many an annual, biennial or perennial weed. In fact, it's a good idea to know before hand into which of those categories your weeds can be classified, for it will make your weed stalking chores a bit easier. Reason? Most annual and biennial weeds occurring in small patches can be yanked as soon as they are large enough and yet before they have begun to produce seed. Even if you pull out the tops of the weeds without getting the roots, you've done enough. The piece of the root remaining in the soil will not sprout again. But that's not true with perennials. Often their roots get new shoots and so for complete eradication you may have to pull one weed several times or be certain that you get the entire root structure. It's best to pull such weeds when the soil is damp so that they can be removed easily. Don't neglect this chore, as weeds can rob your lawn of light, water and mineral nutrients.

Undercut and cut around small patches of undesirable grass with a sharp spade. Lift the undesirable patch and use it as a pattern to cut a replacement piece the same thickness from an inconspicuous place elsewhere in the lawn. Make certain the replacement sod is firmed into place and well watered until it becomes established.

4. Mowing. Mowing lawns is an effective method of keeping weeds in check because it allows the grass to crowd out the weeds and keep them in check. Best mowing height is usually from two to three inches. Although a lower mowing clearance will cut back the weeds decisively, it will also hamper the grass from growing. However, if you have an area of a lawn that is almost entirely weeds, you might want to take advantage of the physical makeup of some perennial weeds. Normally they store a reserve food supply in their underground parts. When the plants begin to blossom, their reserve food supply has been nearly exhausted and new seeds have not yet been produced, that's the time to lower your mower and cut back the weeds to severely weaken them.

In most lawns, however, a higher mowing technique is indicated. Mowing at a height of 2½ to 3 inches shades the soil and protects the bluegrass roots from damaging effects of summer heat. High mowing of common Kentucky bluegrass is an excellent deterrent to the germination and growth of many annual weed species. Some of the newer lawn grasses perform best when mowed two inches or less. Remember that the mowing technique you use on your lawn is one of the most critical maintenance procedures you can practice. Don't use the low mowing technique on sections of grass you wish to preserve. And don't be misled by thinking that if you cut your grass tall that you will have to mow it more often. Regardless of the mowing height, the general rule of thumb you should follow is to cut it frequently enough so that you do not have to remove more than one-third of

[309]

the green leaf area of the plant at each mowing. If you follow this rule, you should mow the low-cut turf more often.

Now we cannot promise you that your turf will look greener and more attractive at the taller height, because this is not always the case. But you can rest assured that your grass will be much healthier, will survive summer heat and drought much better, will resist disease attacks better and will have much fewer weeds in it.

Down at the University of Maryland, scientists compared two plots of ground—one cut at 2½ inches and the other cut at 1 ½ inches.

Weed counts made when the turf was one year old showed that there were only 0.4 weeds per 100 square feet at the 2½ inch mowing height compared to 15.3 weeds for the same area at the 1½ inch height.

Weeds counts made when the turf was two years old revealed the following:

	Weeds per 100 sq. ft.		
Mowing Height	Crabgrass	Broad-leaved Weeds	Total
2½ inches	1.7	6.0	7.7
1½ inches	21.0	32.3	53.3

Now really, how can you afford to mow your turf at the low mowing height? This difference in weeds reflects the weakness of the turf at the low mowing height. The weakness was caused by disease attacks, poor root systems, and overall poor quality turf which allowed the weeds to invade.

5. *Burning.* Often noxious weeds which have

[310]

begun to mature can be burned on the spot. Several small portable weed burners are available for keeping paths, driveways, ditch banks, fence rows, and similar places free from weeds. The burners are effective and easily lit for killing weeds while they're still small. Most operate on several pints of kerosene to scorch the tops of the weeds. Unfortunately, burning does not kill the underground parts and perennial weeds may return. The one plus for flamed-type weed killers is that it's inexpensive (most models sell for under $30), clean and easy. However, use care that the flame is not directly applied to the lawn, for it will also suffer.

6. *Fertilize Organically.* Feeding programs that furnish lawn grasses with necessary organic plant food elements throughout the growing season tend to discourage weeds through competition furnished by more vigorous bluegrass. Fertilize cool season grasses in the fall and spring and as needed during the summer months.

Withhold spring fertilization of warm season zoysia, buffalo, and Bermuda until May 1; stop fertilizing them about August 31.

7. *Use clean seeds.* Most grass seed that you buy at a store contains a certain percentage of weed seed. A reason for that is simple. It's extremely difficult, almost impossible to eliminate all weed seeds from commercial seed mixtures. But there is something that you can do about the seeds you buy. Be aware that grass seed contains one or

[311]

more kinds of noxious weed seed and check the label to determine the per cent of weed seed. Most often cheap seed is the most expensive you can buy because it is high in noxious weeds. Cultivated sod, inspected and treated to reduce weeds, is becoming more plentiful.

Weed Controls Unlimited

Choking weeds that stop up agricultural waterways throughout central Florida are facing a new foe. Instead of toxic weedicides, quarter-inch-long flea beetles of the genus *Agasicles* have been released in canal areas to help control the stubborn alligatorweed. Under investigation by U. S. Army engineers and the USDA for several years, this biological control has been reported exceptionally successful—so much so in tests to date that demand for the imported flea beetles is much greater than the present supply. Aim of the beetle release, point out aquatic plant experts, is not elimination of existing plants, but rather keeping them in check so they won't multiply and further choke waterways in 6 southern states. Five years' experimentation by USDA entomologists showed the flea beetle thrives on alligatorweed only—and does not eat any farm plants or ornamentals.

Weed-eating insects and selective plant diseases are both under close investigation as methods to control weeds—and cut use of herbicide chemicals. USDA scientists have promising "finds" in several weed-diet bugs. Tiny Altica beetles, European natives, are attacking widespread Canada thistle in California, Idaho, Montana and Washington where they've been released. Cinnabar moths and ragwort seed flies have been set loose in Oregon and California to fight tansy ragwort, or stinking willie, a toxic weed. Another western weed, puncturevine, may be destroyed by two weevils that attack stems and seeds of the spiny-fruited plant. Alligatorweed, which clogs southeastern waterways, is yielding to a flea beetle introduced by Florida researchers. Meanwhile, a search for plant diseases that could control native U. S. weeds will be conducted in Italy and South Africa by scientists from Stanford Research Institute under USDA grant. The 2½-year project hopes to find bacteria, viruses and fungi that attack specific weeds that are agriculturally important in the U. S.

Meet Some Troublesome Lawn Weeds

BARNYARDGRASS

A coarse warm season annual grass with a flattened stem especially near the base. Lower portion of the plant tends to be reddish-purple. The seed head branches into 6 or 8 short segments.

CHICKWEED, COMMON

A hardy annual or winter annual with a delicate appearance found in green form most of the year. The small opposite leaves are oval-shaped and

[313]

smooth. Stems are weak and tend to vine. The small star-like flowers are white. Common chickweed is most often found in the shade of trees and shrubs and especially on the north side of buildings. *Mouse-ear chickweed* is a perennial with creeping stems. The leaves, 2-3 times longer than wide, are clammy and fuzzy. Flowers are white; root system is shallow.

CRABGRASS

Crabgrass is one of the most common warm season annual grassy weeds. The stems grow mostly prostrate, branch freely and send down roots where each joint comes into contact with the soil or moist grass. Seed head is divided into several fingerlike segments. Two principal species are (1) large crabgrass sometimes known as hairy crabgrass and (2) smooth crabgrass. Smooth crabgrass tends to be smaller and oftentimes has reddish color on the stems.

Other common names: watergrass.

DANDELION

Cool season perennial common throughout the midwest. Bloom from March to late November. At least two species are common to our lawns.

DOCK

Dock seldom reaches maturity when growing in lawns. The plant forms a large rosette. Curly dock

[314]

is most common. The leaves have crinkled edges. They are often tinted with red or purple color. Pale dock, also known as tall dock, has leaves which tend to be more flat and broad. Both species have flowering stalks that may reach a height of two or three feet.

FIELD BINDWEED

A cool season perennial common throughout most of the United States. It is one of the more difficult weeds to eliminate. The leaf tips and basal lobes are rounded but vary considerably in shape and size. The flowers vary from white to light pink and are about the size of a nickel. The plant readily vines over shrubs and other ornamentals. It spreads by both seed and underground roots.

Other common names: Creeping Charlie; creeping Jenny; wild morning glory.

FOXTAIL

Foxtails are warm season annuals that grow in association with crabgrass. Yellow foxtail has flattened stems that are often reddish colored on the lower portion. The stems of green foxtail is four times as large as green foxtail.

GOOSEGRASS

A warm season annual most often found growing where bluegrass stands are thin. The stems tend to be flattened and near the base are whitish in color. Flower heads are thicker and more robust than on common crabgrass. The extensive fibrous root system makes pulling difficult.

Other common names: Silver crabgrass and yardgrass.

GROUND IVY

A cool season perennial originally introduced as a ground cover. Now a weed in many lawns. Thrives in shade, but will also grow in the sun. Ground ivy produces an abundance of lavender to blue funnel-form flowers in early spring. The square stems may root at each joint where they touch the ground.

MOSS

A low form of plant life consisting of many genera and species. Moss prefers an environment that is cool and moist. It is most often found in shaded areas such as the north side of buildings.

PLANTAIN

Most cool season perennials that form rosettes with prominently veined leaves. The leaves and stems of blackseed (Rugel's) and broad-leaf plantain resemble the miniature foliage and stalks of rhubarb. The leaves are oval shaped and 2 to 3 inches across. Stems are reddish or purple. The rat-tail like seed heads are several inches long.

Buckhorn plantain has leaves about 1″ across. Prominent veins are present. The seed head is one to two inches long and about ⅓″ across.

PROSTRATE KNOTWEED

An annual that thrives from early spring to late fall. Germination often takes place in late March and early April. Grows flat from a long white taproot. Individual plants may have a spread of 2 feet or more. Stems wiry, very leafy; at each joint there is a thin papery sheath. Leaves often have a bluish cast. Seeds are three-cornered, light-brown early and shiny black at maturity.

PROSTRATE PIGWEED

A warm season prostrate annual that grows from a pink taproot. The leaves are very shiny. Stems smooth, light-green to reddish-green may spread 1½ to 2 feet. Seeds are lens shaped, small, and shiny black.

PURSLANE

A warm season annual. Leaves and stems fleshy or succulent, reddish in color. Grows prostrate. Root system tends to be fibrous; stems root wherever they touch the ground, particularly if the

[317]

main root has been destroyed. Flowers small, yellow. Seeds very small, black.

Other common names: Pursley.

QUACKGRASS

A cool season perennial wheatgrass that spreads extensively by underground stems or roots. Leaf blades are twice the width of bluegrass and tend to be more harsh. One of the most distinguishing characteristics is a ring of root hairs every ¾ to 1 inch along the long white underground stems. The lower sheath of the stem is hairy.

Other common names: Couchgrass.

RED SORREL

A low growing, cool season perennial that reproduces by creeping roots and seeds. Leaves are spear shaped and tend to resemble field bindweed. The lacy flowering stalks bloom in May and have a definite reddish color. The seed is small, three-sided and reddish-brown. Remains green from very early March to early winter.

Other common names: Sheep sorrel.

TALL FESCUE

A very coarse cool season perennial bunch grass. Leaf veins are strongly fibrous; when mowed, fibers show on the cut edge especially if mowers are not well sharpened. Mature leaf blades may be one-half inch wide, ribbed above and shiny smooth below. The lower portions of the stems are reddish to purple, particularly in the spring and fall.

VIOLETS

Cool season perennials that are among the first plants to bloom in the spring. Prefer at least partial shade. Flower color varies from very light blue to deep purple. Occasionally become troublesome in lawns.

WHITE CLOVER

A cool season perennial legume that spreads by underground and aboveground stems. May or may not be objectionable in lawns, depending on individual preference. Flowers white, sometimes with a tinge of pink. Seeds will live for 20 or more years in the soil.

CHAPTER XVII

Some Notorious Grassy-Weeds

The Worst Weed of All

CRABGRASS is the worst weed enemy of lawns. It creeps over the surface in such a way that it is untouched by the lawn mower, and because it is an annual, it will reseed itself year after year. Seeds germinate in June and early August.

This unwelcome pest can mar an otherwise perfect lawn by its broad, pale green leaves, which give a very patchy, unhappy appearance to the surface of the grass. When cold weather comes, the creeping stems of crabgrass change to a bronzy, red color, which becomes more intense as the cold increases. The first touch of frost kills the crabgrass leaving unsightly brown patches behind which are open to the inroads of weeds.

When you are dealing with crabgrass you are dealing with a crafty enemy which is going to take every unfair advantage of you it can. So to lick it you've got to do some brain work and advance planning.

The real secret of crabgrass control is contained in this simple formula: *Crabgrass and good lawn grasses thrive on a different set of growing conditions. You can encourage the weed or discourage it by altering its environment.*

Here is what *good* lawn grasses need to grow:

1. A fertile topsoil, preferably no less than 6 inches deep and rich in humus.

2. Cutting at a reasonable height. Perennial ryegrass, one of the most common good grasses, grows 6 feet high in its normal habitat. When it is kept trimmed to an inch or an inch and a half it is going to find the going difficult. So during the hot summer months, when weeds take hold, it helps to trim your grass as high as 3 or 4 inches.

3. An occasional drenching watering.

Crabgrass has a slightly different set of likes:

1. It doesn't grow as strongly on good soil as do good lawn grasses. It cannot stand the competition of ryegrass and bluegrass when those plants have a good soil to back them up.

2. Crabgrass likes to grow low to the ground, so it is not stunted by low mowing. Quite the contrary, low mowing gives it the room it needs to spread out and grow strongly.

[321]

HOW TO FIGHT CRABGRASS

Even though crabgrass is now strongly entrenched in your lawn, you can start right away on a program which will show concrete results this fall.

The program is simple. Just work to make your lawn a better place for the good lawn grasses to grow. Forget for the time being that you are fighting crabgrass, and instead concentrate on helping the grasses you want to grow.

Here is the plan we use on the Organic Experimental Farm. We call it "The Organic Cure for Crabgrass."

1. First, if you have a lawn sweeper, use it after several midsummer mowings to pick up crabgrass seeds that will sprout next year. Put the clippings in your compost heap.

2. Aerate your soil as much as possible, using either a hand aerator or an aerating attachment for your tiller or garden tractor. Don't be afraid to really shake up your soil, because air and moisture are needed below the surface to give encouragement to good grass roots.

3. Spread on your soil liberal amounts of phosphate rock, potash rock and lime, if needed. For an average soil, apply these amounts:

Phosphate and potash rock—10 pounds per 100 square feet.

Lime—5 to 10 pounds per 100 square feet, depending on soil pH. (Larger amount for acid soils,

[322]

less for those nearer neutral pH.) If soil is alkaline, do not apply lime.

Bone meal is also an excellent mineral supplement for lawn soils. Apply in the same proportions as the ground rock fertilizers.

These natural mineral fertilizers will make sure that the good grass you want to grow has ample mineral food.

4. Now comes the most important step—the creation of a good soil structure. It is hard to get across how much can be accomplished in producing a good lawn by improving soil tilth and structure. And the only practical way to do this is to pack plenty of compost, humus, leaf mold, peat or other organic material into your lawn soil.

You should not be concerned about nutrients in the materials you use, because in promoting good growth of grass, nutrient value is secondary to tilth. You have to be a little cautious about spreading sawdust or chopped straw on your lawn (they are low in nitrogen content), but small amounts of those things can be spread without harm.

Of course, it would be better to treat your lawn soil with soil conditioning organic materials before the grass is planted, for that way you could work it in to some depth. But we are talking about *curing* a weed problem on an already established lawn. It is completely possible to improve structure by maintaining a continuous program of spreading organic materials *on top* of your lawn.

Obviously, you don't want to smother the grass,

[323]

so you will have to spread your "structure builders" in installments. That will give the grass a chance to grow a little between spreadings. Basically, what you are doing is *mulching* your lawn, but you still want to encourage the grass to grow through the mulch. Peat moss is one of the best materials for this type of work. Even though a bale costs about five dollars, it goes a long way because of the tremendous ability of peat moss to hold moisture and fluff up the soil. Compost is excellent, but it should be ground or shredded before application.

Other organic fertilizing materials that will go a long way in boosting lawn growth include dried blood, cottonseed meal and soybean meal. These three are especially rich in growth-promoting nitrogen, and should be applied as liberally as needed and if available.

After you have made several of these surface applications of tilth-building organics, you will begin to notice that your lawn has the springy feel you've noticed on the finest park lawns. And the good grasses will be growing with renewed vigor. The soft layer of humus will hold water too, so you won't have to water so often.

PLANTING TIME IMPORTANT

Because crabgrass stops growing in autumn, that's a good reason to start your bluegrass lawn then. One of the best reasons for starting bluegrass lawns in autumn is that crabgrass and other weeds will not be serious pests then. The grass gets a good start, and should be way out ahead of crabgrass by next spring, given a little help from organic fertilizers. Crabgrass won't sprout until spring weather is quite warm, by which time a blue-grass-fescue lawn can be so tight that crabgrass stands little change. Crabgrass won't sprout in the shade of a thick turf.

Inadequate fertilization also tends to weaken the grass, with a resultant reduction in density and subsequent crabgrass invasion. Complete soil testing is the key to proper fertilization. Try to keep the soil pH above 6.5.

Improper watering also contributes to crabgrass invasion. Frequent light watering encourages shallow rooting and promotes weak turf which is susceptible to insect and disease attacks as well as damage from traffic. In addition, watering in this manner encourages the germination and development of crabgrass at the expense of the turf-grasses. The practice of watering deeply (five to eight inches) only when turfgrasses show signs of wilting is a practical approach to a sound watering program.

GROUND COVER STOPS CRABGRASS

There's another promising new way to whip crabgrass — smother it with *Euonymus fortunei Longwood*. This ground cover, from the slopes of

Mt. Tsubuka in Japan, grows so dense that crabgrass seeds can't get enough light to germinate. Able to survive temperatures down to 25 degrees below zero and as high as 105 degrees F., the weed-choking plant can be grown in just about any part of the country, though in extremely high heat there is some sunscald. Low-growing, with small dark-green leaves, it has been found especially suitable in the shade, in partially-shaded areas, or for covering low masonry walls. USDA plant explorers discovered the crabgrass-fighter, now being distributed to experiment stations, arboretums, and nurserymen.

And here is a good method for elimination of crabgrass, sent in by a reader: "On Long Island I had a lawn that was nothing but solid crabgrass when I took over the place, and within 3 years I had entirely done away with weeds without either reseeding or using chemicals. I applied cottonseed meal very heavily just as soon as the frost was out of the ground in the spring, and the natural grass got such a good start that with the aid of clippings, which I always left on, I soon had the crabgrass choked out."

Quackgrass

Like many other weeds, quackgrass has a "Jekyll-and-Hyde" personality. In certain situations, it can be extremely useful. It binds loose soil on banks and steep, sandy slopes very efficiently, preventing erosion and adding organic matter. Also, it will provide good forage where better grasses will not thrive, in some areas of the West.

However, quackgrass in general is a most troublesome pest. Gardeners and especially farmers in the north central states have good reason to hate it. Although it prefers acid, moist soil, it will do well under all sorts of conditions, and it increases by both seeds and rhizomes (underground stems).

Quackgrass grows 18 to 30 inches tall and produces great quantities of seed on straw-colored spikes above the hairy leaves. These seeds can retain their ability to germinate for 4 years or longer. They are difficult to separate from the seeds of many of our common grasses.

The rhizomes, often several feet long, spread laterally in the upper 3 to 6 inches of soil. New plants can be produced at each node (joint), so that the weed quickly honeycombs the soil with a dense, extremely tough sod.

Seeds or pieces of rhizome may be introduced into new areas in topsoil brought in to make new lawns, in manure, mud on the wheels of implements and on shoes or the feet of animals, and in hay or other forage.

CONTROL MEASURES

Constantly removing new top growth will reduce the food reserves in the rhizomes, thus weakening them. So hoe or cultivate weekly during the

[327]

growing season. Always use a sharp hoe or a culti-vator with a sharp blade—tined tools will not com-pletely sever the top growth from the underground parts.

Spading late in the fall will kill many of the rhizomes by exposing them to drying and freezing. (Sometimes in extreme cases, the rhizomes can be raked up and hauled away, but this means a loss of considerable valuable organic matter.) Thereafter, pull stray shoots by hand to prevent re-infestation.

A mulch of plastic, boards or similar materials is also effective. Even better is a deep mulch of organic materials, which, at the same time it is smothering the quackgrass, will add organic matter and have other beneficial effects. A mulch should give a complete kill if left on the ground for one season.

In making a new lawn, heavy mulching or tilling is necessary for a season to eliminate serious infesta-tions. If you choose the tillage method, use a tined cultivator that will lift the rhizomes to the surface and expose them to drying.

Always build up the soil for a new lawn organi-cally, so that the grass will quickly make a tight sod that will crowd out the weed. Keep the lawn wa-tered well to prevent its being weakened by drought, and clip it weekly to a height of one and one-half inches to maintain good vigor.

Sometimes ryegrass, included in lawn seed mix-tures to provide quick cover, is mistaken for quackgrass. However, you can recognize ryegrass

[328]

by its fibrous roots instead of rhizomes, and smooth leaves rather than hairy.

Tall Fescue

A coarse and vigorous grass that is objectionable in fine-leaved turf because of the clumpy type of growth caused by scattered plants of this species. Tall fescue is sometimes included in lawn seed mixtures under either the name Kentucky 31 fescue or Alta fescue. It is frequently present in a very small amount as an unintentional mixture which is very noticeable in the lawn because of its distinct type of growth.

Tall fescue is a clumpy, dark-green, coarse-leaved, fast-growing perennial. It is most obvious in early spring and late fall. Also, under drought conditions it remains greener than bluegrass. It usually starts from some seed included in a mixture (more often sold in cheap, economy brands). Individual plants that survive become obvious as clumps after 2 to 3 years.

To identify, check base of clumps for large, reddish-brown stems. The new leaves are rolled in bud; the old leaves are coarse; and each leaf surface looks like miniature corrugated roofing. It tries to seed in early summer and sometimes in fall by sending up hard-to-mow branched seedheads. Some people may think it is crabgrass, but crabgrass starts from seed each spring and is killed by frost.

[329]

IT'S NOT ALL BAD!

Because of its drought tolerance, rapid and all-season and perennial character, tall fescue is widely used for pasture, erosion control, sod waterways, and pond embankments. In turf it is often used in athletic fields, parking lots, rough roadsides or other large areas where high mowing is done by rotary mowers.

In about 1953 the price of tall fescue dropped; thus, it was added to many turf mixtures. Since 1960 it is being used only in the cheap, or rough seed mixtures. Even in these, bluegrass should always be included so it can fill in around the fescue clumps. Where wanted, two selections of tall fescue, Alta and Kentucky 31, are available. General seeding recommendations as pound per acre are:

	Tall Fescue	Bluegrass
Airports and roadsides	60-80	10-20
Heavy wear and athletic fields	90-200	10-30

Wherever used, tall fescue should be more than 50% of seed mix; otherwise, avoid small percentage and even a few seeds, as other crop, in seed mixtures.

DIG OR IGNORE?

You decide — look over these choices and choose your preference.

A. Just tolerate or ENJOY it

If the clumps are numerous and funds are limited—maybe it's a back lawn—maybe it's not all bad—it's green! Consider overseeding thin or worn areas again with tall fescue.

B. Remove it

1. If just a few clumps—maybe in front lawn, or near the picture window—rake or comb each clump towards its center to determine size and reduce digging. Then, use a shovel, sod cutter, etc., to undercut clump. Go 1 to 2 inches deep to get below the crown where thick stems start.

a. Shake soil off the loosened clumps when it is partially dry to save soil, reseed and smooth area. Keep moist.

b. A preferred way is to fill the holes with small pieces of sod; then firm each into place and water. This is best done in early spring, or mid-fall.

2. Consider *removing* all the infested turf, undercut 1 inch deep, discard and resod area with purchased sod. It may cost less than you think. Check with landscape and sod services.

C. Weaken it

To just reduce the problem, try vertical thinning, or cutting close, plus heavy fertilization. Also, let competition weaken the tall fescue clumps.

1. By hand—by simply chopping into each clump the long leaves, seedheads and old stems may be greatly reduced. Use a knife, a shovel, anyway to get criss-cross slicing. Repeat monthly for one—two years—a manicure!

[331]

2. By machine—Ask at landscape, rental or major equipment supply sources for motorized vertical mowers. At least a dozen brands are available somewhere in the U.S. The vertical blades or tines on these either cut, pull, or comb out old thatch, long leaves and creeping grasses. Best time of use is mid-fall, but repeated monthly use on tall fescue clumps will reduce vigor and weaken clumps.

Clumps of bromegrass, timothy, orchardgrass—any bunchgrass—would offer similar control problems.

Johnsongrass

For the home gardener, an infestation of Johnsongrass has always been bad news because of the difficulty in controlling and eliminating it. In rich organic soil, the roots may be half an inch thick, tuberous, and several feet long. They are brittle and segmented like a tapeworm into sections of half an inch or less. Try to dig them out and they break into many pieces, and each smallest segment will quickly produce a new plant. Let the plant ripen, and each stalk will develop a large loose head of seed, something like sorghum, to be scattered by wind and birds. Individual seed may lie dormant for several years until growing conditions cause it to spring into life.

Penning geese in sugar cane and cotton fields has been much used in the war against Johnsongrass. The geese prefer the tender young shoots of Johnsongrass to the less palatable cotton and coarser sugar cane, and make cheap substitutes for hoe hands. Using geese for weeding has proved successful, although they do require supervision and attention, and must be confined or shifted about in rather small areas to be effective.

Fortunately, Johnsongrass will not stand freezing, and late fall or winter plowing which turns up the roots and exposes them to freezing temperatures helps to keep the grass in check. Not all the roots will be uncovered and killed, of course, but persistent digging, especially where efforts are made to trace out all the roots and sift the soil to gather all the shattered fragments, seems to be the most practical and effective control.

Where freezing is not possible, as in perennial crops, mulching will also do the job. Not mulching as Ruth Stout practices it, though, with 6 to 8 inches of hay. Johnsongrass grows right through and thrives on this kind of mulch. The mulch to use is strips and squares cut from heavy corrugated paper boxes and cartons and laid between the rows in a solid floor, as tight and impervious as linoleum. Such a mulch, made of wood fiber and sizing and often given a light waterproofing, will last through a full growing season before breaking down. And that seems to be what it takes to gain an upper hand over Johnsongrass.

CHAPTER XVIII

Other Lawn Frustrations

LAWN BROWNING

ONE COMMON CAUSE of a browning lawn is cutting too much grass at a single mowing. This is not unusual during vacation season. You go away for several weeks and come back to find grass quite tall. You mow and soon after the lawn turns brown.

Some of the grass will come back if given plenty of water for a period of several weeks. It would be a good idea, too, to refrain from applying any chemicals, as this may cause permanent damage to the already weakened plants making up the lawn.

Insect damage, naturally, will cause browning of the lawn. That may be more obvious after an application of weed or crabgrass killers. The brown-

[334]

ing is due to damage to the roots of the grass plants. The obvious answer is to get rid of the insects.

If the browning is found in scattered patches that seem to gradually get larger, the cause is most likely a fungus disease. The number of these diseases that can attack a lawn are quite numerous. Part of the answer is a well-kept lawn — healthy grass can fight off trouble of this sort.

If you are in the habit of leaving clippings on the lawn after mowing, it would be advisable to remove them until the problem is over. A grass catcher on the mower is one way; you can also use a lawn sweeper or a rake. The reason for this precaution is that certain disease organisms live on dead and decaying portions of the plant. If those are removed, the disease fungus cannot live.

Kindness can also cause browning of the lawn — kindness in the sense that you think you're helping your lawn by applying commercial fertilizer. The result is often brown foliage. That often happens by accident if you neglect to shut off the spreader when turning a corner. If this is the case, apply plenty of water to wash the fertilizer out of the soil and be patient.

The advent of the power mower also gave rise to another reason for brown lawns. If gasoline is spilled on the lawn, it will kill it off in the immediate area. The answer is to never fill the tank when the mower is on the lawn. Take it to the driveway or walk.

[335]

Mother nature is the cause of a great deal of browning. During a drought season when temperatures are high and winds strong, the moisture will be pulled out of the grass plants. Consequently, they turn brown. Water is the answer. If the drought is not too extended, the grass will come back naturally during the cooler weather and gentle rains of the fall. Remember when watering during a drought to thoroughly soak the soil to a depth of several inches. A mere sprinkling on the surface will sometimes drive the roots to the surface and they, in turn, will be killed by the drought.

Some lawns may be damaged to an extent that a complete repairing job will be necessary. To determine if the lawn should be repaired or completely rebuilt, check to see what percentage of perennial grass remains. If there is 50 per cent or more perennial grass coverage, you can repair. If there is less than half perennial grass, dig up completely and put in a new lawn.

POA ANNUA

Poa annua or annual bluegrass is normally considered to be an annual grass although there is evidence that some plants may survive longer. Annual bluegrass has a light, yellow-green color and is characterized by prolific seed production in the spring. Regardless of height of cut, this plant will develop seed heads. Lawns heavily infested with annual bluegrass take on a gray-white cast in the spring due to the great number of seedheads. Annual bluegrass is shallow rooted and cannot withstand high temperatures and severe drought conditions. Loss of annual bluegrass under these conditions may occur in a few hours. Unfortunately, seed produced in the spring has been deposited in the soil and a new crop will germinate in the fall or late winter. Thus, an annual-bluegrass-infested lawn may appear beautiful in the spring and the late fall but be very unsightly in the summer.

GROWING GRASS IN SHADE

The establishment and maintenance of good-quality turfgrasses under shaded conditions often is possible if the basic requirements are known and understood. Trees have extensive root systems (often quite shallow) which enable them to take up huge amounts of water and nutrients, and also dense leaves which decrease the light intensity under the trees. These three factors—competition for water, nutrients, and light—are the basic causes of turfgrass failure under shaded conditions.

In setting up a turfgrass management program, it seems logical that every effort should be made to alleviate or eliminate this competition for water, nutrients, and light.

There are a number of maintenance and es-

[337]

tablishment practices which may improve turfgrass under trees.

1. Use shade-tolerant grasses such as Pennlawn creeping red fescue, Chewing's fescue, Alta or Kentucky 31 tall fescue, and *Poa trivialis* (rough bluegrass).

2. Fertilize the grass frequently at approximately two times the normal rate.

3. Fertilize the trees by drilling or punching holes in the soil at 2 foot intervals in concentric circles extending from the trunk outward to an area equal to the branch spread of the tree.

4. Water deeply and infrequently. Deep watering is essential to prevent movement of tree roots towards the surface.

5. Maintain a soil reaction favorable to the grass. Apply ground agricultural limestone according to a lime requirement test.

6. Remove those trees which are not basic and do not add beauty to the landscape plan.

7. Prune tree branches as much as possible without destroying the function and the beauty of the tree.

8. Prune shallow tree roots as much as possible.

9. Plant new trees wisely, taking into consideration the number and density of the trees. Shade trees should be planted a minimum of 40 feet apart.

10. Plant tree species which present a minimum amount of competition to the grass.

[338]

11. Provide good drainage and aeration to allow proper penetration of nutrients, water, and air.

12. Fall seedings are recommended over spring seedings because of less competition from the trees in the fall.

13. Adjust mowing practices to suit the given grass species. In most instances the clipping height should be considerably higher than it would be for that particular grass in the open sun.

14. Control weeds to improve the appearance of the turf and reduce the competition for light, water, and nutrients.

15. Remove leaves and other debris promptly by raking, sweeping, or mechanically grinding. Leaves allowed to accumulate may smother the grass or provide favorable conditions for disease infestation.

16. Use other types of ground cover where modifications are difficult or the cost is prohibitive. Plants, such as periwinkle, pachysandra, and Baltic ivy are suitable.

BENTGRASS

Bentgrass, often found in commercial seed mixtures, is not compatible with bluegrass and fescue as far as management is concerned. It requires close, frequent mowing, frequent fertilization and irrigation, periodic top-dressing, vertical mowing. Fluffiness of the turf is usually associated with a

[339]

high bentgrass population. Unless bentgrass is subjected to intensive management, it will develop a thatch layer quite rapidly. Once a lawn has become infested with bentgrass, the only solution is to kill out all vegetation and re-establish the lawn to desirable grasses.

SOIL COMPACTION

Soils of poor physical condition or those subjected to play or other compactive forces, especially when wet, form an impervious layer at the surface which prevents water infiltration, nutrient penetration and gaseous exchange between the soil and the atmosphere. Under those conditions turfgrasses tend to thin out and often are replaced by weeds such as knotweed, which flourish on compacted soils. Aerating machines which remove soil plugs or cores, thereby creating an artificial system of large pores, permit moisture, nutrients and air to enter the soil and alleviate the compacted condition.

LOCALIZED DRY SPOTS

Dead or injured spots often develop in turf areas due to insufficient moisture, even though surrounding turf shows no drought injury. Damage from localized dry spots may be due to buried debris such as stumps, stones, bricks, gravel, etc., with the resultant thin layer of soil overlaying

[340]

the area. That thin layer has a low water holding capacity and dries out very quickly. In other cases the presence of a large amount of thatch acts in the same manner as a thatched grass roof and prevents entrance of water into the soil.

SEED MIXTURES

Many lawn problems can be traced back, directly or indirectly, to the original seed mixture. Grasses such as ryegrass, timothy and redtop normally will not persist under lawn management. Bluegrasses are unsatisfactory for use in shaded areas but are excellent in open sun. Fine fescues are well adapted to shade conditions. Tall fescue is an excellent play field grass but is too coarse for lawn use. Bentgrass requires intensive management and is not compatible with bluegrass and fescue in this respect. The selection of a grass seed mixture should be based on the environmental conditions, the use of the area and the management program that will be followed.

DULL MOWERS

Lawns having a gray to brown overcast following mowing are quite common. In most cases that discoloration can be attributed to dull rotary mowers although the same type of damage may occur from dull reel type mowers. Basically, the discoloration is due to the tearing, splitting or shredding

[341]

of the tips of the grass blades. Mowers, regardless of type, should be kept sharp and properly adjusted at all times.

What's Your Lawn Problem?

"What's my lawn problem? The grass doesn't grow!"

That's an answer you're likely to hear if you go around asking people what trouble they have with their lawn. But poor-growing grass is the result: the problem lies elsewhere.

To find out just where, we surveyed lawn specialists all over the country to learn the major problems facing homeowners in their area. More than half the experts listed "low fertility" as the chief troublemaker.

According to D. G. Sturkie, Auburn University agronomist, "the major problem is lack of fertility. The average homeowner applies very little fertilizer to his lawn." W. R. Thompson, Jr. of Mississippi State College's Turfgrass Research Department agrees that "more fertilizers should be used, and if lawns are better fertilized, the grass will be more vigorous and choke out weeds." From Vermont to California came equal stress from experts that lawn growers needed to improve their fertilization methods.

Improvement will best come about from use of slow-acting, organic fertilizers and soil conditioners.

The troublesome qualities of heavy clay, clay loam, silt loam and sandy soils can be largely corrected by application of compost, rotted manure or sawdust, peat, commercial humus, or sewage sludge. These materials actually increase the nutrient-holding capacity of soils as well as improve aeration and moisture retention.

John Harper II, Penn State agronomist, cautions to "always apply fertilizers when the grass leaves are completely dry and water thoroughly immediately after application." It's also good practice to brush grass with a broom or back of a rake after applying fertilizer. Never allow soil conditioners to cake on the soil surface, as this can foster lawn disease, or even smother the grass.

It's generally agreed that most of the fertilizer applied in spring should be spread in March and April, but Penn State's Harper advises "an additional application of organic nitrogen at 20 to 30 pounds per 1,000 square feet in late spring or early summer would be extremely beneficial."

While most lawn soils are benefited by lime, do not apply unless a soil test shows an acid soil. Use 20 pounds raw ground limestone per 1,000 square feet for each ton per acre of lime indicated by a test.

OTHER TROUBLE MAKERS

Following low fertility and poor soil on the experts' list of lawn problems came mowing too close, improper watering, seeding, and weed control.

MOWING IS MORE THAN CUTTING

One turf specialist points out that "mowing is not a simple operation to be regarded merely as a means of removing excess growth. It is a maintenance practice which has far-reaching effects on the appearance and longevity of any turfgrass area."

H. G. Jacobson of Connecticut's Agricultural Experiment Station advises mowing at a height of two to three inches often enough so that clippings can be left without smothering grass. This relatively high cutting is definitely beneficial for Kentucky bluegrass and fescue, because they cannot produce sufficient leaf mass at low heights to sustain growth. If ryegrass is cut too close, too much leaf surface is removed and the plant no longer can carry on enough photosynthetic activity.

Frequent mowing is also important, since infrequent clipping can remove too much leaf surface, will result in excessive browning of leaf tips. Never clip more than one-quarter to one-third of total leaf surface at a single mowing.

NO MIRACLES IN SEED

About the soundest statement on grass seed mixtures we've read in a long time comes from R.

R. Davis, agronomist at the Ohio Agricultural Experiment Station. He writes: "There are no 'miracle' grasses available, and they are not likely to become available in the near future. A good lawn will continue to result from selecting the best available grass or grasses to fit the need, and managing to suit the grass. . . . A new grass variety does not necessarily represent improvement." If you're in doubt about recommended grass mixtures for your area, check with your county agent.

One county agent in eastern Pennsylvania, Glenn Ellenberger, believes that millions of tons of lawn seed are wasted each year because it's merely scattered on top of established lawns that have received poor management. *The seed actually never gets a chance to grow.* It either acts as feed for the birds, lies atop a thatch of grass cuttings from the previous year or gets blown away. "Only in bare spots that have been properly prepared by roughing up the soil, working in a little fertilizer, and tamping in the seed, can you expect much success from a seeding on an old, established lawn," concludes Ellenberger.

WEEDS — SYMPTOMS NOT CAUSES

It may be partial consolation to homeowners who consider weeds as their number one lawn trouble to learn that they've been mistaken. Actually weeds are a *symptom,* not the problem itself. The fact that so many lawns have been built on poor sites that were inadequately (to say the least) prepared is a continuing difficulty . . . evident by a recurring crabgrass or other weed problem.

Most lawn specialists agree that chemicals are not the primary way to clear out weeds. In fact, the University of Illinois booklet on lawns states that *there are no chemicals that will kill or inhibit the germination of weed seeds without killing or severely injuring the grass.*

Good lawn management is the best method of weed control. Aside from that, you can minimize crabgrass spreading by controlling its seed production over several years. Mowing following raking to bring immature seedheads within reach of the mower will aid in checking reinfestation from seed. Use a grass catcher on your mower if seedheads have already matured. Crabgrass does not grow well under shaded conditions; that's why a thick turf, cut no lower than 1½ inches, will check crabgrass growth. Also avoid shallow watering.

MISCELLANEOUS OBSERVATIONS

Following are a few comments on other areas of lawn care:

Connecticut—"Problems often arise from building lawns too high above sidewalks and drives, resulting in water shedding off instead of going down; low humus content of soil leads to severe packing."

California—"Manage turf as a winter crop. Fertilize, aerate, seed, etc., from September 20th to May 1st; from June to September, mow high, avoid fertilizer, don't over irrigate, handle it carefully."

Arkansas—"Leave clippings on lawn and use nitrogen fertilizer three times a year."

New Hampshire—"Encourage soil organisms by using high organic content fertilizers and by leaving clippings on lawn."

The comments in this report are a general round-up of lawn care techniques given by experts across the nation. If you avoid the common mistakes in watering, mowing, and seeding, you'll also avoid the all-too-common problems of lawn failure. If you also follow a sound fertilizing and soil-conditioning program, you'll come up with an attractive lawn.

CHAPTER XIX

Proper Tools a Must

PROPERLY used, today's garden power tools are making it a lot easier to do a complete and thorough job of lawn repair.

Thanks to the ever-increasing number of small riding tractors equipped with 'dozer blades, scrapers, rotary tillers, dump carts and spreaders, the job can now be done in days instead of weeks.

Now, this isn't to say that the mere use of garden power equipment is going to give you a first-rate lawn or rebuild the old one. It's pretty obvious that you can't "buy results" when you buy new equipment. And spreading new seed on unprepared soil isn't going to give you healthy, vigorous turf.

But power tools can help you build the right sort of soil texture and fertility because they are designed to handle bulky, heavy materials and to work them into the soil to a good root-growth depth. They'll also help you correct bad grading and drainage conditions by leveling and moving more soil faster and better than a man can.

The organic gradener, aware that power tools alone cannot do the job, will make a careful diagnosis of the sick lawn before he reaches for a single tool. Here are some of the main reasons why a lawn can fail:

1. Improper drainage
2. Poor topsoil or subsoil
3. Lack of proper or adequate plant food
4. Over-acid soil
5. Compaction, either surface or below.

POWER TOOLS ARE AVAILABLE FOR ALL LAWN REPAIR JOBS

To relieve the above conditions which are mainly physical or even mechanical, an impressive array of garden power equipment has been devised. In addition to the major overhaul operations, power tools are now available which will help you renovate the smaller patches which will respond to such treatment, provided there is adequate soil drainage and the soil pH is satisfactory.

Garden power tools which were first created to handle such strict garden chores as tilling and cultivation have now been diversified to include lawn building and maintenance. As the experienced

[349]

organic gardener knows, the mere possession of power tools will not automatically confer eye-pleasing, healthy stretches of turf and lawn upon the homestead.

However, the organic gardener who works his homestead from "the inside out" will make full use of the new equipment if it will help him get the kind of results he wants—sustained fertility and continued yield over the years.

Double The Life of Your Power Garden Tools

Proper maintenance can double the working life of any garden power tool.

So, if you want to save money, time, trouble, and temper you should practice the following 5-way maintenance program every time you use garden power equipment:

1. DISCONNECT the spark plug before starting operations.

2. CLEAN the entire tool including working parts, casing, framework, and wheels.

3. LUBRICATE it as specified in the manual, checking all moving parts.

4. TIGHTEN all bolts and nuts, checking all joints.

5. CHECK and then ADJUST belts, carburetor timing and spark plug gaps and electrodes.

Keep in mind your mower, tractor, tiller and shredder is a precision-machined tool. You're using and driving it under all kinds of bad conditions, through dust and even mud over rough terrains. So it deserves the kind of watchful pampering you give the family car because it's doing a sound job of getting more work done better in less time without asking any favors. Let's start in with the power mowers.

There are 4 kinds of power mowers today: 1 — the reel, 2 — the rotary, 3 — the hammermill, and 4 — the sicklebar. Regardless of what kind you have, clean it every time you use it. Turn it over so you can get at the undercarriage, following the recommendation of the manufacturer. But first — remember to *disconnect the spark plug*.

Use a flexible, broad-bladed putty knife or a brush with stiff wire bristles to scrape and chip the grass clippings and soil away from the undercarriage and shaft mounting. While you are at it, check for splits, cracks, and stone damage.

It's important to get the grass clippings off because they give off heat when they decompose, which ages the metal housing and causes it to deteriorate. It's also a good idea to wash off the undercarriage with a hose after the motor has cooled and to wipe away all excess grease and oil.

Next, line up your oil cans. There are 3 vital parts of your mower which must always be lubricated and they take oils of different viscosities. The crankcase of the motor usually requires #20 or #30 oil. The heavy-duty gear train in the transmission may go as high as #90 — even higher. The wheels and lighter moving parts will take #20 or even a lighter grade. So be sure to check all the grease and oil cups and listen for undue chatter or vibration as you test the wheels and moving parts.

FOR SAFETY AND ECONOMY

It's obviously bad practice to run any power tool with loose and rattling parts. *So check all bolts and nuts for tightness before and after running the mower.* Most machinists prefer using a box wrench which fits into tight corners and places with lean tolerances. Using such a wrench, go over the handles, the casing and engine mountings, checking for tightness and rigidity. See that all moving parts move smoothly and without unusual vibration.

Next, check all belts for correct tightness between pulleys. In general, there should be about a half-inch of play under light finger pressure in the average belt. Extra tightness does not give greater efficiency, but it does bring harder and faster wear and a lot more heat. So keep a half-inch play in all belting.

When disconnecting your spark plug, take it out of the motor block and check the spark gap. The correct distance is usually from .020 to .025 inch and your gauge will tell you if your plug is working at top efficiency. While you're at it, clean up the electrodes with some fine emery cloth and then set the correct gap, bending the side electrode to make the proper adjustment. If you sharpen your blade, make sure it is symmetrical and in balance. If it is lopsided, it will cause undue wear and strain on the engine and mainshaft to which it is attached.

Finally, it is good periodically to flush out the crankcase and refill with fresh oil. This practice applies also to the air filter and the gas in the gas tank. If you feel equal to it, you can try adjusting the carburetor for maximum efficiency, following the advice of the manufacturer's manual. But, in general, unless you have a friendly neighbor who is a real expert, you're advised to leave engine repair and adjustment to the local internal combustion engine repairman.

The Rotary Tiller

With practically one exception, everything that has been said about the mower applies to the rotary tiller. Both have frames, casings and motors that are subject to strain. But the tiller operates a set of rugged, heavy tines that claw into the soil and chew and mix it with compost and fertilizer.

You should clean the undercarriage and tines every time you're through using the tiller. Long, fibrous weeds wrap themselves around the shaft and tines. Clayey soil wads up under the housing and tends to work its way toward the transmission. It's good to get all this foreign matter away from vital moving parts. You should also sharpen the tines with a file when they become dull and give extra time to all cleaning and oiling chores. Otherwise, take the same care of your tiller that you do with your mower.

THE SHREDDER IN WINTER

There are two tricks to running the shredder on days when the snow is two feet high and on the days when the thermometer sinks to zero. First: clean the rotors and the mixing chamber after every workout and then clean them again before starting the motor. Second: on the very cold days, drain the crankcase and then fill it again slowly with fresh oil heated to about 50 degrees. This treatment warms the machine's innards, easing its mechanisms so it responds promptly to the starter.

One extra remark should be made here about the care and operation of the shredder. Disconnect the spark plug and lock off the fuel tank before you get inside the machine! You'll have to clean off the grids and baffles and you'll be cleaning out the mixing chamber when it is overloaded. But, play it safe and take extra time to make sure all power is disconnected before you open up the machine and go to work.

Proper care of garden power tools will obviously bring better results and a happier garden and gardener. The time spent on cleaning, oiling, sharpening, and adjusting is time well spent, returning dividends in trouble, temper, and money saved as your equipment gives repair-free, efficient operation season after season. — *Maurice Franz.*

Caring for the Gas Motor

Having trouble with your gas motor? A bit of knowhow will beat a strong starter-rope arm every time.

If the engine won't start, make sure there is gas in the tank and that the shut-off valve is open. We find there is plenty of gas going to the carburetor. Remove the spark plug and pour a teaspoonful of gas into the spark plug hole and replace plug. Now crank the engine. If the engine starts and runs for a few turns, the trouble is a stuck float in the carburetor or clogged jets. Rap the carburetor with a wood screwdriver handle to free it. If this does not do the trick, suspect clogged jets. Drain the gas out of the system and pour in about a half-cup of lacquer thinner or commerical gum solvent. Let stand at least an hour. Drain off solvent and refill system with gas. This will cure the trouble unless something is mechanically wrong with the carburetor that will need expert shop attention.

Never operate an engine without checking the air filter. Dust will quickly ruin the engine if the filter is left off, or permitted to run dry of oil. Metal foil filters should be washed in gas and soaked in clean oil. Clogged air filters reduce efficient operation. While the air filter is off for cleaning, check the butterfly valve in the carburetor

(*Text continued on p. 359*)

[355]

There's no need to take your mower to the shop for periodic maintenance when you can do it just as easily at home. Here are some routine
corrective procedures that will add years to the life of your mower.

(1) Remove and clean the spark plug on a wire wheel for efficient firing.

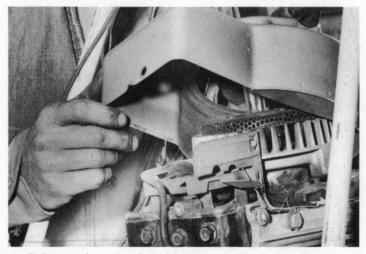

(2) Remove the engine shroud to expose the fly wheel, enabling you to
clean the outside of the engine and check the spark plug wire.

[356]

(3) When you take off the head gasket cover, carbon deposits on the piston head can be seen.

(4) Scrape and clean those deposits from the top of the piston head and replace the cover.

[357]

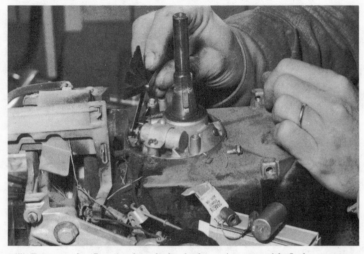

(5) Remove the fly wheel and check the point gap with feeler guage.

(6) Uncover the cooling fins and clean out any grass and debris that may have accumulated.

throat. It should close completely. If it doesn't, turn screws on the valve to accomplish this.

All owners should get into this trouble-forestalling habit. When finished using the engine, close the gas shut-off valve and run the engine until it stops. This empties the carburetor and prevents gumming and the building up of harmful varnish deposits. Keep gas in clean cans. Keep cans full to minimize water condensation. Never use old fuel in gas engines. Old fuel makes for hard starting and quickly builds up gum and varnish in the fuel system. Do not store gas in cans that previously contained paints, syrups or other substances that cannot be completely removed.

Two-cycle engines have very particular fuel requirements which are frequently ignored. This engine requires a gasoline mixed with oil. Many people pour oil into the gas tank, then fill it with gas. As a result, the oil clogs the filter and even works into the carburetor before the gas has a chance to mix thoroughly with it. No wonder the engine won't start on such a poorly prepared fuel.

The proportions for most two-cycle engines is 1 pint of S.A.E. 30 oil to 2 gallons of gas. Outboard motor oil is best to use in two-cycle jobs. Pour the oil into the gasoline. Never pour gas on oil, for this will not give a thoroughly mixed fuel. Cap the container tightly and shake vigorously, turning the container end over end during the process. Never use straight gasoline in a two-cycle engine. Lubrication of internal parts depends on oil vapor contained in the fuel. Always follow manufacturer's oil-to-gas ratio recommendations for utmost efficiency. Don't guess or take chances.

If the engine misses, check the plug wire to see that the terminal is in good contact with the plug. Wire may be frayed and shorting the spark. Tape frayed area or replace with new wire. Wire may be broken at magneto connection. Loose terminals at condenser and magneto will result in missing. Simply tighten screws. But the plug should be checked first. Remove, clean, inspect for hairline cracks in porcelain and regap to recommended specification in owner's manual, or often stated on tab on engine. If plug continues to misfire, replace with new plug.

Loose head bolts will cause missing. Tighten all head bolts. Oil stains on block indicate leaky head gasket. If tightening bolts does not halt missing, install a new gasket. Missing is also caused by a kinked, split or partially clogged gas line. Be sure to check before going farther.

Stuck valves in four-cycle engines, or valves warped or burned will cause missing. Valves stick because of varnish deposits built up on their stems. The varnish prevents free movement in the valve guides. Remove the spark plug. Squirt lacquer thinner through the plug hole and crank engine so that the solvent will reach the valves. If the trouble is sticky valves, this little kink will quickly cure it. Otherwise, new valves will be necessary.

Should you own two- and four-cycle engines, do

not fuel the 4-cycle engines with the same oil-mixed gas that is used in the two-cycle engine. Oily gas quickly fouls plugs and builds up heavy carbon deposits in a 4-cycle engine. Use straight, fresh gas only.

After having checked all these possible troubles and the engine still misses, the sore spot will be a need for new ignition points or an adjustment of the magneto air gap. This calls for shop service since special equipment is needed. And always be sure that the plug is tight on its ring gasket. Finger-tight is not enough since blowby will cause the engine to act as if it were misfiring. This will also make the engine hard to start.

The engine overheats quickly. This is most often the fault of debris-clogged air cooling fins. The heat is dissipated by means of these external fins. If the depressions between them are clogged with dirt, the heat is trapped and cannot escape fast enough. Clean these fins with a brush.

Too lean a carburetor setting will also cause overheating. Turning the adjustment screw to the left increases richness. Keep turning to left until engine runs with full power and smoothness. It is advised that if engine delivers full power and smoothness, not to try for a leaner mixture under the mistaken impression that it will be more economical. Burned valves also result from a lean feed.

Overheating is also caused by a partly closed carburetor choke. Make sure that the choke is fully open when operating the engine. Another

[361]

cause is old oil, dirty and with little viscosity, or oil of an incorrect grade. Drain crankcase and fill with new oil of the grade recommended by the manufacturer. Worn bearings or bushings that cause belt pulleys or chain sprockets to bind will overload the engine, causing it to heat. Check all moving parts to see that they turn freely. Before doing so, remove ignition wire from spark plug to prevent accidental starting of engine.

There is a simple way in which to determine if the engine needs new piston rings and a general overhaul. Pull on the starter rope in a steady motion. If little or no resistance is felt, then the rings are badly worn and must be replaced. This can be double-checked in a simple fashion. If no resistance is felt when the rope is pulled, remove the spark plug. Thrust a short length of wire through the plug hole until it rests on the top of the piston. Now slowly pull on the rope until the piston travels downward to the bottom of its stroke. The wire will go down with it. As soon as the wire starts to come up, stop turning the engine and remove wire.

Pour about two or three tablespoonfuls of oil through the plug hole and replace plug. *Do not attach spark plug wire.* Now spin the engine a number of times. As the oil flows into the spaces created by the worn rings, it acts as a seal. Now a resistance will be felt as the rope is pulled. It indicates that the rings are worn. While doing this, hold the ear closely to the engine. Listen for a hissing sound as the rope is pulled. A burned or leaking head gasket or loose spark plug will be indicated by this means. Tighten plug first. If hissing persists, tighten head bolts. A leaking gasket will have to be replaced.

The piston is not a tight fit in a cold engine. As the engine warms up, the metal expands making an efficient fit. So do not put an engine under load as soon as it is started. Give it a few minutes in which to warm up. This will expand the piston, permitting the engine to put out full power. This practice will also retard wear. 1,700 rpm is a good idling speed. A slower idle does not circulate oil or air efficiently. A low idling speed will often cause an engine to stall under load.

If you have a new engine, let it break in by running an hour or so at idling speed with occasional short bursts of full throttle. This will allow the moving parts to wear in properly. To put a new engine to hard work at once will show up in many troubles later on.

At season's end clean the engine of all dirt before putting away for the winter. Remove and wash the air cleaner free of oil and dust. Mix a 50-50 solution of kerosene and oil that is used in the engine. Shut off gas line at tank. Start engine and pour mixture into air intake of carburetor while air cleaner is off. Run until engine stops. Mixture will coat all moving parts against corrosion. Drain gas from tank and oil from crankcase. Store under cover. Reverse procedure in spring.

[363]

Tractors

Anyone who lives on several acres or more of land and wants to get the most from it will find small tractors to be very efficient. Here are a few jobs it does so well:

Cutting grass, weeds — sickle bar, rotary or gang-reel type mower attachments available.

Hauling rocks, hay, soil, stumps, fertilizer, etc. — utility trailer does this excellently.

Plowing 8 to 10 inches deep — but don't try to use the small tractor for plowing deeply in heavy sod.

Cultivating between vegetable rows.

Loading manure, soil, compost, etc. into trailer — front end loader does a fine job of this.

Snow plowing — an important feature to the man trying to get to work after an all-night snow.

Post-hole digging, paint spraying, sawing wood — attachments for these purposes can be operated from the tractor's power take-off.

Disks and harrows are used only to prepare a seedbed after plowing. Disks on a garden tractor do not have sufficient cutting power to actually work up unplowed soil. Although it is usually advisable to add weights on top of garden tractor disks, the type of seedbed prepared is of excellent quality.

One advantage of the plow-disk method of preparing a lawn seedbed is that the disks will pulverize the soil finely *on the surface*, yet they will not break up the subsurface clods, thus keeping the soil well aerated.

[364]

Versatility is one of the main strong points of the garden tractor, especially when it comes to *pulling* something. The tractor is just what it's name says — a means of *traction*. It does its work by pulling various implements on or through the soil.

A garden tractor can pull a wagon, a sulky, a lawn roller, a planter, a furrower, a fertilizer spreader or a subsoil chisel. It can *push* a snowplow, grader blade, a rotary mower or a rotary tiller attachment. By using a power takeoff, a garden tractor can operate a compost shredder, a saw, a paint sprayer or even a small feed mill. And all these implements are in addition to the plow, disk and harrow — which are standard.

Organic gardeners, who have need to move around bulky mulch materials, compost and fertilizer will find a tractor-pulled wagon a handy tool. It makes the job of cleaning up and of gathering compost material much easier. A rotary mower attachment is also extremely useful to organic gardeners, because it can also be used to shred up light mulch and compost material.

Here are 3 basic rules for tractor operation:

1. Don't expect a garden tractor to do the work of a team of horses.

2. Learn how to care for your tractor properly. You will enjoy using it more if you know that it is always in good condition. Be sure to protect it from the weather. The Department of Agriculture reports that farm and garden equipment usually rusts away before it wears out.

3. Learn how to use your tractor *the right way*.

[365]

Don't be afraid to write to the manufacturer if you have a question. The operator, not the machine, is usually at fault when a job is not being done properly.

A riding tractor is a "must" for stripping topsoil and re-grading the area. Mounting a 'dozer or scraper blade, average small riding tractor will peel back the topsoil and pile it for you to one side, to be held in reserve for mixing with other materials and for a final top-dressing. But first, before stripping the soil, hook on the rotary tiller and turn the weak and sickly grass blades under, breaking them up and mixing them with the soil.

If you have to re-grade, use the tiller to chop up the subsoil, relieving possible compaction and making it more workable for the scraper blade. Be sure to remove all debris or building wastes you may find buried in the subsoil. Such materials can cause poor soil drainage and a sickly lawn. When grading, be sure to slope the subsoil away from the house and avoid working the soil when it is too wet or muddy.

Edgers

There are a variety of edgers you can use to keep your walks and curbs looking trim. The hand edgers normally are of a half-moon design. They can cut stubborn weeds and grass with ease and usually are rugged enough to do a fine job. Some models have a forged one piece blade and shank

[366]

of steel. Often the edge is sharpened all along the half moon. A rugged fine grained ash handle is usually your best buy.

If you're looking for a rotary lawn shears, you'll have several models to choose from. Most are designed for low priced sale. These usually involve a wheel with a blade of disk teeth so that trimming can be done above the trench bottom. There's usually an off-set wheel for good traction. What this type of edger amounts to is literally a scissors on wheels. It's great for shearing weeds or edging around flower beds, trees, walls or sidewalks.

Like most garden tools, there's a power variety. The power edger is usually a gas operated machine that powers a whirling disk which trims off the grass next to the sidewalk. Although more expensive, the power edger provides a professional looking job and are usually used by city maintenance crews and others who are responsible for the appearance of the city grounds or estates.

Aerators

If soil compaction has hit your lawn, spike aerators have been designed to help you get air into the vital root zone and build moisture retentiveness by opening up the turf and removing small plugs of it to stimulate new growth. In the past, this was a rather laborious hand operation using a garden fork or a special hand-aerifier to punch holes in the overdense turf.

[367]

Today, many new and different kinds of aerators are available. These are highly specialized power aerifiers which may be rented from your local garden supply house that punch out and remove rather deep cores of rootlets and soil. There are also manual aerators with rotary spikes which may be hand-pushed over the lawn. And there are aerator attachments which are hooked on to the riding tractor or to a reel-type mower.

Rakes

A variety of rakes can serve the home lawn keeper. They come in handy for general clean-up jobs in yard and garden. The level head rake is designed for preparing and maintaining flower and vegetable gardens, but its level back makes it easy to smooth the ground when preparing it for lawn seeding. The round bow rake, often used for cleaning up around the lawn, holds trash and twigs firmly and releases them easily.

For taking care of leaves in the fall, and removing debris in the spring, a lawn and leaf rake is the thing you need. It will collect the grass cuttings in the summer easily. Most rakes have steel spring teeth that offer strength and flexibility for lawn cleaning. Often a chrome reinforcing spring and retaining bar goes across the teeth for even distribution of pressure. Options include a torsion spring above the spacer bar so that the tines may

[368]

spring back into place after being extended. Lawn rakes come in a variety of styles from bamboo to steel spring.

The newest rake sensation is both a rake and a cultivator. Used with a back and forth motion like a carpet sweeper, it has needle pointed teeth which reach deep down into a lawn to pick up grass smothering debris, and lift up unwanted stolons for mowing. It rips out crabgrass easily. On the forward glide the lawn rake often cleans itself. No lifting involved.

You may think that there's no such thing as a power rake, but you're wrong. Power rakes do the same jobs that hand rakes do, except they eliminate the muscle power. Models start from around $200, with some styles costing close to $700 or more. Although they're not recommended for the small homeowner, they're great for the estate keeper or for football field maintenance.

Hoses

Garden hoses come in different sizes and shapes. Most important in selecting a hose is its inside diameter. But many lawn owners fail to look at that until after they've bought that bright green colored one. Then they may be disappointed in the amount of water their hose can deliver. The smallest diameter sold, 7/16 of an inch, is usually too small for most lawn uses. Standard sizes include 1/2, 5/8, 3/4 inch in diameter. You can also buy a hose of 1 inch diameter but it's seldom sold to homeowners.

Remember this important fact. The output through a hose is in direct ratio to its inside diameter. In 15 seconds a 50 foot length of 1/2 inch hose can deliver more than one gallon. But a 5/8 inch hose delivers almost twice as much, and a 3/4 inch hose provides almost 5 gallons of water in 15 seconds.

Inside diameter isn't the only consideration in picking a hose. The thicker the hose the more it weighs. That means you'll have to tug the hose from spot to spot as you change your watering sites. For example, 50 feet of a 1/2 inch hose can weight 6 pounds (empty) whereas a 3/4 inch hose can weigh 11 pounds when empty and 19-1/2 pounds when full of water. That's quite a chore to lug that much weight around the yard. Consider both diameter and weight in making your selection.

The best decision for selecting a hose is its guarantee. Don't buy one that isn't guaranteed. And avoid those super bargains. Normally they will cost you more than you can imagine.

Seeders — Spreaders

If you want to sow your seed and fertilize like Grandpa did, then you'll probably broadcast it by hand. And, in fact, with a little practice you'll probably become quite good at it. But for many lawn owners who prefer a bit more accuracy in distributing their seed and fertilizer, mechanical seeders are the choice. Most of these machines allow the seeds or fertilizers to drop from the hopper at a set rate, which allows them to be distributed in a fairly uniform pattern over a wide path. Often the operator is instructed to overlap the wheel tracks to avoid skipping spots. Precision machines can be adjusted to distribute as little as one pound of seed per thousand square feet. Most spreaders have rate devices and setting instructions which adjust openings for major types of seed or fertilizer. A mixture primarily of bentgrass takes a smaller setting than one of bluegrass. Largest settings usually go to fescue or ryegrass.

Thatchers

Periodic thatch removal ends "ideal" fungus conditions, and breaks up crabgrass "plantations." It also thins out or rips up the dense matting, permitting light and air to reach the soil. This is very important at seeding time because it allows the new seeds to come in direct contact with the soil and germinate properly.

In the past, breaking up the mat or thatch was a back-breaking chore that sorely taxed the average homeowner's strength and determination. Today, engine-powered "rakes" or lawn "renovators" do the job better in less time and with a lot less personal effort.

[371]

Lawn renovators resemble reel mowers. But instead of a series of helical blades, they operate a horizontal rotating shaft that is belted directly to the engine. Cutting and slicing of the turf is done by a series of short, curved knives that are mounted securely to the shaft and that revolve with it. Depth of cut is controlled by shaft or wheel height adjustment. All refuse cut from the turf thatch should be raked away and removed from the lawn.

The operation of sweeping the sliced matting is eliminated by the power "rake" which, in addition to thinning the thatch, also gathers it. Also resembling the conventional reel mower, the power "rake" operates sets of sturdy tines that, fixed on a revolving central shaft, "do the entire job of loosening, raking and gathering in one fast operation."

Tillers

Rotary tillers consist of the tines or blades that turn and mix the soil, the engine that powers them, the belts, chains or gears that transmit the power, and the frame and handles which house these parts and their controls. There are two main types: those with the tilling unit up front, ahead of the engine, and those with the rotating blades behind the engine. While there are variations in each class, the front tillers are usually simpler and cheaper, while the rear tillers offer more features and combinations of power-plus-control. This extra flexibility is reflected in the price.

[372]

A comparative newcomer to the garden and lawn scene is the extremely lightweight gas or electric-powered tiller or scraper which has been specifically designed to work in small areas and do light tilling or cultivating. It can work quite close to plants without damaging them.

But the conventional tiller, the old workhorse of the garden should not be neglected. Plenty of our readers write in from time to time to tell how they are using their regulation size rotary tillers to re-work the lawn, start new seedbeds, and grade both topsoil and subsoil when necessary.

In any case, you will find that using a rotary tiller is highly advisable because the ground is hard and slightly compacted due to lack of a cover crop of grass. So, use either the new lightweight tiller or the "old regular" to turn the soil under 4 or 5 inches and to prepare a good seedbed.

Sweepers

Since the introduction of rotary mowers, more and more homeowners are allowing clippings to remain on the lawn. Long clippings often do not decompose fast enough and may encourage turf diseases. Good turf management sometimes calls for removal of these long dead clippings.

We are also seeing more lawns that are green at the tips, but at the soil line are dull and brown — just dead grass. Reel and rotary mowers are often fitted with grass catchers to help remove the

[373]

longer clippings, but this means frequent stops to empty the basket.

The real answer to clipping removal is a lawn sweeper, also a highly useful tool for picking up fallen leaves and sweeping paved driveways. Compared with raking, removal of either leaves or clippings with a lawn sweeper requires only one-fifth to one-tenth of the time.

Most lawn sweepers are built on the same general principle—a revolving brush that picks up clippings. Other than sturdy construction, watch for ease of height adjustment control.

CHAPTER XX

Tips For That Showplace Lawn

Walk Ways

You CAN construct your own flagstone walk and terrace while you make your lawn. After the earth has been cleared and leveled, but before it's sown with grass, mark off the places for the path and terrace, using stakes and cord. Next obtain several sheets of pliable sheet metal, and cut them into strips about 4 inches wide, with a length of 10 feet or more. Bend the strips around into circles, fastening the two ends of each together and set these strips on edge in the soil where path and terrace were marked out.

Don't leave the circles as they were, but bend them into irregular forms, like the flat stones of crazy paving. If you press the sharp edges of the

[375]

metal down two or more inches into the soil, the shapes should hold. Arrange the metal moulds to cover path and terrace, leaving an inch or two of space between metal rim and metal rim.

Now you're ready to pour the concrete. Make it very hard, using half cement and half sand. You might want to divide it into several portions, coloring one batch brown, one terra cotta, one dull green and one gray. Into the metal forms pour the mixtures, taking care to place "stones" of different colors in harmonious groupings. Be careful never to pour more than you can handle at once, and take care to leave space, so that you can reach all parts of the work from one side or another.

The concrete takes about four hours to harden. Therefore, when it is half hard, about two hours after pouring, you are ready to work on the "stones." Removing the metal rims carefully, begin to form and model the concrete with a trowel. Bevel the edges off and smooth them, sometimes making them irregular, to look like natural stone. Soon you will have a handsome walk and terrace of crazy paving stones in dull, harmonious colors, restful to the eye and interesting in variety.

After several days, when all the sections are poured and hardened, you are ready for the final touch. Shovel out a wheelbarrow load of the sifted compost and grass seed on to walk and terrace. Then with a straw broom sweep the misture into the crevices which you left between the paving stones. When the cracks are full and smoothed, give all a gentle sprinkling with the hose. In a few days the grass will be growing green and thick between the stones, and you will have a path and terrace which seem to be an ancient, settled, part of an old, old garden.

Night Shading

Outdoor home areas can look better at night than in the daytime. Carefully planned, creative lighting of those areas puts them at their best advantage. Outdoor lighting need not be expensive

Where Lawn Joins Walk & Drives

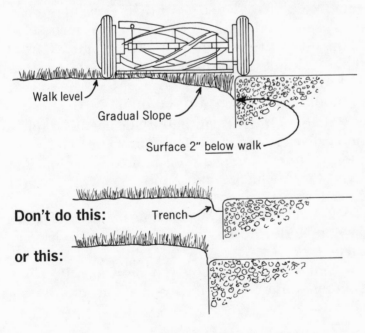

Walk level

Gradual Slope

Surface 2" below walk

Don't do this: Trench

or this:

[377]

or elaborate to be effective; single covered bulbs placed in the proper places can make an unusual and attractive setting. Areas and scenes that aren't usually visible after dark can become useful and attractive with the proper lighting and a flick of a switch can produce a charming garden scene out of a sea of darkness.

Beauty is only one use for outdoor lighting. Work, play, family entertaining, safety and protection are all legitimate uses for exterior lighting. Many activities of work and play are more comfortably done after sunset during spring, summer, and fall when the air is cooler. For play, it's best to use a light source well above eye level of the players to keep direct light out of their eyes. Lights can be placed on a building or pole for this purpose.

Intruders are less likely to enter lighted areas than dark ones. We suggest placing light switches in bedrooms and other convenient places so that outdoor lights may be turned on quickly.

Whether outdoor lighting will be useful or solely decorative, it can always be attractive. Here are some pointers for planning lighted areas outside from the Michigan State University Agricultural Extension Service:

— Accent the most interesting features of your garden; hide the less attractive areas by leaving them dark.

— Side or back lighting can be dramatic; front lighting is more likely to produce flat, uninteresting effects.

[378]

— Plan for year-round effects. Every season provides interesting material for outdoor lighting.

— Create interesting patterns with light. Watch reflections, shadows, shades of foliage for their best uses.

— Vary the light strength and use indirect lighting whenever possible. An evenly lighted area seldom creates an interesting picture.

— Control the amount of light. Do not try to produce a daytime appearance. Too little lighting is better than too much, since a soft flow is better than a glare.

Remember to give consideration to neighbors when outdoor lighting is to be installed. You might want to place shields on lights or, better yet, place them where they will not disturb others.

Underground circuits are the most permanent and satisfactory for outdoor lighting, but must be protected from insect and rodent damage, be capable of withstanding freezing and thawing weather and must be protected against damage from moisture and digging.

Circuits above ground are less attractive and less permanent than the underground type but are easier to install and maintain. Those circuits may consist of overhead wires supported by posts, trees or buildings, or of wires hidden on the backs of walls and fences. For temporary use, specially treated extension cords may be used, but are not recommended because of the danger to people and equipment when wiring is exposed.

[379]

commonly used for large plazas or terraces. Great care should be taken so that only the highest grade flag is used. The color of the stone will determine quality. Poor quality stone is light gray in color and comes from near the surface of a shallow quarry. Its lack of density will result in spalling and chipping. High quality flagstone is usually a deep blue-gray color and its high density will yield a maintenance-free surface.

As a surface material, brick can produce interesting color, texture and patterns. If it is installed on a bed of sand or "stone dust," it must be carefully laid with tight joints to prevent weed growth. Brick should not be laid on concrete in cold climates. Because of its porous nature, it will absorb water which will freeze in winter, causing the bricks to loosen.

Retaining Walls

The three basic types of walls used to reduce steep grades are:

    a. Concrete Walls with or without Veneers

    b. Dry Walls

    c. Cribbed Walls.

Concrete Walls with or without Veneers. Poured concrete walls with stone or brick veneer should require next to no care because it combines the sturdiness of concrete with the durability of a brick or stone surface. Drains or "weeps" should be provided through the wall to prevent the buildup of water pressure and subsequent buckling. Special attention must also be paid to proper installation of expansion joints to allow for movement in the concrete due to temperature changes. The exposed face of a plain concrete wall is always subject to surface deterioration. If a tight budget forces you to delete the stone or brick veneer, provide a stone shelf slightly below finished grade for the future addition of a veneer in the event the exposed surface should eventually fail.

Dry Walls. Dry walls (stone walls without mortar) are not recommended for minimum maintenance on home grounds. If dry walls must be used, the individual stones should be massive enough to prevent the removal of the stones by vandals. Finally never build a dry wall higher than 5 feet in area subject to extreme frost action.

Cribbed Walls. The bulky nature of concrete cribbing is associated with heavy landscaping of highways and railroad embankments and, therefore, should not be a part of home development. In addition, the voids in the cribbing are always subject to the development of weed growth.

Exterior Steps. Exterior steps should be avoided when possible, but if they are required, they must be less steep than indoor steps. A satisfactory "rule of thumb" for exterior step construction is a maximum riser height of 6 inches and a tread depth of 14 inches.

For safety and durability, stone steps are the unanimous choice. It has a better non-skid surface, and can withstand mechanical and salt damage.

[383]

Handrails. Handrails should be used alongside all exterior steps, but they can be a major maintenance problem if they require frequent care and painting. The best material is an anodized aluminum rail which requires no painting and, unlike regular aluminum, resists corrosion. Never install aluminum rails in iron pipe sleeves, for iron, in direct contact with aluminum, will cause the aluminum to deteriorate. The easiest and best method of installation is to drill the holes for upright members directly in the surface of the stair treads.

Ground Covers For Lawn Problems

Does your lawn have bare spots that even Houdini couldn't grow grass on? Are you constantly yanking weeds from your flagstone steps, or distorting your sacroiliac, clipping those odd angle corners of the lawn or garden borders? No matter how hard you work, these things never look quite right.

The problems needn't plague the gardener who knows there are *ground covers that will succeed where all else fails.*

Almost all the common ground cover plants are as vigorous as weeds. Of course, you wouldn't expect grass to grow on a windswept or rainwashed slope; neither will most ground covers. You could plant really tough monsters like crown vetch or gout weed in such spots, but they grow with such abandon you'd have a hard time holding them in check. Preparing the soil for a suitable ground cover is wiser than planting potential pests.

Dig to a depth of at least 8 inches, removing all weeds and foreign material. Mix in a 2-to 3-inch layer of organic material such as compost, peatmoss, rotted manure or aged sawdust. Soak well a few hours before planting.

Since ground covers are higher in initial cost than seeding a lawn, there are many schools of thought on how to economize. Some gardeners prefer to set plants a good distance apart, thus using a smaller number of plants, and battle weeds in the longer interval the plants take to cover. Others buy seed, seedlings, or rooted cuttings from nurseries in order to produce the ground cover more cheaply at home. But if these are planted directly outdoors, many will die, giving a ragged effect to the bed. It's better to start them in your "home nursery" or pots, carefully shading and watering, before setting them out.

Some economy-minded gardeners transplanted wild plants from nearby fields and woods.

The ideal method is to set small plants close together. The proper distance apart depends on the rate of growth and size of the plants at planting time. Three to 8 inches apart is correct for most ground covers, while some vines can be up to 36 inches apart.

What height should your ground cover be? Tall vines and some shrubs up to 2 feet tall are suit-

[385]

able for large open areas and some slopes, while small areas like the flower garden borders or odd angle corners where the lawn mower can't reach, call for something low with delicate foliage.

Ground covers can also be planted under and around permanent garden furniture where it's difficult to cut grass. Once established, ground covers need no coddling. But while they are getting started they do deserve some care. Water occasionally during the first season. Top-dressing with compost, humus or well-rotted manure will supply the nitrogen needed for dense growth, to cover the ground without any "holes." As the plants grow, they will strangle any crabgrass or plantain.

The value and practicality of ground covers are all too often ignored. More and more gardeners are coming to realize their importance in keeping garden and lawn chores to a minimum.

None of the so-called ground covers can cover the soil as closely as a good grass turf. They are not recommended for any area where there is traffic—none of them will stand up to wear. Walks must be built through areas covered by plants other than grass, because almost any ground cover will succumb to trampling.

Most ground cover is established by planting sprigs or cuttings. These should be spaced no more than 12 inches apart. While many of them are not particular about soil requirements, they will spread more quickly and make a more luxuriant growth if the soil is prepared as for bulbs. Those most commonly used are listed below.

Aaron's-Beard. Hypericum calysinum, or creeping St. John's wort, is an evergreen undershrub that grows to 1 foot in height. It bears a few 2-inch blossoms during the summer. It is hardy in most of the southern parts of the country. It is recommended for shady places and will not thrive in full sun. Sandy soil is its preference, but it will grow on any loose soil that is well-drained.

Airplane Plant. Also known as anthericum to which it is closely related, the airplane plant is a tropical lily plant which grows only 6 to 8 inches tall. It spreads fairly rapidly if planted 10 to 12 inches apart in partial shade. Two different species of the genus Chlorophytum can be used interchangeably as ground cover in the frost-free sections: *C. comosum* and *C. elatum,* the latter having white-striped leaves and growing somewhat taller than the former. Both are native to South Africa and are tender to freezing. They are drought-resistant and may be grown in the more arid sections as well as the humid frost-free portions of the far South. They are propagated by division.

Bugle. Ajuga genevensis may be grown in full sun or partial shade. Bugle is a prostrate member of the mint family which bears 6-inch blue flower spikes in spring, a few persisting on into the summer. It roots from leaf axils and is easily and rapidly spread from cuttings. It has attractive, slightly

[387]

puckered bright green leaves. *A reptans,* the common bugle, has a variety with metallic-colored leaves which is very attractive. Although winter-hardy into the northern sections of the country, bugle is also easily grown as far south as the most tropical areas.

Creeping Juniper. Juniperus horizontalis is one of the few conifers used as ground cover. It is sometimes also called savin. Varieties may be obtained which are only a few inches tall, others grow almost upright at first and later become procumbent, with long trailing branches. The scaley, evergreen leaves are bluish-green in the species, but are steel-blue to yellow-gold or even whitish in varieties.

Creeping juniper is at its best in the northern zones, and may be grown south about to the latitude of New Jersey. It makes good ground cover in rocky or sandy soil, preferably moist, but it will tolerate some dryness. It may be propagated from cuttings, layering or seeding with special techniques.

Crown Vetch. Coronilla varia is useful when planted on banks. It is a member of the pea family, with dense heads of pinkish-white flowers which bloom from time to time throughout the summer. It is a sprawling perennial creeper, hardy in the northern sections. It may be used in the perennial border for its flowers, but is more often planted to serve as a ground cover, especially in the northeastern states. It is propagated by seeds or cuttings.

[388]

Dichondra. *Dichondra carolinensis* (ponyfoot or lawnleaf) is a tiny, low creeping plant found in the Gulf States near the coast, or sometimes in greenhouses, where it is used as ground cover. Its pad-like leaves seldom grow taller than 3 inches, and when they do, they may be mowed. It is considered a weed in many parts of the South, but may be valuable as a ground cover until it is attacked and destroyed by a fungus. It does best in moist, shady areas and cannot withstand continued high temperatures in the open. It is easily damaged by foot traffic.

Propagation is either vegetatively (if you know someone who is thinning it out) or by seed. Four to 8 ounces will seed 1,000 square feet. Dichondra is vulnerable to disease, especially in humid areas. It should be tried only on an experimental basis until its worth has been proven in the situation you may have in mind. It spreads rapidly in either sun or shade and may prove to be a nuisance if it escapes control.

Ivy. The ivies provide everygreen ground cover and may sometimes be prevailed upon to climb over walls or rocks. Several different species of the genus *Hedera* are useful in the North or South. *H. helix,* English ivy, is the one most often encountered in the North. It is an evergreen vine which will grow either in dense shade or in full sun. It is especially recommended for covering steep banks or bare spaces around trees. It grows under city as well as under country conditions. It

[389]

is occasionally necessary to prune English ivy, where it finds conditions especially to its liking. It may become too high and matted to make a satisfactory ground cover unless it is kept under control.

All the ivies thrive best in rich, moist soil. They are propagated by cuttings, layers or seeds which do not germinate until the second year. Many different varieties of *H. helix* are available, with variegated leaves, large or small leaves, tall or small in habit, etc. These are at their best in Washington or north. In the southern states and in California, Algerian ivy, *H. canariensis,* fills the same niche.

Ivy is easy to propagate from cuttings. It is already supplied with aerial rootlets which will convert the roots if given a chance. It may be rooted in sand indoors or in open frames or a propagating bed at any time of the year. After it has rooted, it makes a rapid growth, covering a bank or shaded area in a single season.

Japanese Honeysuckle. Lonicera japonica is only one of the many honeysuckle vines that might be used for ground cover, but it happens to be the one most often used because it has naturalized itself in this country. It is a rapid-growing climbing or recumbent vine whose yellow, pink, red or white blossoms perfume the countryside when they are fully in bloom. Some flowers appear in late summer, but most of the bloom occurs in June. Japanese honeysuckle is semi-evergreen;

that is the leaves remain green on the vine until midwinter in the North. Among the many varieties with differently colored flowers, there is one whose leaves are variegated with yellow markings.

Honeysuckle is a rampant grower that should be introduced into the home grounds with caution. It is capable of strangling small trees and shrubs, over which it twines itself to their tops. On the ground, honeysuckle vines quickly form a tangle of woody stems which chokes out anything beneath.

The chief value of honeysuckle on the home lot is to hold a steep bank, if the area can be isolated from other plantings. The vines will quickly spread to cover any area until they reach some sort of natural barrier. Honeysuckle may be dug from the woods or fields and transplanted to the garden, or it may be propagated from seeds, from layers or from cuttings. Greenwood cuttings must be rooted under glass.

Japanese Snakebeard. Ophiopogon japonica, also known as Mondo and lily-turf, is one of a genus of small lilies with grasslike leaves. It grows 8 to 12 inches high and bears purple or white flowers. It can be planted in either sun or shade and thrives in poor soils. It spreads slowly, so does not become a nuisance. But because of the slow spreading, it should be planted fairly close, to make a good sod in a reasonable length of time. Snakebeard is propagated by division, the pieces being planted 3 to

[391]

6 inches apart for ground cover. It can be grown in the Far South and is hardy north through New York state.

Japanese Spurge. Pachysandra terminalis, is one of the best evergreen ground covers in the areas between the cooler portions of the Gulf States and southern New England. In this area, it will grow in either sun or shade and is perfectly hardy. Further south, it grows only in the shade and needs considerable attention to watering to survive. It is a low-growing plant that spreads by underground suckers and has attractive, glossy dark-green leaves. It grows in ordinary soil and makes a dense cover under large trees where grass will not grow. It is also sometimes used on pocket handkerchief-size city lawn areas, where mowing is not practical.

Spurge is easily propagated from cuttings taken in the summer. They may be rooted in a cold frame or may be planted rather thickly directly where they are required for ground cover, if they are shaded and kept well watered. Cuttings should be spaced 4 to 6 inches apart. Plants may be set one foot apart.

Lippa. Lippia canescens, which is used as a grass substitute in frost-free portions of the Southwest, is first cousin to our house plant, lemon verbena. It is a creeping plant with dark green leaves an inch or less in length. If kept mowed, it makes a turfy sod capable of crowding out not only all weeds, but also Bermudagrasses. Lippia can be used only in areas where the temperatures never go to freezing. It is killed by freezing temperature and may be injured by temperatures somewhat above freezing. It is also susceptible to nematode damage, which makes it impractical in Florida. About the only places where it can be planted to advantage are the southern portions of Arizona and California. Lippia is established by planting sods which may be spaced one foot apart. They spread and cover rapidly. Lippia honey is attractive to bees.

Partridgeberry. Mitchella repens, is a ingratiating little evergreen vine with small round or oval glossy leaves and a tidy habit of growth. It does well in the shade, but will do even better in the sun in the East if it is kept moist. It likes fertile soil with plenty of organic matter and with a pH near neutral. It produces pairs of fragrant pinkish-white flowers in spring which are followed by pairs of bright red berries in fall and winter.

Partridgeberry is easily propagated from cuttings, which root at the joints. It may be found growing wild along stream banks in the central portion of the East, but it should be dug with discrimination, because in many places, it is disappearing from the wilds. Dig less than half of any planting you may find, if you go to the woods for it. Plants may also be obtained from nurseries that specialize in wild flowers.

Periwinkle. Vinca minor is sometimes called myrtle, though that name is more properly applied to a shrub, *Myrtus communis,* a member of a different family. Periwinkle is a hardy low-growing evergreen that spreads by creeping stems. It has small dark green glossy leaves and blue-violet flowers in spring.

Common periwinkle will form a dense mat that shades out weeds and grasses when conditions are to its liking. It grows best in moist soils that are high in organic matter. It prefers dense shade, but it will grow satisfactorily under dry conditions and in full sun. Variegated forms are available.

Periwinkle is established by division or cuttings which may be planted at any time when the soil is not frozen. Spaced 4 to 8 inches apart, the pieces will take hold and cover within a year or two. The plant is easy to control, so it may be used near borders or beds of more delicate subjects.

Purple-Leaved Wintercreeper. Euonymus fortunei coloratus, is one of the finest vines that can be used for ground cover. It is an evergreen, hardy except in the coldest portions of the country, though in the northern areas above Philadelphia, it should be given some winter protection.

Wintercreeper derives its name from its small leaves which turn purple in autumn and winter, with a paler shade of purple or lavender beneath. It climbs by means of rootlets, which take hold in the soil if it is permitted to creep, making new plants that may be separated as layers from the parent plant. It will grow in almost any soil or with any exposure, but in rich soil may climb as high as 15 to 20 feet. It has attractive, lobed fruit in late summer, following its inconspicuous greenish-white flowers.

Trailing Spiderwort. Tradescantia zebrina, also known as widow's tears and wandering Jew, is a tropical creeper grown mostly in greenhouses for filler in hanging baskets in the North. In the South where temperatures seldom drop below freezing, it may be grown outside as a ground cover. Leaves may be variegated, with purple underneath or may be entirely green. It spreads rapidly and, though it may be damaged by temperatures under 26 degrees, in the warm sections a few sprigs often escape the cold to start the bed over again. It is easily propagated by cuttings, which may be planted 4 to 6 inches apart for quick cover. It prefers the shade to the sun.

Wedelia. A salt-resistant tropical creeper, Wedelia is perennial in southern Florida, but can be grown in a few other places in the United States. It will grow in any soil, in sun or shade, but will drop its leaves if the temperature goes down to 28 degrees and dies out at 20 degrees. It spreads rapidly and may tend to become a nuisance in a climate that suits it.

Wedelia has 2- to 4-inch leaves growing from more or less woody stems and in summer sends up a few yellow daisies. It is established from cuttings.

White Clover. Trifolium repens, is regarded by some as a desirable ground cover and by others as a lawn weed. It belongs to the family of legumes,

[395]

so it is of some benefit to the grass because of the nitrogen its nodule bacteria are able to take from the air and transform to a compound needed by the plants. Clover often grows in patches in the lawn, giving the sod an uneven appearance. Some people object to the white flower heads, which interrupt the solid green lawn. Clover, of course, is relished by honey bees and may be planted for that reason if for no other. However, another disadvantage is that it disappears during hot, dry weather, leaving bare spots in the turf. Contrary to claims made for it, clover cannot crowd out crabgrass.

CHAPTER XXI

Basic "Dos and Don'ts"

HERE, in a short space, is a review of basic principles of lawn management. Check with these rules until they are firmly implanted. They can spell out the difference between a successful lawn and a frustrating failure.

Preparation

Quality grasses cannot thrive on an infertile, hard-packed, or rubbish-filled soil. A loose, porous structure is needed, into which air, water, and roots can penetrate. Grass can stand a moderate amount of competition, but cannot battle against many surface tree roots.

DO — start properly to build a lawn on a new lot, and that includes a decent burial for a contractor's quick-grow seeding. — spade, till, or plow and disk at least 8 inches deep. — remove all debris, plaster scraps, and large stones. — work up an old lawn in the same way if it is tired, hard-packed, and sparse. — skip areas of exposed tree roots and plan on a ground cover. — leave areas next to house walls for shrubs or flowers.

DON'T — try to improve a hard, worn-out, or poor-grass lawn by mere scratching over. — turn under builder's scraps or large stones. — work up only a few inches deep, leaving tight subsoil beneath. — chop up roots of valuable trees or shrubs.

Humus

A successful lawn grows on a soil well supplied with vital organic matter. Subsoils are dead soils, as are many of our depleted topsoils. There are a number of good ways to add essential humus.

DO — get a soil analysis report that includes recommendations for humus improvement. — spread the required amount of organic material and work in at least 6 inches deep. — take advantage of any available compost, leaf mold, or mushroom soil; or use one part of these and part ground corncobs or sawdust. — keep in mind that peat, and trade-name peat or sedge products, are excellent soil builders.

DON'T — try to build a lawn on a poor-humus soil, or think that it is an economy to avoid the purchase and handling of organic materials. — try to guess about the humus content of your soil. — believe that a dark colored soil must indicate good humus content. —try to use synthetic soil conditioners to take the place of humus. —use fresh manure. —rely on sewage sludge as a soil builder. —be taken in by local black-dirt merchants.

Lime

Lime is both a plant food and a natural soil conditioner. The right amount of lime promotes good biological activity in a soil and makes nutrients properly available. Too much or too little lime causes poor grass vigor.

DO —work in the proper amount of ground limestone, as recommended by a soil report, to at least a 6 inch depth. —top-dress an established lawn with lime, but only when and as needed. —use a spreader for even application.

DON'T —lime by guesswork or by general recommendations for your area. —use hydrated or quick lime. —work in lime only a few inches deep for a new lawn. —spread lime hit-or-miss by hand. —get lime on soils for acid-loving shrubs.

Plant Food

A vigorous lawn is a heavy feeder, but it is particular about the kinds of plant food it receives. Many a lawn has been ruined by superficial applications of soluble fertilizers that burn the grasses and are then soon leached away. Materials that give a slow but steady supply of nutrients are the rule.

DO —feed your lawn as recommended by a qualified soil test report. —work in the required plant food several inches deep for a new lawn, following incorporation of lime and organic materials. —use phosphate rock, granite dust or greensand, and rich organic materials for basic plant food buildup as called for. —top-dress an established lawn with complete organic plant food at least once a year. —supplement the complete feeding with an organic nitrogen-carrier in fall or early spring. —use a spreader.

DON'T —try to fertilize your lawn by guesswork or kitchen-sink testing. —use chemical liquid feeding formulas. —use inorganic farm fertilizers or miracle-claiming lawn and garden fertilizers. —scatter lawn feeding materials by hand, some here, some there.

Seed Bed

A fertile, humus-rich soil, well loosened, is the basis for good seed germination. Once the preliminaries are done, preparation of a seed bed is a simple matter.

DO —rake over the newly worked-up soil to form a fine, firm, crumbly seed bed. —remove most small stones and sticks. —roll lightly before seeding if necessary to firm. —broadcast seed evenly at 5-lb. per 1,000 square feet, spreading half while walking in one direction and half at right angles to the first direction. — roll lightly after seeding. — seed your lawn in early fall, or early spring as a second choice. — patch up bare spots in an established lawn by raking loose and re-seeding. — remove fall leaves before they form a mat.

DON'T — settle for a coarse, loose, or lumpy seed bed. — skimp on seed, or spread it double thick. — try to seed on a windy day. — seed in late spring or in summer. — throw away or burn leaves after they are raked up.

Seed

There are over 1,500 species of grasses in the United States, but only a few are suitable for lawns. Some are coarse and quick-growing, like ryegrass. Some die out in hot weather, like Canadian bluegrass. Some stand up well and spread rapidly, like Merion bluegrass and the bents. Some grow in the shade, like the fescues, and some in full sun, like Kentucky bluegrass. Some must be started from stolons, especially in hot, dry climates. The inclusion of clover is a matter of choice.

DO — buy the best quality lawn seed for your section of the country, sunny or shady as appropriate. — make sure that the germination rate of the seed is good, and that the chaff and weed-seed content of the mix is low. — use the seed the same year you buy it.

DON'T — buy so-called bargain seed, containing

a high percentage of ryegrass, timothy, red top, or Canadian bluegrass. — buy unproven, wonder-promising lawn seeds. — try to produce a good lawn by mowing field grass. — expect even the best seed to grow on rock-hard, infertile soil.

Water

A good lawn soil should be like a sponge, absorbing and holding large amounts of water, and giving it off to the grass as needed. Adequate soil humus and a thick sod create an excellent reservoir. The critical times for moisture are the weeks following seeding and very hot, dry spells.

DO — keep a newly seeded lawn watered moderately at all times until the new grass is well established. — water an established lawn when necessary, by deep and thorough soaking. — keep in mind that big trees are water-hogs, and must be provided for.

DON'T — water an established lawn with a light spray. — set a sprinkler in one place all day. — depend on nature entirely to keep lawns supplied with water in a dry climate. — be in a hurry to water an established lawn in a normally moist climate.

Weeds

The best weed control is a thriving sod. Performance fails to match claims for the many weed control materials. Treat your lawn right, in other respects and weeds will be the least of your problems.

DO —rebuild your lawn if necessary, instead of trying to rejuvenate a wornout or temporary sod. —add humus, lime, and fertilizer to encourage ideal grass development. —mow 1-1/2 to 2 inches high, and keep your mower sharp. —mow in a counter-clockwise circular pattern, and let the clippings lie. —mow frequently in seasons of rapid growth.

DON'T —count on spray killers to keep your lawn weed-free. —expect a poor sod to complete satisfactorily against weeds. —neglect liming and fertilizing as needed. —give your lawn a crew cut, unless it is a fine bentgrass turf. —let grass become rank before cutting. —gather up clippings, unless very coarse. —use magic formulas to hold back grass growth.

Reconditioning

Often an established lawn that is in fair shape can be successfully reconditioned. The truly sad cases should be started over, as set forth already, but there are many instances where no such drastic work is needed.

DO—find out by a soil test report what lime and fertilizers are needed for your lawn, to ensure optimum grass growth. —aerify with a spike-tooth or spooning tool if soil is hard. —spread leaf mold,

[403]

peat, or similar coarse organic matter if needed, and rake back and forth into holes made by aerifier. —remove coarse clumps of undersirable grass and weeds. —rake the surface soil loose before re-seeding.

DON'T—waste time reconditioning a lawn unless it is properly limed, fertilized, and loosened. —scatter seed on an impenetrable surface, where it will die after germinating. —think liquid soil conditioners can be sprayed on the surface to loosen structure.

Envoi

Unless you are a greenskeeper and spend all day fussing about grass, your lawn won't be perfect.

DO—follow the foregoing suggestions as much as possible.

DON'T—be a fussbudget and end up with an ideally manicured lawn and a case of ulcers.— *Edward Harrington*

Time Saving Tips

With proper design and proper application of materials, many difficult and time consuming problems can be eliminated or appreciably reduced. The following list contains some of the more obvious recommendations for reducing maintenance—many of which can be added to the home grounds at any time:

[404]

1. Provide for continuous mowing by avoiding sharp corners and angles around plant beds and building corners.

2. Use concrete, brick or stone mowing strips against buildings, walls and under fencing to eliminate hand trimming.

3. Keep lawn areas flush with paved surfaces such as walks and terraces to avoid unnecessary trimming and provide easier movement of maintenance vehicles.

4. Eliminate hand trimming around trees by using grass barriers or metal edgings. This will also reduce tree damage from mowers.

5. Use a section of flush paving around lawn obstructions such as fire hydrants, light poles, sign posts and sewer vents. This can eliminate hand trimming and speed-up power mowing.

6. Avoid impossible-to-mow situations. Use low maintenance groundcover on steep slopes and bumpy or rough areas.

7. Locate water outlets conveniently. Handling of excessive lengths of hose should not be required to water lawns and plants. The absolute minimum in maintenance would be an automatic sprinkler system.

8. Provide for the free movement of maintenance-equipment from one area to another. All roads, walks, ramps and entrances should be planned wide enough to accommodate equipment.

9. Avoid trying to grow grass in "impossible situations"—in heavily shaded areas, heavily traveled areas or under roof overhangs.

[405]

Index

[409]

INDEX